ECONOMIC ISSUES
Rhetoric and Reality

MICHAEL WALDEN
North Carolina State University

PRENTICE HALL, Englewood Cliffs, NJ 07632

Library of Congress Cataloging-in-Publication Data

Walden, M. L. (Michael Leonard)
    Economic issues : rhetoric and reality / Michael Walden.
        p.   cm.
    Includes index.
    ISBN 0-13-300245-4
    1. United States--Economic policy--1993- 2. United States-
-Economic conditions--1981-   I. Title.
HC106.82.W35 1995
338.973--dc20
                                                          94-44024
                                                               CIP

Acquisitions editor   *Teresa Cohan*
Production editor   *Maureen Wilson*
Cover designer   *Tom Nery*
Buyer   *Marie McNamara*
Editorial assistant   *Liz Becker*

 © 1995 by Prentice-Hall, Inc.
A Simon & Schuster Company
Englewood Cliffs, New Jersey 07632

Printed in the United States of America

10 9 8 7 6 5 4 3 2 1

ISBN 0-13-300245-4

Prentice-Hall International (UK) Limited, *London*
Prentice-Hall of Australia Pty. Limited, *Sydney*
Prentice-Hall Canada Inc., *Toronto*
Prentice-Hall Hispanoamericana, S.A., *Mexico*
Prentice-Hall of India Private Limited, *New Delhi*
Prentice-Hall of Japan, Inc., *Tokyo*
Simon & Schuster Asia Pte. Ltd., *Singapore*
Editora Prentice Hall do Brasil, Ltda., *Rio de Janeiro*

To my wife, Mary, for your constant support and understanding.
The topics in this book should encourage
your budding interest in economics.

Contents

Introduction

It seems as if economic issues are in the news constantly today. From who's getting rich and who's getting poor, to taxes, to welfare policies, to deregulation, to the alleged decline of U.S. manufacturing, to analyzing health care reforms, some economic issue hits the headlines everyday. Although some of these economic issues may seem remote, most of them do affect us in the wallet or in the types of jobs that are available.

This book is about economic issues facing the nation today. We'll cover the waterfront, including government size (how it has grown and where government spends money), the deficit (is it about to sink us), taxes (who pays them), health care (what reforms make sense), welfare (how the cycle of poverty can be broken), and jobs (where to find them). We'll bring the issues out of the headlines and look at them in terms of causes, consequences, and possible solutions.

The tools for studying the issues are obviously from the discipline of economics. However, don't panic, this book isn't a course in economic theory—I'll leave that to courses in microeconomics and macroeconomics. Actually, you don't need any formal training in economics to understand this book. All you need is a healthy interest in economic issues.

I will use some standard economic concepts in the study of the issues. Two in particular are used, the role of incentives and the role of markets. Incentives are the key to understanding any economic behavior. Incentives simply refer to the payoff people or businesses receive for doing something. Incentives can be in the form of a payment received, savings achieved, or satisfaction gained from an action. The simple message is that people and firms will do more of something if the economic payoff for doing it increases. Similarly, people and firms will do less of something if the economic payoff for doing it decreases. As you will see, applying economic incentives will go a long way in understanding behavior in such disparate areas as health care, poverty and welfare, and the savings and loan bailout.

The role of markets is a more subtle concept but no less important. An economic market describes the interaction of consumers and businesses in the trading of goods and services. Prices of products and services in a market are determined by the interaction of desires (demands) of consumers and costs of production faced by businesses. Changes on one side of the market usually cause a reaction on the other side of the market. For example, a change in consumer desires for a product sets in motion forces which affect producer costs and, ultimately, change the product's price. An understanding of markets is crucial to comprehending many economic issues.

In presenting and discussing the economic issues, this book emphasizes facts over opinion. Most readers will have established opinions about the issues, but these opinions may or may not be consistent with the facts. In the presentation of the issues, I'll reinforce the economic analysis with evidence and facts and let the reader be the judge.

The book is "user-friendly." The issues are presented in thirteen chapters grouped into five parts. The chapters can be read in any order. Numerous figures and tables present evidence, information, and relationships to make the issues more understandable.

So you're off on your journey into economic issues. I think you'll view these issues in a more informed way after your excursion is completed.

Acknowledgments

Many individuals contributed to the completion of this book. First and foremost I thank my colleagues at North Carolina State University, especially Craig Newmark and E. C. Pasour, Jr., who read various versions of the book and made valuable comments. I'm grateful to the following people for their reviews of the manuscript and helpful advice: Steve Robinson, The University of North Carolina at Wilmington; James L. Barbour, Elon College; Richard P. F. Holt, Elon College; Lars G. Sandberg, Ohio State University; and Anthony Zambelli, Cuyamaca College. I also thank the many listeners to my radio call-in program appearances who encouraged me to put my analysis of economic issues on paper. Evelyn Clegg deserves high praise for typing of the manuscript and her preparation of the figures. Evelyn always came through to meet my deadlines. Finally, I thank the wonderful professionals at Prentice Hall, especially Stephen Dietrich, economics editor, and Bill Wicker, senior acquisitions editor, for their faith in the project and their guiding hand in seeing it to completion.

I. STANDARD OF LIVING ISSUES

The first and foremost concern of most Americans is how well they're doing. Earning enough income to meet personal and family needs and dreams, putting enough aside in savings for a "rainy day" and the kids' college education, and keeping debt under control are issues which most citizens worry about. The scary thing about these issues is that they're not totally under the individual's control. The family standard of living can be "booming" when the overall economy is booming, but through no fault of the individual, everything can fall apart when an economywide recession hits.

In this section we'll examine three standard of living issues. First, we'll address the overall issue of "how we're doing," including what's happened to income wages, the middle class, and the relative economic positions of women and minorities in recent years. Is the American Dream broken or is it still attainable?

The second chapter examines those economic forces beyond our direct control that profoundly impact our economic lives. These are the ups and down in the overall economy, which I call the "economic roller coaster." Has this roller coaster become bumpier? Why can't government prevent the "downs" in the economy? Are recessions now the standard in the economy rather than the exception?

The third and last chapter in this section examines recent saving and debt behavior of both consumers and businesses. Have we become a nation of spenders rather than savers? Was the 1980s the decade of debt? Have we lost our traditional values of frugality and saving for the future? Fortunately, as you will see, the answers are no.

1

How are we doing?

One of the most contentious issues of the 1980s has been whether the "rich got richer and the poor got poorer." The popular perception is that this indeed was the case, and it represented a drastic break with America's historical past in which any citizen, despite his or her initial standing, could "make it" in America. Was the American Dream broken in the 1980s, and can only the rich get ahead today? Has the middle class shrunk, and are wage earners doomed to a subsistence living? What happened to the rate of pay of women and minorities in the 1980s relative to the pay of white males? Did women and minorities advance or fall further behind? Also, has America overall gotten poorer relative to other nations?

WHAT'S HAPPENED TO INCOME?

There are a number of issues related to the question of Americans' income over the past two decades: What's happened to average income? What's happened to the income of high-, middle-, and low-income Americans? And what's happened to the gap between the income of the rich and the income of the poor, so-called income inequality? I'll address each of these in order.

What Happened to Average Income?

Critics of the 1980s like to compare the average (median) income of American families between selected years in the 1970s and selected years in

3

the 1980s. For example, Kevin Phillips states that virtually no increase in real (inflation-adjusted) median family income occurred between 1973 and 1987.[1] In 1987 dollars, Phillips shows that real median family income was $30,820 in 1973, $30,025 in 1977, and only $30,853 in 1987; thus, in almost 15 years there was virtually no improvement in the average real income of the American family.

There are two problems with Phillips's comparisons. First, they mask changes that were occurring in the years between the comparison points. The years from 1978 to 1982 were disastrous for American families because high inflation rates of the period reduced the purchasing power of families' incomes. In addition, the 1980–82 recessions (a reaction to the high inflation rates) reduced the take-home pay of families. Yet, after this disastrous period, the real median income of American families rose. Even the data cited by Phillips show that real median family income rose from $27,591 in 1982 to $30,853 in 1987, a 12 percent increase.[2] Once the recessions of the early 1980s were over, family income resumed its traditional rise. In Figure 1-1, the line "Real Median Family Income" tracks the data used by Phillips.

The second problem with the family income comparisons used by Phillips and others is the adjustment for inflation. This may seem like a technical point, but it is extremely important, so stay with me! Of course, in comparing incomes over time, it is necessary to adjust for changes in the cost of living, or inflation, from year to year, since a higher cost of living reduces the purchasing power of dollars. Typically, the Consumer Price Index (CPI), is used to adjust for inflation. Prior to 1983, the CPI included the sales value of homes as a component. However, since a small percentage of families buys a home every year, most economists agreed that the sales

Figure 1-1   Alternative Measures of Economic Well-Being (1970 = 100)

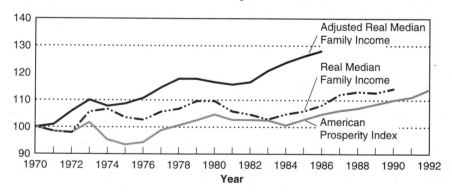

Sources: U.S. Bureau of the Census, *Money Income of Households, Families and Persons in the U.S., 1987*, U.S. Government Printing Office, 1989; Richard McKenzie, *The Fortunate Fifth Fallacy*, Center for the Study of American Business, Washington Univ., St. Louis, Occasional Paper 101, February 1992; Melynda Wilcox, "An Exclusive Look at How We're Doing," *Kiplinger's Personal Finance Magazine*, April 1993, pp. 49–56.

value of a home should not be in the CPI. A new CPI has been developed which uses a comparable "rental value" as the cost of homeowning.[3] This CPI shows significantly lower inflation rates in the late 1970s when house values were rapidly rising.

The family income data used by Phillips use the old CPI. When the new CPI is used to adjust actual family income, a more positive picture emerges ("Adjusted Real Median Family Income" in Figure 1-1). Professor Richard McKenzie goes even further in the adjustments. McKenzie notes that since families have been getting smaller in size, family income should be adjusted for changes in family size.[4] Also, the income data cited by Phillips and others do not include the value of noncash income, such as the value of employer-provided health insurance, other fringe benefits, and government supplements. These have become increasingly important as a component of total worker compensation, rising from 12 percent of wages and salaries in 1970 to 20 percent in 1986.[5] When these two adjustments are also made, the rise in average real family income in the 1980s is even more dramatic.

The bottom line appears to be this. Once past the recessions of 1980 to 1982, real family income resumed its growth. In the 1970s, real family income was hurt by a severe middecade recession (1973–75) and by high inflation rates in the latter part of the decade.

The discussion thus far has focused on income, whether cash or noncash, as a measure of family well-being. But is this the most comprehensive measure? Current income measures an individual's or family's financial resources earned this year. It doesn't measure the net financial resources an individual or family has accumulated over the years in the form of savings or investments. This is called net worth, or wealth. Net worth of an individual or family simply measures the value of assets minus the value of liabilities (for example, loans owed). Net worth of an individual or family represents resources which can be used now or in the future.

Kiplinger's American Prosperity Index combines both spending and net worth of households to measure their well-being.[6] All dollar amounts are adjusted for inflation for year-to-year comparisons. The index once again shows that, following the 1980–82 recessions, average household well-being improved (Figure 1-1). Interestingly, the index moved upward even during the recession years of 1990 to 1991. This is because, although household spending sputtered during those years, net worth of households dramatically improved as households paid down on debts.

There's one way in which the critics of the 1980s are correct. By any measure, the rate of growth of household well-being in the 1980s was substantially lower than the rate of growth in the 1950s and 1960s.[7] This is an issue related to the overall growth of the economy, which I'll address later.

What Happened to Incomes of the Rich and Poor?

Critics of the 1980s may concede that average income rose during the decade. However, this can occur, they say, simply as a result of the incomes of the rich rising so much so as to counteract the stagnation or decline of incomes of the poor. To cite support for this argument, Phillips and others report that the average real family income of the poorest 20 percent of families fell by over 8 percent between 1977 and 1988, while the average real family income of the richest 1 percent of families rose by almost 50 percent over the same time period.[8]

These comparisons suffer from the same problems discussed when tracking average family income: They hide year-to-year changes, they use the wrong inflation adjustment, they ignore family size changes, and they count only cash income. When only the first two problems are corrected, both McKenzie and the Bureau of the Census show that real household income of all income groups rose during the expansion period of the 1980s. For example, between 1983 and 1989, real household income rose 11 percent for the poorest 20 percent of households, income rose between 10 and 12 percent for the middle 60 percent of households, and income rose almost 19 percent for the richest 20 percent of households.[9]

If these figures are accurate, although they show that all "income boats" rose in the 1980s, the incomes of the rich rose the most. That is, if the cliché "the rich got richer and the poor got poorer" doesn't exactly apply, then maybe "the poor got richer, but the rich got much, much richer" applies. This would mean that the income gap between the rich and the poor grew, or, in other words, income inequality grew in the 1980s. In fact, much has been written about this alleged increase in income inequality in the 1980s.[10]

But again, what appears to be the case on the surface may not be accurate once the surface is peeled away. There are two big problems with following income groups. The first problem is with the upper-income group. Since real incomes, in general, rose during the 1983–89 period, it took higher real incomes to be in the top 20 percent group than it did at the beginning of the period. This "uplifting" of the boundary of the upper-income group would, therefore, naturally contribute to the bigger income gain of the top-income group.[11]

The big changes in the income tax laws in the 1980s, particularly the reduction in marginal tax rates, also contributed to the bigger income gains by the top-income group. This is not necessarily because the tax rate reductions allowed the rich to make more money but because the tax rate reductions motivated the rich to take money out of tax shelters and declare it as income for tax purposes. A study by Feenberg and Poterba has addressed this issue and finds that an increase in reportable income by the rich, particularly after 1986, was a major reason for the bigger income gains by the rich in the 1980s.[12]

The second problem with tracking income groups over time has to do with who is being tracked. When, for example, it is stated that the real incomes of the richest 20 percent of households rose 19 percent from 1983 to 1989, most readers probably think that the same households are being compared over that time period. But this is usually not the case. Tracking statistical income groups doesn't necessarily mean tracking the same households. Two studies have conclusively demonstrated that there is substantial income mobility in the American economy.[13] For example, one study showed that almost 15 percent of the households that were among the poorest 20 percent of households in 1979 were among the richest 20 percent of households in 1988.[14] So, when we talk about the "rich" and the "poor" in two different years, we're not necessarily talking about the same households.

This problem was corrected in a study by the Urban Institute, a Washington, DC think tank.[15] The study tracked the income changes of the same families from 1977 to 1986. The findings are summarized in Table 1-1. Although the results aren't directly comparable to other data because of the study's time period, the results are startling because they show just the opposite of the conventional wisdom. Poorest families realized the largest real income percentage gains, while the richest families saw the smallest percentage gains. These data illustrate the problem of drawing conclusions about household income changes from aggregate statistics that don't track the same people over time.

It appears as if the rhetoric of income changes of the 1980s that the "rich got richer and the poor got poorer" is not the reality. More careful analysis shows that once the recessions of the early 1980s were past, income gains were made by all income groups.

WHAT'S HAPPENED TO WAGES?

Along with the concern about what happened to real incomes during the 1980s is a complementary concern about what happened to real wages during the decade. In some ways, examining trends in real wages gives a better picture of the economic well-being of families. Families can always maintain or increase their income by working more hours or working a second job even if their hourly pay falls. The hourly pay, the wage rate, tells what workers are paid apart from how many hours they work.

The concerns about wages during the 1980s parallel the concerns about incomes. These concerns are represented by Professor Lester Thurow, who states that real hourly wages for nonsupervisory workers fell 12 percent between 1973 and 1990.[16]

Once again, we must be careful about which statistics are used and what those statistics mean. First, we must be careful not to use different mixes of full-time and part-time workers when analyzing trends over time. This is because the wages of part-time workers are usually lower than the

Table 1-1   Real Income Gains of Families by Beginning Income Group, 1977–1986

Poorest 20% of families	+77%
Second 20% of families	+37%
Third 20% of families	+20%
Fourth 20% of families	+10%
Richest 20% of families	+5%

Source: Isabel Sawhill and Mark Condon, "Is U.S. Income Inequality Really Growing?" *Policy Bites*, no. 13, June 1992, Washington, DC, The Urban Institute.

wages of full-time workers. This problem is most easily handled by examining the wage trends of only full-time workers.

Second, we must recognize that more educated workers and more experienced workers generally earn higher wages, so the changing mix of education and experience over time must somehow be accounted for when studying wage trends. If, for example, wages have fallen as a result of an influx of relatively inexperienced workers to the labor force, then this should not imply that workers are worse off.

Finally, as we discovered with income trends, it can be misleading to pick two years and compare incomes or wages, especially when those years span a number of ups and downs (expansions and recessions) in the economy.

A study by Murphy and Welch corrects these problems in examining wage trends.[17] Murphy and Welch use wages only for full-time workers, and they developed a technique to adjust these wages for changes in the education and experience mix of the workers.

Murphy and Welch indeed find that, like Thurow, average wage rates fell from 1973 to 1989 (the last year covered in the Murphy/Welch study) by 7.4 percent (real wage index in Figure 1-2). But most of this drop occurred during the period from 1973 to 1983, a period marked by three recessions and double-digit inflation. From 1983 to 1989, Murphy and Welch's wage rates adjusted for education and experience rose, albeit modestly, by 1.2 percent.

Robert Myers, former chief actuary of the Social Security Administration, uses comprehensive data from the social security system to reach a similar conclusion. Myers finds that real wage income rose until 1973, then fell until 1983, but from 1983 to 1989 rose 1.1 percent annually.[18] Myers's data, however, are not adjusted for changes in the education and experience mix of workers.

Figure 1-2   Trends in Real Wages and Real Compensation (1970 = 100)

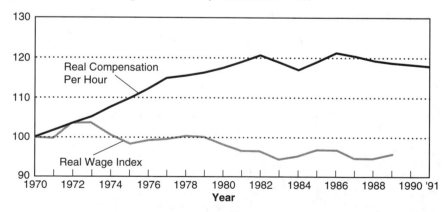

Sources: Kevin Murphy and Finis Welch, "The Structure of Wages," *Quarterly Journal of Economics,* 107, no. 1, February 1992, 285–326; Bureau of Labor Statistics, *Monthly Labor Review,* vol. 115, no. 6, June 1992, Table 45.

There is one empirical point about wages on which all the studies agree: Real wage growth was much slower in the expansion years of the 1980s than in the 1950s and 1960s. For example, Murphy and Welch's data show that average real wages rose 2.3 percent annually from 1963 to 1973, but rose less than 1 percent annually from 1983 to 1989. Similarly, Myers's data show that average real wages also rose 2.3 percent annually from 1947 to 1973, but rose only 1.5 percent annually from 1983 to 1989. This parallels the slowdown in income growth that was pointed out earlier.

Another finding that everyone agrees with is the increasing returns to education that arose in the 1980s. For example, after adjusting for changes in experience, the average hourly wage of college graduates exceeded the average hourly wage of high school graduates by 37 percent in 1979 but by 58 percent in 1989.[19] Also, the United States isn't alone in this phenomenon, with the returns to education also increasing in the 1980s in most industrialized countries.[20] Needless to say, the increasing returns to education in the 1980s have sparked much interest and "head scratching" by economists. To date, the best explanations given for this are: (1) increased foreign competition from lower-skilled foreign workers in the 1980s, which helped to depress wages of lower-skilled, lower-educated U.S. workers; (2) the development and spread of computers in the workplace in the 1980s, which put a premium on educated workers who could apply the computers; and (3) the slower growth of college graduates in the 1980s caused by the "baby bust" of the late 1960s and 1970s.[21]

There's one final ruffle to our wage story, and it concerns a fundamental issue: What really is the best measure of the "pay" from a company to a worker? So far we have been talking about wages as the measure of pay. But companies also pay workers in the form of fringe benefits, such as retirement contributions, health insurance, and vacation and sick leave. Although workers don't receive these benefits in cash, they are a form of compensation. And, as already noted, the relative importance of fringe benefits in the total compensation of workers has increased.

When real (inflation-adjusted) total compensation per hour, which includes wage and salary income plus the value of fringe benefits, is plotted, then we can see that it has steadily increased over the past quarter-century. (Figure 1-2 shows real compensation per hour in manufacturing.) An issue of concern for workers is, however, the increasing part of this compensation that is going to benefits rather than being received in cash. This is an important issue when discussing health care and health insurance.

WHAT'S HAPPENED TO THE MIDDLE CLASS?

The observation that the returns to education, in particular, have been increasing has produced a concern about the class structure of American society. One of the traditional features of American society has been a large middle class, which acted as a buffer or glue (depending on your perspective) between the upper and lower classes. But with higher-educated citizens getting progressively bigger income gains and with, by some measures, higher-income households achieving the largest income gains in the 1980s, some observers of the economic scene have said that the relative size of the American middle class has shrunk.[22]

Before we can determine whether this is indeed true, we must answer a more fundamental question: What is the middle class? *Class* is a multidimensional concept, which includes economic, social, and psychological elements. The social and psychological elements are beyond our consideration, so we will concentrate on an economic definition of *middle class*.

The most widely used economic measure of middle class is that it includes households with annual incomes between $15,000 and $50,000 in 1989 dollars (that is, with dollars adjusted for purchasing power in 1989). This roughly corresponds to "rich" households (those with more than $50,000 income) making more than six times the poverty level, and "middle-class" households making more than twice but less than six times the poverty level.[23]

Using this definition of middle class, several data sources do indeed show a shrinking middle class over the past two decades. For example, the Census Bureau shows that almost 63 percent of families were middle class in 1970. This share fell to 59 percent in 1980 and to 53 percent in 1989. Another study tracked the *same* households over time and found the same trend: 57 percent of households were middle class in 1970, the proportion was down to 54 percent in 1980 and further down to 52 percent in 1986 (the last year of the study).[24]

This is the bad news if one is worried about the middle-class glue in society. However, the good news is that the same studies find that the decline in the relative size of the middle class is matched by an increase in the relative size of the upper-income group, while the relative size of the lower-income group has remained remarkably constant. For example, the Census Bureau finds the upper-income group increasing from 20 percent in 1970 to 22 percent in 1980 to 29 percent of households in 1989, while the lower-income group remained constant at approximately 18 percent of households. Similarly, the study tracking the same households over time found the upper-income class increasing from 18 percent in 1970 to 20 percent in 1980 to 23 percent in 1986, with the lower-income class remaining constant at about 26 percent of households. It is also important to note that the same trends are found for African-American households. (The annual data on the relative size of the household income groups are given in Appendix Tables A–C.)[25]

Thus, although not everyone will define income classes in the same way, the most accepted definition does show a shrinking middle class, but one that has been squeezed up rather than down. This does mean, however, relatively fewer households to hold together the rich and the poor.

WHAT'S HAPPENED TO WEALTH?

There are a number of ways to measure economic well-being. The wage rate measures what a person earns per hour of work. The compensation rate measures what a person earns per hour of work, including the value of benefits. Income, a product of what a person earns per hour and the number of hours of work, measures total earnings during a year.

I've alluded to another measure of well-being when discussing Kiplinger's American Prosperity Index, and this is wealth, or net worth. Wealth, or net worth, simply measures the value of assets, or investments, minus the value of debts. Wealth represents a store of value which an individual or household can use to purchase goods or services in the future. Therefore, changes in wealth for a household are an important indicator of how well a household is doing economically.

A charge leveled at the 1980s is that increases in wealth were concentrated in the hands, or accounts, of the rich.[26] Yet a look at two serious studies of the issue suggests otherwise. The most comprehensive study of wealth is done by the Federal Reserve System every six years. A comparison of the 1983 and 1989 studies shows that the biggest *percentage* increases in wealth over the period were actually made by middle-income Americans earning between $20,000 and $50,000 annually. These households increased their wealth 28 percent between 1983 and 1989, compared to an increase of 6.6 percent for households making over $50,000. However, low-income households (incomes under $10,000) did have the smallest percentage gains at 3.3 percent. Of course, higher-income households had greater dollar gains in wealth because they started with a larger base. It is also interesting to note that the Federal Reserve study found greater percentage gains in wealth for nonwhite households than for white households.[27]

Once again, the Federal Reserve study follows statistical income groups and not the same households, and so it may give somewhat misleading results. A study by Duncan, Smeeding, and Rodgers tracked the wealth of the same households from 1984 to 1989. They found that the poorest households (the 20 percent of households with the lowest incomes) had the same percentage increase in wealth (55 percent) as the richest households (the 10 percent of households with the highest incomes). Consequently, the ratio of wealth of the richest households to the wealth of the poorest households remained unchanged at 39 from 1984 to 1989. The study also found that African-American low- and middle-income households experienced greater increases in wealth than white households.[28]

WHAT'S HAPPENED TO FEMALES AND AFRICAN-AMERICANS?

Have women and minorities, particularly African-Americans, moved closer to men and whites in pay equality in recent years, or have they fallen further behind? Pay equality means receiving the same pay for the same job for two individuals with the same education, training, and work experience.

Let's begin with women. The female/male earnings ratio for full-time workers rose substantially in the 1980s from 60 percent in 1980 to over 70 percent in 1990 (Figure 1-3). Furthermore, this rise in the relative pay of women in the 1980s occurred after very little movement in the ratio in the 1960s and 1970s.

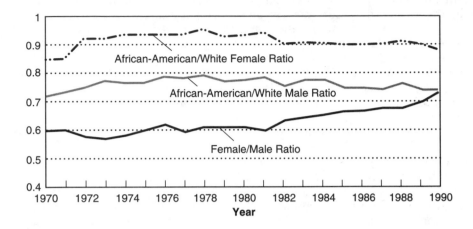

Source: Elaine Sorensen, *Gender and Racial Pay Gaps in the 1980s: Accounting for Different Trends, Final Report*, contract No. J-9-M-0-0079, U.S. Dept of labor, The Urban Institute, Washington, DC, October 1991.

Figure 1-3   Gender and Race Pay Ratios

More detailed comparisons show that female/male pay ratios rose for all categories of job experience. For white females and males with less than nine years of experience, the female/male pay ratio rose seven percentage points between 1981 and 1988; for white females and males with 10 to 19 years of experience, the increase was six percentage points; and for white females and males with over 20 years of experience, the increase was also six percentage points.[29]

What are the reasons for this good news about women's pay relative to men's pay? There are at least four reasons. First, women's experience has increased relative to men's experience. For example, in 1980 working women aged 35 had 11.7 years of experience; in 1990 working women aged 35 had 14.5 years of experience.[30] The average work experience of (white) men actually declined between 1979 and 1985.[31] Since the labor market values work experience because it is generally related to increased productivity, the rising work experience of women has helped move their pay closer to that of men.

Second, the time spent by working women out of the work force declined in the 1980s, whereas it increased for men.[32] Employers prefer workers who don't take long periods away from work, since such absences may reduce worker productivity. Therefore, the reduction in women's absences from the workplace improved their pay position.

A third important factor behind the decreasing pay gap between women and men in the 1980s is that females' occupations have become more like males' occupations. The increasing education and experience of females have allowed them to move into higher-paying occupations previously dominated by males. The index of occupational segregation, a measure of the percentage of women who would have to change jobs in order for the occupational distribution of women and men to be the same, fell from 65 percent in 1970 to 57 percent in 1987.[33]

Finally, there is evidence to suggest that discrimination against women in the labor market declined in the 1980s.[34] The support for this is the finding that differences in female and male pay not explained by differences in economic fundamentals, such as education, experience, and occupation, declined in the 1980s.[35]

The news for the relative position of African-Americans isn't as good. As Figure 1-3 shows, the African-American/white pay ratio slipped slightly in the late 1970s and 1980s after rising in the early and mid-1970s. (Actually the rise had been ongoing since at least the 1940s.)

The numbers in Figure 1-3 are averaged across workers with different experience and education levels. A more detailed analysis, which shows pay ratios by age (a proxy for experience) and education groups of men, reveals that the news isn't all bad. African-American/white male pay ratios increased in the 1980s for half of the age/education categories and decreased for half of the categories (Table 1-2). Pay ratios were more likely to increase for older workers, and pay ratios were more likely to decrease for younger workers.[36]

So what's going on here? The answer is complicated by the fact that the educational level and occupational attainment of African-American workers became *more* like those of white workers during the 1980s. For example, between 1979 and 1985, African-American men's educational attainment increased an average of 1.1 years compared to 0.5 years for white men; for African-American women, educational attainment increased an average of 0.7 years compared to 0.4 years for white women.[37]

Table 1-2   African-American/White Male Earnings Ratios by Age and Schooling

	THREE-YEAR AVERAGE	
AGE AND YEARS OF SCHOOL	1977–1979	1986–1988
Ages 25–34		
0–11 school yrs.	74.5	81.6
12	79.6	75.5
13–15	85.4	82.1
16+	96.4	85.1
Ages 35–44		
0–11 schools yrs.	76.0	80.4
12	79.5	74.4
13–15	84.3	81.3
16+	77.1	81.0
Ages 45–54		
0–11 school yrs.	72.8	72.5
12	72.0	74.0
13–15	74.0	82.0
16+	73.6	81.7

Source: June O'Neill, "The Role of Human Capital in Earnings Differences Between Black and White Men," *Journal of Economic Perspectives*, 4, no. 4 (Fall 1990), 36, All rights reserved, used with permission.

Instead, two shifts accounted for the majority of the deterioration of the pay ratio for some African-Americans in the 1980s. One was employment shifts. In the 1980s union coverage fell for both African-Americans and whites, but the decline was greater for African-Americans. Since union workers earn more, on average, than nonunion workers, this shift hurt African-Americans. The proportion of African-Americans working in manufacturing also declined relative to that for whites. Again, since manufacturing jobs have often paid more than their alternatives, this shift also hurt the pay of some African-Americans, particularly young African-Americans.

The second shift has been the most important, and this is one we have already discussed. This is the increase in the returns to education which occurred in the 1980s. That is, in the 1980s employers put a higher value on education than they had in previous decades. O'Neill estimates that the return to an additional year of college for all workers aged 20 to 34 increased by 0.3 percent annually from 1977 to 1987.[38] Although, as stated earlier, African-Americans increased their educational level relative to whites in the 1980s, the *average* educational level of African-Americans is still less than the average educational level of whites. Therefore, the increase in the returns to education in the 1980s benefitted whites more than African-Americans and contributed to a bigger pay gap between African-Americans and whites. Again, this was particularly the case for young African-Americans.

What about racial discrimination? Is there any evidence that racial discrimination increased in the 1980s and contributed to the increasing pay gap between African-Americans and whites? Although a sure answer is difficult to give, the evidence suggests that racial discrimination did *not* increase in the 1980s. Two recent studies of racial earnings differences in the 1980s found no evidence of increased racial discrimination.[39] For example, O'Neill's analysis of 1987 male racial pay differentials found that 99 percent of the pay gap between African-Americans and whites could be accounted for by differences in education as measured by completed school years and test scores and differences in work experience.

So the tales of sex and racial pay differences in the 1980s are different. Females made progress compared to males, but the evidence on African-American progress is mixed. However, the overriding theme is that economic fundamentals are driving these changes. The negative impact that the increasing return to education has had on the earnings of some African-Americans highlights what everyone has heard by now at least 100 times: Education is the key to financial reward for the vast majority of Americans, and the financial rewards from more education have never been higher.

HOW ARE WE DOING COMPARED TO OTHER COUNTRIES?

Americans like to compare themselves to their fellow citizens and also to foreign citizens. In the two decades following World War II, Americans were always ahead of foreign citizens economically, since many foreign countries had their economies devastated by the war.

But in the 1970s and 1980s America's economic lead over the rest of the world shrunk. Two countries in particular, Japan and Germany, closed the economic gap with the United States. Where do things stand now, and what happened in the 1980s? Is America's economy still the world's leader, or have we been overtaken by others?

This is not an easy question to answer. Comparisons of economies and standards of living between countries are difficult for several reasons. Each country measures its output in its own currency, so exchange rates between currencies must be applied before a comparison is made. The prices of inputs and other factors of production vary between countries. Also, tastes and preferences of citizens, which obviously influence what is produced and consumed, are different between countries.

It takes careful consideration and analysis of all these factors to be able to compare standards of living of different countries. Research by Summers and Heston has been the most detailed in this area.[40] They have reached the important conclusion that the United States was still the leader in output of goods and services per person in 1988 (the last year of the study) among the world's major economies. Other countries closed in on the U.S. lead in the period immediately after World War II, but in the 1980s the U.S. lead was maintained or slightly increased.

Another way of making international comparisons of standards of living is to look at the U.S. share of total world output of goods and services. The U.S. share of total world output did fall in the 1960s and 1970s primarily due to the rebuilding from World War II in other countries, but the U.S. share stabilized and actually rose somewhat in the 1980s, ending the decade at 34 percent. U.S. output did fall relative to Japan's output in the 1980s, but U.S. output rose relative to Germany's output in the 1980s.[41]

The predominant economic position of the United States in the immediate postwar period should not be used as the standard of comparison, since this was an unusual and unrepresentative period. Countries that were strong economic producers before World War II, particularly Japan and Germany, are again strong economic producers and competitors once the ashes of the war were cleared. This should not be surprising or a cause for alarm. For what it's worth, careful analysis shows that the United States is still the world's economic leader. What is more important is whether the United States has the proper policies and support system for successfully competing in the future.

SO WHAT ARE THE REAL PROBLEMS?

National economies never stand still. New competitors are always arising and existing competitors are always dying. Innovations and new technologies are constantly being developed, which make "better mousetraps" and which shift the competitive edge to those with the new technologies and away from those without.

All this economic flux makes for winners and losers. The 1980s was no different. The biggest change occurring in the 1980s was what many would consider to be a positive change, and this was the increasing returns to education. The wage gap between those with education and those without increased dramatically in the 1980s. Professors Bound and Johnson conclude that the development of computer-driven technology, which requires an educated user, was the major factor behind the increased income premium for education.[42] Although this benefitted those with education and serves as a great motivator to students to stay in school and excel, it has been bad news for those individuals who have not acquired a necessary amount of education. These individuals will fall further behind in an education-driven workplace.

Another apparent problem arising out of the 1980s is the growing gap between the cost of worker compensation to the employer and the wages and salaries received by the worker. The difference between the two is worker benefits, such as the cost of vacation and sick leave, retirement pensions, and health care benefits. As benefits, particularly health care, have become increasingly expensive, a bigger share of worker compensation has gone to benefits and a lesser share has gone to wages and salaries. The problem is that most benefits don't put cash in workers' hands now. Many workers would probably prefer to take the value of their benefits in cash now and forgo the benefits in the future. The issue is whether workers can be "trusted" as the best judge of their own welfare. Can workers be trusted to make the best decisions about how much health care they need and how much retirement saving they should do? If the answer is yes, then "cashing out" the value of benefits could make workers happier with no additional cost to employers.

NOTES

1. Kevin Phillips, *The Politics of Rich and Poor* (New York: Random House, 1990), Appendix C. Similar statistics are presented in Lawrence Mishel and Jared Bernstein, *The State of Working America* (New York: M.E. Sharpe, Inc., 1993).
2. Ibid.
3. U.S. Department of Commerce, Bureau of the Census, *Households, Families, and Persons in the United States: 1990* (Washington, DC: U.S. Government Printing Office, August 1991), p. 193.
4. Richard B. McKenzie, "The 'Fortunate Fifth' Fallacy," Center for the Study of American Business, Washington University, St. Louis, Occasional Paper 101 (February 1992). McKenzie does not adjust for changes in the number of workers in the family; that is, some of the increases in real family income in the 1980s could have occurred from an increase in two worker incomes. However, although the percentage of married women in the labor force increased from 52 percent in 1983 to 58 percent in 1989, this increase was much more modest than the increases from 30 percent in 1960 to 41 percent in 1970 to 50 percent in 1980 (U.S. Bureau of the Census, *Statistical Abstract of the U.S.*).
5. Ibid.
6. Melynda D. Wilcox, "An Exclusive Look at How We're Doing," *Kiplinger's Personal Finance Magazine* (April 1993), pp. 49–56.

7. For example, from 1953 to 1968, Kiplinger's American Prosperity Index rose an average of 3 percent annually, compared to rising only an average of 0.5 percent annually from 1969 to 1993.

8. Phillips, *The Politics of Rich and Poor*, p. 17.

9. McKenzie, pp. 3–5; U.S. Department of Commerce, Bureau of the Census, *Current Population Reports, Series P60-183, Studies in the Distribution of Income* (Washington, DC: U.S. Government Printing Office, 1992). In another study, McKenzie found that spending by the poorest 20 percent of households rose faster than spending by other households during the 1984–1989 period (Richard McKenzie, "The Rich Got Richer But So Did the Poor: Spending Patterns in the 1980s," Center for the Study of American Business, Occasional Paper 109, August 1992).

10. See, for example, U.S. Department of Commerce, Bureau of the Census, *Current Population Reports, Series P-60, No. 177, Trends in Relative Income: 1964 to 1989* (Washington, DC: U.S. Government Printing Office, 1991); Congressional Budget Office, CBO Staff Memorandum, *Measuring the Distribution of Income Gains* (Washington, DC, March 1992); David Cutler and Lawrence Katz, "Rising Inequality? Changes in the Distribution of Income and Consumption in the 1980s," *American Economic Review*, 82, no. 2 (May 1992), 546–551.

11. Alan Reynolds expands on this point in "The Middle Class Boom of the 1980s," *The Wall Street Journal*, March 12, 1992, p. A12.

12. Daniel Feenberg and James Poterba, "Income Inequality and the Incomes of the Very High Income Taxpayers: Evidence from Tax Returns," Working Paper No. 4229, Cambridge, MA, National Bureau of Economic Research (December 1992).

13. Isabel Sawhill and Mark Condon, "Is U.S. Income Inequality Really Growing?" *Policy Bites*, no. 13 (June 1992), Washington, DC, The Urban Institute; U.S. Department of the Treasury, Office of Tax Analysis, *Household Income Mobility During the 1980s: A Statistical Assessment Based on Tax Return Data*, Washington, DC, June 1, 1992.

14. U.S. Department of the Treasury, *Household Income Mobility During the 1980s*.

15. Sawhill and Condon, "Is U.S. Income Inequality Really Growing?"

16. Lester Thurow, *Head to Head* (New York: William Morrow and Co., 1992), p. 53.

17. Kevin Murphy and Finis Welch, "The Structure of Wages," *Quarterly Journal of Economics*, 107, no. 1 (February 1992), 285–326.

18. Robert Myers, "Real Wages Went Up in the 1980s," *The Wall Street Journal*, August 21, 1990.

19. Murphy and Welch, "The Structure of Wages," p. 300. Juhn, Murphy, and Pierce also find that real average weekly wages for the most skilled workers have risen in the 1970s and 1980s, whereas real average weekly wages for the least skilled have fallen since 1973 [Chinhui Juhn, Kevin Murphy, and Brooks Pierce, "Wage Inequality and the Rise in Returns to Skill," *Journal of Political Economy*, 101, no. 3 (June 1993), 410–442].

20. Lawrence Katz, "Understanding Recent Changes in the Wage Structure," *NBER Reporter* (Winter 1992/3), pp. 10–15.

21. Lawrence Katz and Kevin Murphy, "Changes in Relative Wages, 1963–1987: Supply and Demand Factors," *Quarterly Journal of Economics*, 107, no. 1 (February 1992), 35–78; John Bound and George Johnson, "Changes in the Structure of Wages in the 1980s: An Evaluation of Alternative Explanations," *American Economic Review*, 82, no. 3 (June 1992), 371–392.

22. Phillips, *The Politics of Rich and Poor*, p. 15.

23. Greg Duncan, Timothy Smeeding, and Willard Rodgers, "W(h)ither the Middle Class? A Dynamic View," paper prepared for the Levy Institute Conference on Income Inequality, Bard College, June 18–20, 1991, p. 19.

24. U.S. Department of Commerce, *Statistical Abstract of the U.S.*, 11th ed. (Washington DC: U.S. Government Printing Office, 1991) Duncan, Smeeding, and Rodgers, "W(h)ither the Middle Class?"

25. Ibid.

26. Paul Krugman, "Like It or Not, the Income Gap Yawns," *The Wall Street Journal*, May 23, 1992, p. A13.

27. Arthur Kennickell and Janice Shack-Marquez, "Changes in Family Finances from 1983 to 1989: Evidence from the Survey of Consumer Finances," *Federal Reserve Bulletin*, Board of Governors of the Federal Reserve System, 78, no. 1, 1–18.

28. Duncan, Smeeding, and Rodgers, "W(h)ither the Middle Class?", pp. 13–15.

29. Francine Blau and Andrea Beller, "Black-White Earnings Over the 1970s and 1980s: Gender Differences in Trends," *Review of Economics and Statistics*, 74, no. 2 (May 1992), 276–286.

30. James P. Smith and Michael Ward, "Women in the Labor Market and in the Family," *Journal of Economic Perspectives*, 3, no. 1 (Winter 1989), 9–23.

31. Elaine Sorensen, "Gender and Racial Pay Gaps in the 1980s: Accounting for Different Trends," Final Report, contract no. J-9-M-0-0079, U.S. Department of Labor, The Urban Institute, Washington, DC (October 1991), p. 22.

32. Ibid.

33. Francis Blau, "Occupational Segregation by Gender: A Look at the 1980s," paper presented at the American Economic Association meetings, New York (December 1988).

34. Sorensen, "Gender and Racial Pay Gaps," pp. 24–25.

35. James P. Smith and Finis Welch, "Black Economic Progress After Myrdal," *Journal of Economic Literature*, 27, no. 2 (June 1989), 519–564.

36. June O'Neill, "The Role of Human Capital in Earnings Differences Between Black and White Men," *Journal of Economic Perspectives*, 4, no. 4 (Fall 1990), 25–46.

37. Sorensen, "Gender and Racial Pay Gaps," p. 22.

38. O'Neill, "The Role of Human Capital," p. 37.

39. O'Neill, "The Role of Human Capital," p. 22; Blau and Beller, "Black-White Earnings Over the 1970s and 1980s," pp. 276–286.

40. Robert Summers and Alan Heston, "The Penn World Table (Mark 5): An Expanded Set of International Comparisons, 1950–1988," *Quarterly Journal of Economics*, 106, no. 2 (May 1991).

41. Richard McKenzie, "America: What Went Right," *Policy Analysis*, no. 172, June 1, 1992, Cato Institute, Washington DC, p. 11.

42. Bound and Johnson, "Changes in the Structure of Wages in the 1980s," pp. 371–392.

2

The economic roller coaster

Although Chapter 1 stressed the importance of education in determining an individual's economic status and success, either unfortunately or fortunately, we don't totally control our economic future. You may work as hard as you possibly can and do everything right and "by the book," and still there are periods of time when you may not succeed, and, in fact, you may fall back. What's happening in this case is that the "economic roller coaster" is rolling over you. By economic roller coaster I mean the irregular, yet persistent, ups and downs in the economy. The economy does not grow in a straight line, but grows in fits and spurts with intermittent stalls and outright stops. You may be doing everything right in your career and still be dragged down by one of these stalls and stops. So you don't totally control your economic life.

This chapter addresses a number of issues about the economic roller coaster. Have the downturns in the economic roller coaster become milder or worse? Also, why can't government prevent the stalls, stops, and downturns in the economy and keep the economy growing on an even keel? Was the recession of 1990 to 1991 fundamentally different than previous recessions? Finally, when we look beyond the roller-coaster ups and downs in the economy at long-run economic growth, is there reason for concern about the American economy? Is our long-run economic growth rate sputtering so that our standard of living, and our children's standard of living, will not be increasing as in the past? We'll delve into each of these questions in the pages ahead.

IS THE ECONOMIC ROLLER COASTER GETTING BUMPIER?

In the 1980s the economy expanded continuously for 93 straight months, the second longest period of economic growth in U.S. history. Maybe this spoiled us because when the economy stopped growing in 1990, many people (and, importantly, many commentators) thought the economic world had come to an end. Unfortunately, Americans have short memories because if they had consulted their economic history, they would have found that the economic ride is far from smooth and, in fact, is quite bumpy.

It is commonly accepted by economists that the economy goes through cycles of ups and downs called *business cycles*. One complete business cycle is composed of an expansion phase when the economy is growing (growth is in *real terms*, that is, after taking out inflation) and a recession phase when the economy is shrinking (again in real terms). Two sample business cycles are shown in Figure 2-1. During the expansion phases, jobs are growing and people generally feel good about the economy. During the recession phases, jobs are harder to find and people feel bad about the economy.

As the figure shows, expansions blend into recessions, and recessions blend into expansions. Expansions begin with the economy growing at a rapid pace. This is sometimes called a *boom*. As the expansion begins to die, the growth rate of the economy becomes smaller and eventually becomes negative. This is when the recession begins. As the recession ends, the economy's growth rate slowly turns from negative to positive.[1]

Figure 2-1 Sample Business Cycles

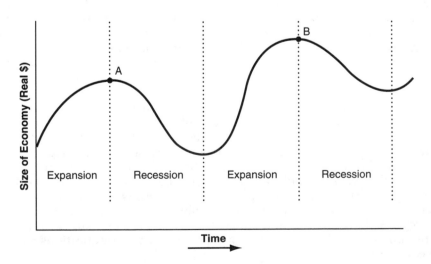

You can clearly see from Figure 2-1 how the economic roller coaster can overwhelm us. When the roller coaster heads down into a recession, most of us get pulled down with it in some way no matter how hard we work. Many people lose their jobs, others have their hours or wages cut, and others lose money on their investments. This is inevitable as long as the economic roller coaster exists and as long as we cannot perfectly predict when the downturns occur.

Considering all this, you might think that the economy never makes progress. Fortunately, the economy does make progress because the recessions tend not to wipe out all the gains made during the expansion. That is, the recessions tend not to be as deep as the expansions are high. You can see this in Figure 2-1 where the peak of the second expansion (B) is higher than the peak of the first expansion (A). Since World War II there have been nine business cycles and nine recessions. Yet, from 1945 to 1991, the total real (inflation-adjusted) income generated in the economy increased threefold, and the real income per person in the country increased 67 percent.[2]

"OK," you might say, "I'll accept this. But since life, in general, appears to have gotten more complicated, surely the economy has gotten tougher. After all, that's what some politician (no party designation intended) tells me every four years."

So have the economic downturns become longer and more frequent, and has the economic ride become bumpier? Although you may be tempted to say yes, the real answer is no! The perception that the "bad times" have become more frequent couldn't be more wrong. One of the biggest and most beneficial changes in our economy since World War II is that recessions have gotten shorter and expansions have gotten longer. This can easily be seen by looking at Figure 2-2. In Figure 2-2, the shaded areas are recessions and the unshaded areas are expansions. Recessions were obviously more frequent and expansions less frequent before 1945 than after 1945.

Let's be more specific. Before World War II, the average recession lasted 20 months and the average expansion lasted 25 months, whereas after World War II, the average recession has lasted only 10 months and the average expansion has lasted 50 months. Stated another way, 40 percent of the pre-World War II period was spent in recessions, whereas only 20 percent of the post-World War II period has been spent in recessions.[3]

So the evidence strongly suggests a shift since World War II to longer expansions and shorter recessions. But what about the bumpiness of the business cycle? That is, are the ups and downs in the business cycle less severe in the post-World War II years compared to the pre-World War II years? Has the economic ride become less or more bumpy?

There has been disagreement among economists about the bumpiness of the business cycle in the periods before and after World War II, but today the pendulum seems to be on the side of less bumpiness. Balke and Gordon painstakingly reviewed the studies on economic volatility and also conducted their own research. To be fair, they excluded the depression years of the 1930s and the World War II years, since both were very bumpy eco-

1855 1865 1875 1885 1895 1905 1915 1925 1935 1945 1955 1965 1975 1985 1995

Note: Recessionary episodes are shaded.

Source: Francis X. Diebold and Glenn P. Rudenbusch, "Shorter Recessions and Longer Expansions," *Business Review*, Federal Reserve Bank of Philadelphia (November/December 1991), p. 15.

Figure 2-2 *Expansions and Recessions, 1855–1991*

nomic periods. They found that all the studies pointed to the 1869–1928 period being between 26 percent and 113 percent more volatile economically than the postwar period of 1947 to 1986.[4]

So the evidence points to the post-World War II period being both economically more stable and having longer periods of growth than the prewar period. But why? That's a good question, which has not been easily answered by economists. Two reasons are typically offered. One popular with economists states that economists in the post-World War II period know more about how the economy operates, and this knowledge has been transferred to economic policymakers. For example, economists now know the importance of the Federal Reserve in supplying sufficient credit to the economy to pull out of a recession. The Federal Reserve did not do this during the 1930s and, of course, the Federal Reserve did not exist during the nineteenth century.

Second, some economists think that structural changes in our economy have increased economic stability and reduced the bumpiness of the economic ride. There are three factors involved here. First, consumers have had greater access to credit in the postwar period. This has allowed consumers to continue to borrow even during recessions. Such borrowing and spending during recessions have reduced their severity.

The second structural factor is the use of new technical knowledge by firms to better manage inventories. This is important because a buildup of inventories during expansions can be a cause of job layoffs in recessions. Firms like to keep products in stock (inventories) during expansions so they can readily meet customer demands. However, when a recession hits and customer demand declines, firms don't need as many inventories, so they decrease production of products and lay off workers. Furthermore, the greater the extent to which firms have built up inventories during the expansion, the greater they will shut down production during the recession and the more workers they will dismiss. If firms can more accurately forecast demand, they will be better able to match production to customer demand and avoid a large buildup of inventories. New technical knowledge, especially using computers, has enabled firms to do this better in the postwar period.[5]

Finally, service and trade employment tends to be more stable than manufacturing employment because firms have traditionally been more likely to lay off manufacturing workers during recessions than service and trade workers. Because service and trade employment has grown relative to manufacturing employment since World War II, the employment picture has become more stable compared to the prewar time period. This improved stability in employment has led to improved stability in income, which in turn has lessened the severity of recessions.

So we've made the business cycle more stable—but why can't we eliminate it, and in particular, why can't we eliminate the recessions? I'll get to this question, but first let's look at the most recent recession of 1990 to 1991 in more detail.

HOW BAD WAS THE 1990–91 RECESSION?

Most of you reading this book will remember the 1990–91 recession. This is the recession which ended the 93-month economic expansion of the 1980s. It was the recession that ended the Bush administration and helped elect Bill Clinton to the presidency. It was the recession which some said put the economy in the worst shape in 50 years.[6]

There are two purposes to this section. First, you'll learn more about recessions, how to tell when they begin and when they end, and how to measure their severity. Second, we'll compare the 1990–91 recession to previous recessions to see if the most recent recession was more or less severe and to see if it was different in any fundamental way.

Recessions begin when the overall economic growth rate turns negative, meaning the economy begins to shrink in size, and ends when the economic growth rate turns positive, meaning the economy begins growing again. By convention, the economic growth rate must be negative for two consecutive quarters (six months) for an official recession to be declared. A nonprofit organization of professional economists, the National Bureau of Economic Research, is charged with declaring the beginnings and endings of recessions.[7]

The severity of a recession is measured by the percentage of shrinkage in the size of the economy during the recession. The size of the economy is again measured by the concept of gross national product (or gross domestic product), which is simply the total income generated in the economy during a specified period (such as a year). Recessions that shrink the economy by a greater percentage are considered more severe than recessions that shrink the economy by a lesser percentage.

Although the percentage shrinkage in GNP is the main measure of a recession's severity, economists also look at other complementary measures, such as the increase in the unemployment rate and the percentage declines in consumer spending and in investment.

With this background, how bad was the 1990–91 recession compared to other recessions? The answer is shown in Table 2-1. By almost all the measures, the 1990–91 recession was milder than previous recessions. In terms of length, the recession lasted eight months compared to an average of 11 months for other postwar recessions and 14 months for all recessions since 1919. The decline in real (inflation-adjusted) gross national product was only one-third as severe as the average for other postwar recessions and only one-sixth as severe as the average for all recessions since 1919. Likewise, real investment fell less, the unemployment rate rose less, and real net exports rose more in 1990 to 1991 compared to previous recessions.[8] Only real consumption fared worse during the most recent recession compared to previous recessions.

But was the 1990–91 recession different in ways not reflected in these statistics causing people to view it as more severe? The answer is yes, and it primarily has to do with the type of job losses. During the typical recession, blue-collar or production workers suffer greater relative increases in unemployment than white-collar (managerial, technical, professional, and sales) workers. This occurred for two reasons. First, blue-collar jobs are more directly tied to production level than white-collar jobs. Therefore,

Table 2-1 Recessions Compared

PERCENT CHANGE IN:[a]	1990–91 RECESSION[b]	OTHER POST-WORLD WAR II RECESSIONS	OTHER RECESSIONS SINCE 1919
Length in months	8	11	14
Real GNP	−0.8%	−2.4%	−5.4%
Real Consumption	−0.6%	+0.4%	−0.5%
Real Investment[c]	−11.0%	−19.5%	−27.8%
Real Government Purchases	+1.1%	+1.7%	+3.3%
Real Net Exports	+115.9%	+10.9%	+17.5%
Unemployment Rate	+1.3% pts.	+2.7% pts.	+4.5% pts.
Interest Rate[d]	−2.0 pts.	−2.1% pts.	−2.0% pts.

[a]Percent changes are annualized averages over the period; changes for unemployment rate and interest rate are total percentage point changes over the period.

[b]July 1990 to March 1991.

[c]Real private gross domestic investment.

[d]Three-month commercial paper rate.

Source: Thomas E. Hall, *Business Cycles: The Nature and Cause of Economic Fluctuations* (New York: Praeger, 1990), pp. 15–17; U.S. Department of Commerce, *Survey of Current Business*, 1991.

when production levels fall during a recession, relatively more blue-collar jobs were traditionally cut than white-collar jobs. Second, the pay of white-collar workers has been more flexible than the pay of blue-collar workers. Thus, rather than having their jobs cut during a recession, white-collar workers could keep their jobs but see their bonuses or profit sharing decline.

The relative immunity of white-collar workers to recessions appears to have changed in the 1990–91 recession. In an analysis of the six recessions since 1960, Groshen and Williams found that, consistent with the measures in Table 2-1, the increases in the unemployment rates for both white-collar and blue-collar workers were not as severe in the 1990–91 recession as in the other recessions. However, for the first time in the six recessions studied, in the 1990–91 recession the percentage increase in the unemployment rate for white-collar workers was *greater* than the percentage increase in the unemployment rate for blue-collar workers (see Table 2-2). Also, whereas in the other five recessions white-collar employment continued to grow during the recession (by an average of 1.8 percent), during the 1990–91 recession white-collar employment barely increased (by 0.3 percent). Therefore, the 1990–91 recession was relatively harder on white-collar workers.[9]

The other way that the 1990–91 recession was different was in the division between permanent and temporary job losses. The Bureau of Labor Statistics divides job losses into those classified as permanent and those classified as temporary.[10] Unfortunately, these data only go back to 1977, so they span only three recessions. Comparing the 1980, 1981–82, and 1990–91 recessions, there's clearly a trend which became even more pronounced from 1990 to 1991. In the 1990–91 recession, 72 percent of the rise in the unemployment rate was due to permanent job losses. This is in comparison to permanent job losses accounting for 65 percent of the job losses from 1981 to 1982 and 47 percent of the job losses in 1980. So although the total unemployment rate in the most recent recession peaked at a much lower level than in the previous 1981–82 recession (7.8 percent from 1990 to 1991 compared to 11 percent from 1981 to 1982), the higher percentage of permanent job losses from 1990 to 1991 certainly increased its severity.

Table 2-2   Impacts of Recessions on White-Collar and Blue-Collar Unemployment

RECESSION	PERCENT INCREASE IN UNEMPLOYMENT RATE:		RATIO OF WHITE-COLLAR INCREASE TO BLUE-COLLAR INCREASE
	WHITE COLLAR	BLUE COLLAR	
1960–61	28.1%	37.9%	0.74
1969–70	61.0	68.1	0.90
1973–75	69.6	126.1	0.55
1980	11.2	41.0	0.27
1981–82	39.6	67.5	0.59
1990–91	25.4	23.9	1.07

Source: Erica Groshen and Donald Williams, "White- and Blue-Collar Jobs in the Recent Recession and Recovery: Who's Singing the Blues?" *Economic Review*, 28, no. 4 (1992), Federal Reserve Bank of Cleveland, pp. 2–12.

WHY CAN'T WE ELIMINATE THE BUSINESS CYCLE?

Now we're ready to address this very important question. You've now learned that the ups and downs in the economy (the business cycle, or economic roller coaster as I've termed it) are the norm and not the exception in economic life. Although the frequency of recessions and the bumpiness of the economic ride have been reduced since World War II, the economy has still moved one step back for every four steps forward in the postwar period. Why can't we eliminate that one backward step and always move forward in our economic trek?

The real question is why we have recessions, and this is a very good question indeed. As usual, economists don't agree on the answer, but we have plenty of possibilities.

Some economists argue that expansions naturally sow the seeds of their own recession. As expansions continue, more and more capital goods such as office buildings, factories, and housing developments are built. Eventually, there are too many of these capital goods relative to the demand for them, so an oversupply exists, and the value of capital goods begins to fall. The falling values of capital goods cause businesses and consumers to reduce spending and bring on a recession. During the recession, capital good construction slows considerably or stops. Eventually this creates a shortage of capital goods, and construction speeds up and a new economic expansion begins. Some economists think the 1990–91 recession is a good example of this theory.

Other economists emphasize the role of the Federal Reserve System in the business cycle. The Federal Reserve System is the central bank of the United States, and as such, it has a great deal of control over the money and credit supplies of the country. The Federal Reserve can encourage an expansion by creating more money and credit, but if this is overdone, higher inflation rates and higher interest rates occur. Then, in order to reduce inflation and interest rates, the Federal Reserve puts the brakes on the money and credit supplies. But this makes it harder for businesses and consumers to borrow money, and so borrowing and spending slow and a recession results. The 1981–82 recession, which followed the high-inflation years in the late 1970s, is a good example of a recession induced by the Federal Reserve.[11]

Recently, economists have emphasized the role of special events, so-called "shocks" to the economy, in causing recessions. Disruptions to oil supplies, reductions in labor supply due to low birth rates, new business regulations, and changes in production technology are examples of shocks which, if severe enough, can send the economy into a recession. Certainly the Arab oil embargo of 1974 helped cause the 1974–75 recession.[12]

So if we know what causes recessions, then why can't the government take suitable actions to "head them off at the pass"? Well, some economists do think that government policies should act as a counterbalance to the business cycle, and particularly to recessions. In fact, it has been the official policy of the federal government since 1946 to do just that. The idea is that when the economy goes into a recession, the federal government should spend additional money and/or cut taxes (this is called fiscal poli-cy), and the Federal Reserve should pump additional money and credit into the economy (this is called monetary policy), in order to avert or at least to moderate the recession. Likewise, when the economy is booming, the feder-al government would reduce spending and/or raise taxes, and the Federal Reserve would slow the growth of money and credit in order to temper the boom and keep inflation in check.

These actions are generally called *stabilization policy*, and they look good on paper. But many economists are skeptical of stabilization policy, and some go so far as to claim that stabilization policy can actually make the business cycle bumpier![13] Stabilization policy is based on the premise that government economists can tell where the economy is in the business cycle at any point in time, and the government can take action quickly to moder-ate the cycle. But in reality this isn't the case. In reality, it takes most eco-nomic forecasters, both inside and outside the government, several months (maybe up to a year) to determine a new trend in the economy. This means it may be several months before the government can change fiscal and mon-etary policy to address the new trend in the economy. By this time, the recession or expansion may be over (remember that the average postwar recession has lasted only 11 months).

For example, suppose the economy goes into a recession, which lasts the average 11 months. However, it takes the government a year from the start of the recession to establish that it has occurred. At this point, the recession is actually over and an expansion is beginning. But, because the government has just detected the (now over) recession, antirecession fiscal and monetary policies are put in place. However, these policies are begun during an expansion, which the government hasn't yet detected. Therefore, the antirecession policies are unnecessary and actually speed up the expan-sion and increase the chance of higher inflation.

It is for this reason that some economists claim that activist govern-ment policies, designed to smooth the economic ride, actually make the ride rockier. These economists argue that a better economic policy would be for the government to maintain stable fiscal and monetary policies (that is, a stable rate of growth of the money and credit supply and stable tax and spending policies) and accept that the economy will go through ups and downs.[14] Unfortunately, we don't yet have the knowledge or ability to pre-vent this roller coaster.

But remember, even though the economy does go through a con-stant roller coaster, expansions have won out over recessions and the econo-my has tended to grow over time. However, there is increasing concern about the speed of this long-run growth. Let's look at this issue next.

HAS LONG-RUN GROWTH SLOWED?

Long-run economic growth refers to the rate at which the economy grows when averaged out over several business cycles. For example, in Figure 2-1, the long-run growth rate would be measured from point A to point B. Since expansions have been much longer than recessions in the postwar period, this long-run economic growth rate has been positive.

Currently there is a concern that the long-run economic growth rate in the United States has slowed from what it used to be. Many analysts and commentators are worried about the apparent slow recovery of the U.S. economy from the 1990–91 recession.[15] Why should the average citizen be concerned if the annual long-run economic growth rate is 2 percent rather than 3 percent? Big deal! What would all the fuss be about a difference of one percentage point?

Well, the fuss is that a difference of one percentage point can have a big impact on how fast the average person's standard of living grows over time. The faster the long-run economic growth rate, the faster the average citizen's standard of living increases. For example, if the annual long-run economic growth rate is 3 percent rather than 2 percent, then after ten years the average citizen's standard of living will be 55 percent higher; after 20 years it will be 65 percent higher; and after 30 years it will be 77 percent higher! Think of all the additional products you could buy and the more you could do if your standard of living (e.g., your real income) was 77 percent higher. This should be enough motivation for you to be interested in the issue of long-run economic growth.

There are many who are concerned that the long-run economic growth rate in the United States has significantly fallen in recent years. For example, DeLong and Summers calculate that the average annual long-run economic growth rate in the 1970s and 1980s was only 0.9 percent compared to an average of 2.3 percent during the 1950s and 1960s.[16] If the recent long-run economic growth rate continues, then the average standard of living will be only two-thirds of what it would have been in 30 years if the growth rate during the 1950s and 1960s had prevailed.

But is this the correct comparison? Should the long-run economic growth rate of the 1950s and 1960s be the standard? There are two reasons to think not. First, all industrialized countries have experienced a drop in their long-run economic growth rate in the last 20 years. For example, Japan's average annual long-run economic growth rate in the 1970s and 1980s was only 49 percent of its rate in the 1950s and 1960s, and Germany's rate in the 1970s and 1980s was only 39 percent of its rate in the 1950s and 1960s. Also, using more recent comparisons, the United States is one of only two industrialized countries (with Canada) that experienced an increase in the long-run economic growth rate in the 1980s compared to the 1970s.[17]

More importantly, if a longer view of economic growth in the United States is taken, then it is not obvious that recent growth is slow. Figure 2-3 is constructed from data calculated by Professor Robert Barro. Barro has been careful to calculate growth rates per *person*. This is important because, obviously, everything else equal, the faster population growth is, the faster economic growth will be. Barro's numbers show that there has been no noticeable decline in the average annual long-run economic growth rate in the United States in recent years. Barro estimates that the U.S. economy has been growing at an average annual real rate of 1.6 percent since 1880. Part of the reason for the observed faster growth rates in the 1950s and

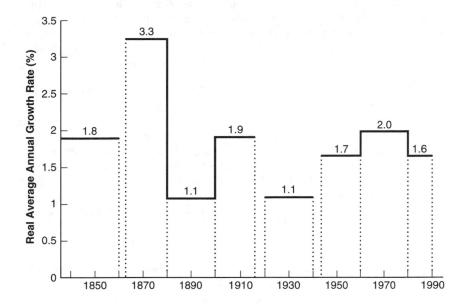

Source: Constructed from data in Robert Barro, *Macroeconomics*, 4th ed., New York, John Wiley & Sons, Inc., 1993, p. 285.

Figure 2-3   Long-run Economic Growth Rates in the United States

1960s reported earlier was the faster population growth rates in those decades. Between 1947 and 1960 the U.S. population grew at an average annual rate of 1.7 percent; in the 1980s the U.S. population grew at an average annual rate of only 1 percent.[18]

So it does not appear that recent long-run economic growth in the United States is abnormally low.[19] The comparison of recent growth to the 1950s and 1960s is misleading because growth in those decades appears to be abnormally high; growth then was probably high due to the recovery of the private economy from World War II. Also, growth in the 1970s was certainly lower than average because of the two oil price shocks in that decade.

Nevertheless, both recent (1970s and 1980s) and postwar long-run growth in the United States has been below the growth rates of many other industrialized countries. If we want to raise our long-run economic growth rate, what can we do? There's no shortage of prescriptions. The standard prescription to increasing long-run economic growth is to increase investment in new technologies, new factories, and new state-of-the-art equipment.[20] Although certainly there is always room to increase these activities, there is no evidence that these types of investments have slowed recently in the United States.[21] For example, factory and equipment spending as a percentage of the total economy (gross national product) actually rose in the 1980s. (I'll provide detailed statistics on this in Chapter 6.)

Another focus is on investment in worker skills and education. Professor Barro finds that a 10 percent increase in educational attainment is associated with a 0.2 percent increase in the annual long-run economic growth rate.[22] Clearly, better educated and skilled workers are more productive workers, and more productive workers increase the long-run economic growth rate.

Tax and regulatory policies in the United States and their impacts on economic growth have come under increasing criticism. In the 1980s the tax on long-term capital investments (the capital gains tax) was increased, many business investment deductions were limited, and the effective corporate income tax was doubled. There is also evidence that the costs to businesses of complying with government regulations, which fell in the early and mid-1980s, rose in the late 1980s and early 1990s. This is important because Professor Thomas Hopkins of the Rochester Institute of Technology has found a negative correlation between regulatory costs and long-run economic growth.[23] This can occur through the impact of higher regulatory costs increasing the costs of business and reducing profit margins.

Finally, Professor Barro has recently focused on the role of government spending and its size relative to the size of the economy on long-run economic growth. With empirical support for his argument, Barro states that larger relative government spending on transfer programs to redistribute income is associated with lower long-run economic growth rates.[24] The reason is that transfer programs can reduce incentives for individual work effort. Barro also finds that government investment in infrastructure is unrelated to economic growth.

These findings suggest an agenda for increasing long-run economic growth. Certainly education and worker training are important, and efforts should be made to improve the quality and results of public education and worker training programs. As we will see in Chapter 4, these programs have not suffered from a lack of financial resources, so improvement may not necessarily come from spending more money.

Tax and regulatory policy should be reexamined for their impact on long-run economic growth. Presumably, regulations are passed with beneficial goals in mind (such as reducing pollution, increasing worker safety, and increasing job access for all Americans). However, it should be recognized that these regulations impose costs on businesses and may very well slow economic growth. The costs and slower economic growth should be compared to the estimated benefits of the regulations in deciding on the merit of the regulations.

Finally, the relative size of government spending should be reviewed not only for its impact on taxes and the deficit, but for its potential impact on long-run economic growth. If larger government slows the growth of the private economy, then long-run economic growth is enhanced if government size is controlled. Of course, controlling the size of government can also have beneficial effects on the tax burden and deficit. We'll discuss these issues in Chapters 4 and 5. But first, let's turn to another aspect of our standard of living, that is, how much we're saving and how much we're going into debt.

NOTES

1. The business cycles discussed here are typically four to six years in length. Some economists and historians argue that the economy also goes through longer waves of growth, with the business cycles within these long waves. See Brian Berry, *Long-Wave Rhythms in Economic Development and Political Behavior* (Baltimore: The Johns Hopkins University Press, 1991).

2. Data are from the *Economic Report of the President*.

3. Francis X. Diebold and Glenn P. Rudebusch, "Shorter Recessions and Longer Expansions," *Business Review*, Federal Reserve Bank of Philadelphia (November/December 1991), p. 15.

4. Nathan Balke and Robert Gordon, "The Estimation of Prewar Gross National Product: Methodology and New Evidence," *Journal of Political Economy*, 97, no. 1 (February 1989), 38–92. Much of the debate about volatility of the business cycle hinges on the quality of pre-World War II data. See Christina Romer, "Is the Stabilization of the Postwar Economy a Figment of the Data?" *American Economics Review*, 76, no. 3 (June 1986), 314–334.

5. For a documentation of improved inventory management, see "Companies' Slimmed-Down Inventory Picture," *The Wall Street Journal*, November 3, 1992, p. A2.

6. See Alan Reynolds, "The Worst Lying About the Economy in the Past 50 Years," *The Wall Street Journal*, October 21, 1991, p. A16; and Robert Hall and John Taylor, "Economic Scare Stories," *The New York Times*, October 16, 1992, p. A31.

7. For a discussion of the procedures used by the National Bureau of Economic Research to date recessions, see Robert Hall, "The Business Cycle Dating Process," *NBER Reporter*, Cambridge, MA, National Bureau of Economic Research (Winter 1991/92), pp. 1–3.

8. The unemployment rate in the 1990–91 recession continued to rise after the official end of the recession in March 1991. It peaked at 7.8 percent in July 1992. This still represented only a 2.2 percentage point increase from the 5.6 percent rate in August 1990, and still made the rise in the unemployment rate during the 1990–91 recession smaller than during the previous average recession.

9. Erica Groshen and Donald Williams, "White- and Blue-Collar Jobs in the Recent Recession and Recovery: Who's Singing the Blues?" *Economic Review*, 28, no. 4 (1992), Federal Reserve Bank of Cleveland, pp. 2–12.

10. U.S. Bureau of Labor Statistics, *Monthly Labor Review*, Current Labor Statistics, Table 8.

11. The classic works on monetary policy and business cycles are Milton Friedman and Anna Schwartz, *A Monetary History of the U.S., 1867–1960* (Princeton: Princeton University Press, 1963); and Milton Friedman and Anna Schwartz, *Monetary Trends in the U.S. and U.K., Their Relation to Income, Prices, and Interest Rates, 1867–1975* (Chicago: The University of Chicago Press, 1982).

12. See Robert Barro, *Macroeconomics*, 4th ed. (New York: John Wiley and Sons, Inc. 1993), p. 23; John Long and Charles Plosser, "Real Business Cycles: A New Keynesian Perspective," *Journal of Economic Perspectives*, 3, no. 3 (Summer 1989), 79–90.

13. See Milton Friedman, "The Effects of a Full-Employment Policy on Economic Stability: A Formal Analysis," in *Essays in Positive Economics*, (Chicago: University of Chicago Press, 1953), pp. 117–132; Gerald Dwyer, Jr., "Stabilization Policy Can Lead to Chaos," *Economic Inquiry*, 30, no. 1 (January 1992), 40–46.

14. Allan Meltzer, "Limits of Short-Run Stabilization Policy," *Economic Inquiry*, 25, no. 1 (January 1987), 1–14.

15. Adrian Throop, "The Slow Recovery," Federal Reserve Bank of San Francisco Weekly Letter, No. 92-33, September 25, 1992.

16. J. Bradford DeLong and Lawrence Summers, "Macroeconomic Policy and Long-Run Growth," in *Policies for Long-Run Economic Growth* (Kansas City, MO: Federal Reserve Bank of Kansas City, 1992), pp. 93–128. However, Darby thinks that recent growth has been underestimated due to problems in measuring the output of services. See Michael Darby, "Causes of Declining Growth," in *Policies for Long-Run Economic Growth*, pp. 5–14.

17. DeLong and Summers, *Policies for Long-Run Economic Growth*, p. 96.

18. Barro, *Macroeconomics*, pp. 284–285.

19. Meltzer comes to the same conclusion using slightly different data than Barro; Allan Meltzer, "Commentary," in *Policies for Long-Run Economic Growth* (Kansas City, MO: Federal Reserve Bank of Kansas City, 1992), pp. 141–148.

20. DeLong and Summers, *Policies for Long-Run Economic Growth*, pp. 114–116.

21. Lawrence Kudlow, "Commentary," in *Policies for Long-Run Economic Growth* (Kansas City, MO: Federal Reserve Bank of Kansas City, 1992), pp. 135–140.

22. Robert Barro, "Human Capital and Economic Growth," in *Policies for Long-Run Economic Growth* (Kansas City, MO: Federal Reserve Bank of Kansas City, 1992), pp. 199–216.

23. Thomas Hopkins, *Cost of Regulation*, RIT working paper, Rochester Institute of Technology, 1991.

24. Robert Barro, "Economic Growth in a Cross Section of Countries," *Quarterly Journal of Economics*, 106 (1991), 407–443. Peden and Bradley also find a negative relationship between government size and productivity in the private economy; see Edgar Peden and Michael Bradley, "Government Size, Productivity, and Economic Growth: The Post-War Experience," *Public Choice*, 61, no. 3 (June 1989), 229–246. Karras estimates that the optimal size of government is 20 percent of gross domestic product; see (Georgios Karras, "Employment and Output Effects of Government Spending: Is Government Size Important?" *Economic Inquiry*, 31, no. 3 (July 1993), 354–369.

3

Saving and debt

Americans have been criticized for their saving and debt habits in recent years. In fact, the 1980s has been called the "decade of debt" because allegedly both consumers and businesses built up mountains of debt. Some see this as irresponsible behavior, which will eventually come back to haunt the country. These critics see the increase in debt as an indication that Americans are a short-sighted people who only "live for the moment."[1]

The flip side of the alleged debt buildup is the alleged shrinkage in saving by Americans. Statistics are frequently quoted indicating that the rate at which Americans are saving for the future is at very low levels compared to historical rates.

Borrowing, which creates debt, and saving are related. By saving, a person is putting aside resources today for use in the future. Conversely, by borrowing, a person is transferring resources which will be earned in the future for use today. If borrowing is up and saving is down, then does this mean that Americans are indeed throwing aside all concern for the future and only living for today? These important questions and issues are addressed in this chapter.

HOW MUCH ARE WE REALLY SAVING?

Consumers save for a variety of reasons. A young couple might save for a future down payment on a new house. A teenager might save money earned from an after-school job to buy a car. Middle-aged consumers save for their retirement years. What all these motives have in common is that saving reduces consumption today in order to increase consumption sometime in the future. That is, the young couple saving for the house down payment could have spent that money today on a vacation or on new clothes. Instead, they will go without the vacation or new clothes in exchange for buying a new house in the future. They are trading off less current consumption for more future consumption.

There's nothing inherently "good" about saving and "bad" about not saving, simply because there's nothing inherently "good" about more future consumption and "bad" about more current consumption. Consumers make decisions about saving based on their current economic situation, their expected future economic situation, and the rewards for saving. Young consumers, especially those just beginning their career and with young children, typically save little because demands for current consumption are so great and income is low. In contrast, middle-aged consumers, who are at the peak of their career and whose children are "gone from the nest" and on their own, typically save more because demands for current consumption are low and retirement (when work income will fall to zero) is right around the corner.

Economists also argue that consumers' saving behavior responds to the rewards for saving. The primary economic reward for saving is the real after-tax interest rate, which is simply the interest earned on savings after subtracting what must be paid in taxes and after subtracting that part of interest earnings eaten up by inflation. The latter component is important because inflation reduces the purchasing power of future dollars. A dollar today will purchase a dollar's worth of goods and services. But if inflation over the next year is 10 percent, then a dollar next year will only buy 90 cents worth of goods and services.

An example will help clarify the real after-tax interest rate. Suppose you save money in an investment and earn 10 percent interest after a year. Suppose you will pay 30 percent of the interest earnings in taxes. This is equivalent to 3 percent of the interest earnings, so you are left with 7 percent after taxes. Now suppose that during the year the inflation rate was 5 percent, meaning that the average increase in the prices of goods and services was 5 percent. This means that by saving your money and not spending, you have suffered the cost of seeing prices rise by 5 percent. This reduces your after-tax return of 7 percent by another 5 percent to only 2 percent. Therefore, your reward for saving, after accounting for both taxes and inflation, is only 2 percent. This is the real (for after inflation) after-tax interest rate. The point is that consumers will be motivated to save more as the real after-tax interest rate increases.[2]

There is a bigger role for savings in the economy besides that which allows consumers to adjust their consumption over time by moving resources from the present to the future. This is the role of savings in the economy's overall economic growth. For businesses to be able to borrow money to invest in new technology and equipment, consumers must supply the money for borrowing through their savings (or, alternatively, foreign consumers must supply the money for borrowing).

With this background, what can be said about saving by Americans in recent years? The savings rate that is most often quoted is the *personal savings rate*. The personal savings rate purports to show that fraction of consumers' after-tax income that isn't consumed today. Indeed, as shown in Figure 3-1, the trend in the personal savings rate has been down since the early 1970s. In 1989 the personal savings rate hit a low of 4 percent, compared to rates consistently between 6 and 10 percent in the 1960s and 1970s.

Before taking the dismal record of savings indicated by the personal savings rate at face value, consider the fact that the personal savings rate doesn't include all types of savings. The biggest source of savings by Americans is the equity buildup in their homes (home equity is the difference between the market value of a home and the balance owed on the mortgage).[3] The personal savings rate doesn't include the savings that homeowners accumulate each year when the equity in the home rises. Also, the personal savings rate does not directly measure changes in stock and bond values, which certainly also add to savings if they increase.

Another significant component of savings not included in the personal savings rate is the savings employees and employers make in the form of social security contributions. Social security is a form of forced savings, required by the government, which Americans make for their retirement. This is even more true since the changes made to social security in the 1980s, which altered it from a pay-as-you-go system to a system which accumulates surpluses for future retirees.

Figure 3-1 shows two alternative measures of savings rates, which correct the flaws of the personal savings rate. The savings rate by individuals is compiled by the Federal Reserve System and includes savings from changes in home equity and stock and bond investments. In 1990 this rate was 8.9 percent, and the rate has shown little trend over the past 45 years.

Figure 3-1   Alternative Savings Rates

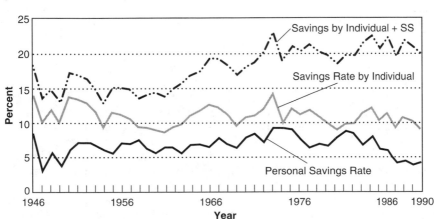

Source: *Economic Report of the President.*

However, an even more dramatic impact on the savings rate is seen in Figure 3-1 when social security contributions are added to the savings rate by individuals. By this measure, Americans are saving at almost a 20 percent rate, and this savings rate has been much higher in the 1970s and 1980s than in the 1950s and 1960s.[4]

Other economists who have studied savings rates have found similar results; that is, Americans are saving as much or more than in previous decades. For example, when economists at the Federal Reserve Bank of Boston added home equity savings to other savings, they found savings rates in the 1980s were actually higher than rates in the 1950s, 1960s, and 1970s.[5] Professor Robert Eisner uses a different methodology to find savings rates much higher than those commonly reported. Robert Blecker uses increases in inflation-adjusted household net worth as savings and finds savings rates in the 1980s at 11 percent annually.[6]

As suggested earlier, the demographic makeup of a country likely has an impact on savings rates, and some studies have suggested that the relative increase in low-savings demographic groups (young households and old households) in the United States in the 1980s lowered the savings rate in that decade. This should change in the future. Meyer estimates that the proportion of the U.S. population in the prime saving years (thought to be between 45 and 64 years old) will increase from 18.5 percent to 28 percent of the population between 1990 and 2010. At the same time, the share of the population in the low-saving years (thought to be under 20 years old or over 65 years old) will decline from 40 percent to 38 percent between 1990 and 2010. Meyer estimates that these demographic changes alone will increase the U.S. savings rate by 3.5 to 4 percentage points by the year 2010.[7]

If it is decided by politicians, policymakers, and economic advisors that consumers should save more, then tax policies could be changed to boost savings. The first thing to do would be to only tax investment rates of return that exceed the inflation rate, that is, only tax the real rate of return. In our example at the beginning of this section in which the consumer earned a 10 percent interest rate on savings and the inflation rate was 5 percent, this would mean taxing only the real return of 5 percent rather than the total return of 10 percent.

The second tax policy to change would be to stop the double taxation of dividends paid by corporations to stockholders. Under current tax law, corporate dividends are taxed twice, first by the corporate income tax as the dividends are earned at the corporate level, and second by the personal income tax when the dividends are passed on to stockholders. Since corporations are merely collections of individual shareholders, it would make the most sense to end the corporate taxation of dividends and only tax them at the individual level. Of course, in line with my first suggestion, only real (inflation-adjusted) dividends would be taxed.

Therefore, when studied in more detail, it appears that Americans have not lost their frugality, and saving is alive and well in the United States. But what about the flip side of saving—borrowing? Are we collectively "up to our eyeballs" in debt? I turn to this issue next.

HAVE WE OVERLOADED ON DEBT?

Borrowing is the flip side of saving. When consumers save, they transfer current resources to the future. When consumers borrow, they transfer expected future resources to the present and are able to increase current consumption at the expense of lower future consumption. Borrowing and saving both allow consumers to move resources to points of time where their use has the highest value to the consumer.

As already emphasized, demographics have a big influence on borrowing as well as on saving. Specifically, relatively young consumers in their twenties and thirties, who are raising children and buying houses, cars, and appliances, are the biggest borrowers.[8] They find it valuable to transfer expected future resources to the child-rearing and household-building years.

Other factors influence borrowing. The real after-tax interest rate, a factor which influences saving, affects borrowing in the opposite direction. The real after-tax interest rate is the price of borrowing a dollar for a year. For example, if the real after-tax interest rate is 4 percent, then the consumer must pay 4 cents in interest costs annually for every dollar borrowed. Therefore, the higher the real after-tax interest rate, the more expensive is borrowing and the less borrowing that will take place. Conversely, the lower the real after-tax interest rate, the less expensive is borrowing and the more borrowing that will take place.

Finally, consumer or business income or wealth will allow the support of more debt. For example, a $50,000 debt to someone earning only $10,000 annually will probably create debt problems for that individual, whereas a $50,000 debt to someone earning $150,000 annually will likely create no debt problems. This means it's always important to evaluate debt in relation to income or wealth.

So what has happened to private borrowing and debt in America? Have both consumers and businesses lost all grasp of common sense and borrowed "up to their collective eyeballs"? There's no question that private debt has expanded rapidly. For example, consumers increased their debt a whopping 166 percent between 1980 and 1990, from $1.5 trillion to $4 trillion! Businesses were not far behind, with business debt rising from $1.3 trillion in 1980 to $3.4 trillion in 1990, a 161 percent increase![9]

By these measures, it is easy to conclude that consumers and businesses have gone on a borrowing spree. But as I've emphasized, looking at debt is only half of the issue. The other half of the issue is the income or assets used to support the debt. Debt can responsibly increase if the income or assets owned by consumers and businesses likewise increase.

A commonly tracked measure of the relative size of consumer debt is the ratio of consumer installment debt to consumer income. Consumer installment debt is debt used to purchase cars, appliances, furniture, and any other consumer durable good except houses. The ratio of consumer installment debt to consumer income did rise to record levels in the 1980s, but the record was not that far out of line with previous highs. At the end of the economic expansion of the 1970s, the installment debt to income ratio was 13.5 percent. At the end of the economic expansion of the 1980s, the installment debt to income ratio was 16 percent, but by 1993 the ratio had fallen to 14 percent.[10] Some economists attribute the rise, albeit modest, in the consumer installment debt to income ratio to the increasing availability of credit cards in the 1980s.[11]

Other measures of the relative size of private debt show even more modest increases. This measure is the ratio of debt to assets. Assets, of course, are the value of what a consumer or business owns. The notion is that the greater the size of assets, the more debt a consumer or business can carry. Figure 3-2 shows this ratio for both consumers and businesses. The ratio for consumers shows a gradual rise over the past 40 years, but with no noticeable acceleration in recent years. (The consumer debt to asset ratio rose from 13.4 percent in 1980 to 16.3 percent in 1989.) The ratio for businesses shows a large increase in the 1980s, but this followed a big drop in the ratio in the 1970s.[12] The ratio of business debt to assets in 1989 stood at 43.8 percent, changing little from 41.1 percent in 1970.

Also, it appears that demographics certainly had an impact on debt in the 1980s. The percentage of households in the prime borrowing years (ages 25 to 44) rose from 24 percent in 1970 to 28 percent in 1980 to 33 percent in 1990.[13] However, as these baby boomers become middle-aged in the 1990s and beyond, aggregate debt ratios may fall.

Although relative U.S. debt ratios are not far out of line with historical trends, but how do U.S. debt ratios compare to debt ratios for other countries?

Total debt, including both private and public (government) debt as a percent either of total assets in the country or as a percent of national income, is not the highest in the United States. In fact, the U.S. trails Japan and Germany on both measures.[14]

Figure 3-2   Total Debt as a Percent of Total Assets

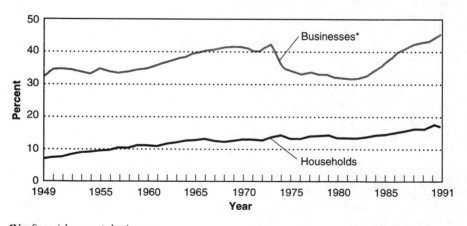

*Nonfinancial corporate businesses.

Source: Board of Governors of the Federal Reserve System, *Balance Sheets for the U.S. Economy, 1945–92,* March 1993.

One other bothersome aspect of debt is whether a buildup of debt can become too much of a burden to consumers so that consumers must reduce spending on products and services in order to service the debt. The reduced spending then causes a recession. So can debt buildup eventually send the economy into a downturn?

Economists who have studied trends in debt and in the national business cycle have thrown cold water on this concern. They find that changes in debt *follow* changes in the general economy rather than lead those changes.[15] Consumers take on more debt when the economy is improving, and consumers reduce their debt burden after the economy sours. The state of the overall economy is the dog wagging the debt tail, rather than the reverse.

So, yes, consumer and business debt have increased in recent years, but when compared to either the increase in income or the increase in assets, the jump has been slight and not out of line with historical trends.

NOTES

1. For a critical view of the debt buildup of the 1980s, see Larry Reibstein, et al., "Tapped Out for the Holidays: The Personal Debt Crisis," *Newsweek*, December 10, 1990, p. 54; Christopher Ferrell, "Learning to Kick the Debt Habit," *Business Week*, March 12, 1990, p. 112; and Fred Bleakley, "A Decade of Debt Is Now Giving Way to the Age of Equity," *The Wall Street Journal*, December 16, 1991, p. A1.

2. For evidence that saving behavior responds to the real after-tax interest rate, see A. Lans Bovenberg and Owen Evans, "National and Personal Saving in the United States," *International Monetary Fund Staff Papers*, 37, no. 3 (September 1990), 636–669.

3. Robert Avery and Arthur Kennickell, "The Household Balance Sheet," *Cornell Consumer Closeups*, 1988–89, no. 4, Dept. of Consumer Economics and Housing, Cornell University.

4. A related issue is whether the Japanese savings rate is higher than the U.S. savings rate. The comparison is made difficult because of differences in data and accounting measures in the two countries. See Fumio Hayashi, "Is Japan's Saving Rate High?" *Quarterly Review*, Federal Reserve Bank of Minneapolis (Spring 1989); and Robert Dekle and Lawrence Summers, *Japan's High Saving Rate Reaffirmed*, Working Paper No. 3690 (April 1991) Cambridge, MA: National Bureau of Economic Research.

5. Alicia Munnell Leah Cook, "Explaining the Postwar Pattern of Personal Saving," *New England Economic Review* (November/December 1991), pp. 17–28.

6. Robert Eisner, "The Real Rate of U.S. National Saving," *Review of Income and Wealth*, series 37, no. 1 (March 1991), 15–32; Robert A. Blecker, "The Consumption Binge Is a Myth," *Challenge* (May–June 1990), pp. 22–30.

7. Stephen A. Meyer, "Saving and Demographics: Some International Comparisons," *Business Review*, Federal Reserve Bank of Philadelphia (March/April 1992), pp. 13–23. Bovenberg and Evans also find large impacts of the demographic composition of the population on the savings rate.

8. Households under the age of 45 have total debt to financial asset ratios two to ten times larger than households between ages 45 and 65. See Douglas Pearce,

"Rising Household Debt in Perspective," *Economic Review*, Federal Reserve Bank of Kansas City (July/August 1985), pp. 3–17.

9. Board of Governors of the Federal Reserve System, *Balance Sheets for the U.S. Economy, 1945–92* (March 1993). Business debt is for nonfarm nonfinancial corporate businesses.

10. U.S. Dept. of Commerce, *Survey of Current Business*, various issues.

11. Richard McKenzie and Christina Klein, *The 1980s: A Decade of Debt?* Center for the Study of American Business, Policy Study Number 114, October 1992, St. Louis, Washington University. McKenzie and Klein cite that the number of credit cards in use rose from 526 million in 1980 to 957 million in 1989.

12. McKenzie and Klein cite the energy crises and rising inflation rates as reasons for the drop in the business debt/asset ratio in the 1970s. (Ibid., p. 21.) Worthington shows a similar pattern for business debt when measured by the ratio of debt to gross domestic product or the ratio of interest payments to cash flow; see Paula Worthington, "Recent Trends in Corporate Leverage," *Economic Perspectives*, Federal Reserve Bank of Chicago (May/June 1993), pp. 24–31.

13. Pearce, "Rising Household Debt in Perspective," and Bureau of the Census, current population reports.

14. In 1990, total debt as a percent of national income was 80 percent higher in Japan than in the United States. Also in 1990, nonfinancial corporate debt as a percent of national income was over three times higher in Japan and 75 percent higher in Germany than in the United States; see Howard Harve and Charles Pigott, "Determinants of Long Term Interest Rates: An Empirical Study of Several Industrial Countries," *Quarterly Review*, Federal Reserve Bank of New York (Winter 1991–92); and John Paulus, "The Debt Non-Problem," *The Wall Street Journal*, July 19, 1991, p. A10.

15. Keith Carlson, "On the Macroeconomics of Private Debt," *Review*, The Federal Reserve Bank of St. Louis, 75, no. 1 (January/February 1993), 53–66.

II. GOVERNMENT

It seems as if almost everyone complains about government spending and taxes. Some say that government spends too little, and others say it spends too much. And, of course, government spends too little on things each of us likes. What has really been happening to government spending?

It takes taxes to run government, and who likes taxes? But how big is the tax burden, and who pays it? Also, there have been major changes in the tax system, especially at the federal level, in recent decades. What impacts have they had? Is there a better tax system than what we now have?

Then there's that ever present deficit and national debt. Aren't they going to destroy our country? How did they arise and what can be done to control them?

We'll take on government and taxes in the next two chapters. Hopefully, we'll brush aside the hysteria and bring common sense and facts to the discussion.

4

How big is government?

Complaining about the size of government is probably the number-one hobby of Americans. Almost everyone thinks that government wastes money by spending it on worthless projects. Of course, the same people think that government spends too little on projects that *they* think are worthwhile!

The gripes about government have seemed to increase in direct proportion to the increase in the federal budget deficit and national debt. This has led to the common statement that the "nation is financially bankrupt."

The concerns about government size and government debt are real and important. Just how big is government and what does it spend its money on? Is government too big, or is it too small? Are the government deficits and the national debt about to sink us, or our children and grandchildren? What can be done to control government spending? These and other issues will be addressed in this chapter.

HOW HAS GOVERNMENT GROWN?

Is the best way to measure the size of government by the number of dollars government spends, by how many people government employs, by how many people who receive government benefits, or by some other measure?

Two measures economists use to gauge the size of government are total government spending in inflation-adjusted dollars and government spending as a percent of the total economy. The first measure is the easiest to understand. We simply look at the number of dollars spent by government each year, being careful to adjust those dollars for changes in the cost of living over time. (We did the same thing when comparing incomes and wages over time in Chapter 1.) That is, we can expect government to spend more each year just to keep up with rising prices, just as households must spend more each year to keep up with rising prices in order to maintain the same standard of living. Thus, in order to continue providing the same total output of services, government must spend more as the prices of the services rise. We don't want to count this additional government spending, which is necessitated by rising prices, as real new government spending. Instead, just as we did for household incomes and wages, we adjust actual government spending each year by an inflation index to take out the impact of higher prices each year. The resulting inflation-adjusted number is called *real spending*.

The other approach to measuring the size of government takes a slightly different approach. This approach looks at the percent of spending in our economy that is done by government. In other words, of all the spending that is done in our economy, what percent is done by government and what percent is done by the private sector? The broadest measure of total spending in the economy is the gross national product. Thus, the second approach to measuring the size of government is to measure government spending as a percent of gross national product (GNP).[1]

In measuring the size of government, we will lump all levels of government (federal, state, and local) into one group called *total government*. There are two reasons for doing this. First, there are significant flows of funds between governments, meaning that funds which are raised at one level may be spent at another level. (For example, some monies raised by the federal government are transferred to the states and spent by state governments.) Also, government functions are not divided between the levels of government in the same way in all states. (For instance, most education spending is done by the state in North Carolina, whereas most education spending is done by local governments in Ohio.) Second, it is appropriate to be concerned about the size of government at all levels combined, since any government spending represents a transfer of monies and responsibilities from private hands to public hands.

With all of this said, what do the measures show? The size of government as represented by the two measures is illustrated in Figure 4-1. The scale on the left-hand vertical line measures the size of government in real (that is, inflation-adjusted) dollars, and the scale on the right-hand vertical line measures the size of government as a percent of gross national product. Both measures say the same thing, but to differing extents. In real dollars, total government spending has increased threefold in the past three decades. Similarly, as a percent of GNP, total government spending has grown from 27 percent in 1960 to 35 percent in 1990. This may not seem like much, but it means that if the 27 percent ratio had been maintained in 1990, government would have spent $440 billion less in 1990! As we shall see, this is much more than the federal government's budget deficit in that year.[2]

One ruffle to these measures of the size of government has to do with the inclusion of self-financing government retirement programs. The most prominent of these programs is social security, but there are also state and local

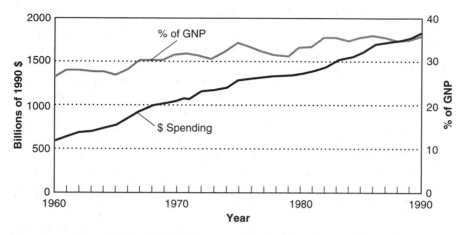

Source: *Economic Report of the President*, U.S. Government Printing Office, February 1992.

Figure 4-1   Two Measures of the Relative Size of Government

government retirement programs for their employees. Social security is, of course, the federally managed retirement program for most citizens. The point is that since these programs are self-financing (for example, social security taxes finance the social security system) and since they have been developed for a single purpose (retirement income), they should be considered separately from other government spending.

Whether you buy this argument or not, let's see what difference it makes in the growth of government. Is the relative growth in government over the past 30 years due to the growth of social security and similar government-managed retirement programs, or has government continued to grow even aside from these retirement programs? The answer is that government has continued to grow even without the social security and associated government retirement programs. Without these retirement programs, total government spending increased from $517.8 billion in 1960 to $1,468.3 billion in 1990 (all in 1990 purchasing power dollars). Likewise, omitting government retirement program spending, total government spending as a percent of GNP rose from 23 percent in 1960 to 28 percent of GNP in 1990. Relative government spending on retirement spending did double between 1960 and 1990 (rising from 3.5 percent of GNP in 1960 to 7 percent of GNP in 1990). But, as we have just seen, this increase did not account for all of the relative increase in the size of government.

So, any way you cut it, government spending in the United States has grown in the past three decades.[3] The government has been taking relatively more resources out of private hands and spending those resources. Some say this is a bad sign because it may have adverse consequences for the private economy. Indeed, in Chapter 2, I discussed studies which found a negative relationship between the relative size of government and a country's economic growth rate. Right now, let's address what government has been spending these resources on. I answer this question in the next section.

WHAT IS GOVERNMENT SPENDING MONEY ON?

Citizens disagree not only about how much government spends in total, but also about what government spends money on. Some think too much is spent on defense, others think too little is spent on the armed forces. There's wide disagreement about spending on social programs and how much should be spent in these efforts. Foreign aid spending is another contentious issue.

In looking at what government spends its money on, I use spending as a percentage of the total annual economic pie, or gross national product. To review, this measure tells us how much of our national income each year is devoted to the various government spending categories. Also, initially we will examine spending of all government levels (federal, state, and local) combined.

Figure 4-2 shows the major categories of total government spending as a percent of gross national product (GNP) for the decades of the 1960s, 1970s, and 1980s. Most of the categories are self-explanatory, but a couple need further explanation. Public welfare spending is all spending in support of needy persons, including medical care. The biggest component of the health category is the federally funded Medicare program for citizens over age 65. Defense also includes spending for international relations.

A picture (or graph) is worth a thousand words, but in this case, I'll only hit the highlights. The most noticeable feature of Figure 4-2 is that relative spending in all categories except two has trended upward in the past 30 years. This reflects the growing size of government, which we examined in the first section. The category that has had the greatest decline in relative spending is defense. In the late 1980s, defense spending as a percent of GNP was 30 percent lower than what it was in 1960. Relative defense spending did rise in the early and mid-1980s with the Reagan defense buildup, but with the Cold War over, defense spending as a percent of GNP is scheduled to fall further in the 1990s. The rela-

Figure 4-2 Total Government Spending by Category as a Percent of GNP

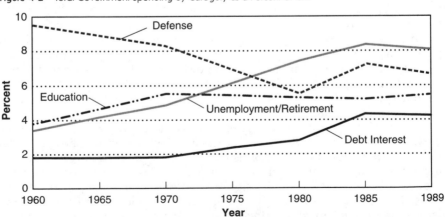

Source: Graph prepared by author from raw data taken from The Tax Foundation, *Facts and Figures on Government Finance*, Washington DC, 1992.

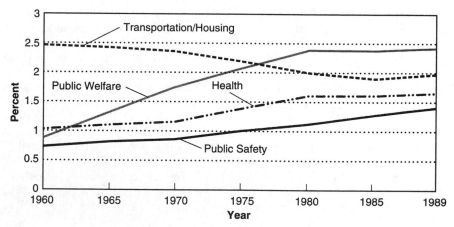

Figure 4-2 (continued)

tive size of the transportation/housing spending category has also declined, primarily due to the completion of the interstate highway system in the 1980s.

In the other categories of spending there is remarkable consistency. Relative spending rose in the 1960s and 1970s and remained relatively stable in the 1980s. For example, relative spending on education rose from under 4 percent of GNP in 1960 to over 5 percent of GNP in the 1980s; relative spending on public welfare rose from under 1 percent of GNP in 1960 to almost 2.5 percent of GNP in the 1980s; and relative spending on health rose from 1 percent of GNP in 1960 to over 1.5 percent of GNP in the 1980s. Also notice that relative spending for interest on government debt more than doubled from 1960 to the 1980s but remained relatively constant after 1985.[4]

There has been a long-running debate in the country between advocates of government spending on defense and supporters of government spending on social programs (the "guns" versus "butter" debate). The numbers show that as a percent of national income, the nation actually devoted more of its resources to social programs and less of its resources to defense in the 1980s than in the two previous decades. Also remember that since real (inflation-adjusted) national income (GNP) rose over the 1960s, 1970s, and 1980s, even a constant percentage of national income devoted to a program will result in more *real* dollars of spending. For example, in constant 1989 dollars, government at all levels spent $75 billion on education in 1960 but spent $280 billion in 1989. Also, government at all levels spent only $17 billion (1989 dollars) on public welfare in 1960 but spent $126 billion in 1989, over a sixfold increase. (The real dollar spending amounts for all programs are given in Appendix Table D.)

Of course, the federal government is the largest of our governmental units, and much of the discussion about government spending focuses on the federal government. So what has the federal government been spending money on, and do the trends here parallel the trends for all governmental levels combined?

The answer is that trends in federal government spending have followed the same trends outlined previously for total government spending for the simple reason that federal government spending is 63 percent of total government spending. For example, federal spending on education rose from 0.15 percent of GNP in 1962 to 0.45 percent of GNP in 1970 and has hovered between 0.4 and 0.5 percent of GNP since then. Also, a look at the numbers shows that federal poverty spending, including spending on job training, low-income housing, food stamps, general income support, and health care for the poor (primarily Medicaid) did not fall in the 1980s compared to earlier decades. In fact, federal poverty spending as a percent of GNP rose from 0.86 percent of GNP in the 1960s to 2.10 percent of GNP in the 1970s to 2.42 percent of GNP in the 1980s.[5] On the other hand, spending on international affairs, which includes foreign aid, has steadily fallen from almost 1 percent of GNP in 1962 (bigger than national poverty spending then) to only 0.28 percent of GNP in 1991.

One category of federal spending has steadily climbed during the past decades, and this is spending for interest on the national debt. Federal interest spending has crept from a little over 1 percent of GNP in the early 1960s to almost 3.5 percent of GNP in the early 1990s. Some critics of federal spending claim this is a sign of impending disaster for federal fiscal policy. This is the issue to which we now turn.

IS THE FEDERAL DEBT ABOUT TO SINK US?

By most citizens' standards, the federal budget deficit and the national debt are viewed as prime examples of Washington's incompetence and inability to manage fiscal affairs. Some people are almost hysterical about the deficits and debt, claiming that both will sink the country and doom everyone to a future of poverty. Others argue that the deficits and debt are a sign that taxes must be raised; in contrast, the argument is just as forcefully made that the deficits and debt are a sign that federal spending must be cut. Needless to say, the deficits and debt are the number-one government fiscal issue in many peoples' minds.[6]

Before we embark on our journey into red ink, some definitions must be established. Citizens frequently use the terms *deficit* and *debt* interchangeably. They are not the same, but they are related. The federal government runs a deficit when it spends more money than it receives in tax revenues. To raise the additional money, the federal government borrows the funds. The funds can be borrowed from almost anyone, including U.S. citizens, foreign citizens, and governmental agencies. The amount by which federal spending falls short of federal tax revenues, and hence the amount which must be borrowed by the federal government in a given year, is called the deficit. The deficit is thus an annual number.

In contrast, the national debt is a cumulative number. The national debt is the sum of all federal borrowing which has been done to date and which hasn't been repaid. A simple way to think of the national debt is as the accumulation of all past deficits.

How Big Are the Deficits and Debt?

The numbers about the deficits and debt which horrify people have been re-counted many times. In the 1980s the annual deficit ballooned from under $50 billion annually to almost $300 billion annually. In fact, the federal govern-ment has not run a budget *surplus* since 1969. As the annual deficit has sky-rocketed, so too has the total national debt, rising from $1 trillion in 1980 to over $4 trillion by the end of the decade. Even if the Clinton administration's economic plan works exactly as designed, the national debt will increase by another $1 trillion by 1997. Don't these numbers clearly indicate that the fed-eral budget is a mess, the federal government is "broke," and the federal fis-cal mess is ready to "take down" the whole country?

Not necessarily. The first thing we must do is correctly measure the deficits. There are four major problems with the deficit and debt numbers just cited. First, the numbers only include federal deficits and debt and ignore the fiscal position of state and local governments. Since state and local govern-ments have run surpluses in most years, their fiscal position has tended to off-set some of the federal deficits and debt.

Second, the popular numbers ignore that part of federal borrowing which is for capital (e.g., long-lasting) projects. Borrowing for capital projects is acceptable in the private sector. For example, when a company wants to build a new building, it generally borrows money. Households also borrow money to buy homes. It's reasonable to borrow money to pay for long-lasting projects and repay that money over the life of the project. This means that fed-eral borrowing for projects like roads, bridges, and aircraft carriers is much more legitimate than borrowing for salaries or transfer payments.[7]

Third, the popular numbers about the deficits and debt don't consider them in relation to the size of the economy. Just as a business with $2 million in annual sales can more easily afford a $10,000 debt than can a business with only $100,000 in sales, the American economy can afford higher deficits and debt as the economy grows.

Fourth, the commonly cited debt and deficit numbers only look at one side of the ledger and ignore the other side—government assets. A family, business, or government is only "broke" if its debts (or liabilities) exceed its assets. What really counts is the difference between the assets and liabilities, that is, the net worth.

The left-hand side of Figure 4-3 measures the annual budget deficits after adjusting for state and local government surpluses and federal capital spending, and expressing the annual deficit as a percent of the size of the na-tional economy (gross national product).[8] Positive percents represent a bud-get surplus, while negative percents mean a budget deficit occurred. The results show that, after these adjustments, the government actually ran bud-get *surpluses* until 1975. Since 1975, budget deficits have been run in half the years, but the annual adjusted deficits have all been less than 3 percent of GNP.

The right-hand side of Figure 4-3 measures total government debt as a percent of GNP after accounting for state and local government surpluses. The results show that the relative size of the debt has risen since 1981. However,

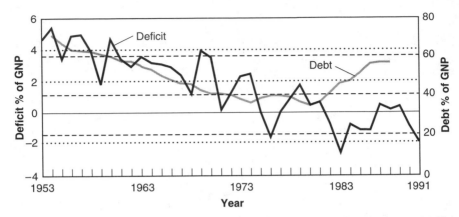

Sources: U.S. Office of Management and Budget, *Budget of the U.S. Government, FY 1993*, Historical Tables, February 1992; U.S. Dept. of Commerce, *Survey of Current Business*, June 1993.

Figure 4-3   Relative Sizes of Government Deficits and Debt

the relative size of the debt was not at an all-time high in the late 1980s. Government debt as a percent of the economy was larger in most of the decade of the 1950s than in the late 1980s.[9]

I haven't addressed the fourth criticism of the national debt hysteria, which states that the numbers ignore government assets. The government does own many valuable things, such as roads, bridges, parks, buildings, land, mineral rights, military hardware, gold, cash, and loan assets. When total government (federal, state, and local) debt is subtracted from the value of total government assets, the good news is that the result is positive. That is, if government at all levels sold all of its assets and then paid off all its debts, government would still have money left over. In fact, the latest estimates (1989) show that the value of total government assets is about 35 percent greater than total government debt. This surplus of government assets over debt is as large as at any time between 1945 and 1970.[10]

There is some bad news about government net worth (assets minus liabilities). If *federal* government debt is subtracted from federal government assets, the result is currently (1988) negative. Thus, it can technically be said that the federal government is "broke," although the federal government also had debt larger than assets between 1945 and 1955.

You might be breathing a slight sign of relief now, but let me first burst your bubble before blowing it back up. Let's focus only on the federal government. The federal debt is actually only one part of the total money which the federal government has promised to pay in the future. As Table 4-1 shows, the biggest component of future money the federal government has promised to pay (called liabilities) is social security. Table 4-1 shows that total federal liabilities are greater than federal assets by almost $8 trillion (in 1987).

But Table 4-1 also shows some good news. Federal government net liabilities, which is the burden to future taxpayers, as a percent of GNP actu-

Table 4-1   All Federal Government Net Liabilities as a Percent of GNP

	6/30/74	9/30/81	9/30/87
		(BILLIONS $)	
Liabilities			
Social Security	$2,460	$5,858	$5,580
Federal Debt	343	784	1,898
Pensions	188	842	1,027
Other	194	391	593
Total Liabilities	$3,185	$7,875	$9,098
Total Assets	327	690	1,146
Net Liabilities	$2,858	$7,185	$7,952
As % of GNP	202%	241%	180%

Source: T. E. Daxon, "Shrinking Mortgage: Ronald Reagan Was a Friend to Future Taxpayers," *Policy Review*, no. 47 (Winter 1989), pp. 68–69; used with permission. All rights reserved.

ally fell between 1981 and 1987 and are significantly lower than in 1974. This resulted primarily from the social security reforms of 1983, which increased social security taxes and reduced future benefits by raising the retirement age and taxing more social security benefits.[11]

Before concluding this section, one myth about who owns the government debt should be laid to rest. It is not true that foreigners own most of the federal debt, and that by owning this debt, they keep a strangehold on our country. In 1991, foreigners owned 16.4 percent of federal net debt, actually slightly lower than the 17.2 percent share owned by foreigners in 1981.[12] U.S. citizens own the vast majority of federal debt through their ownership of U.S. treasury securities and U.S. savings bonds as investments. This means that if the federal government simply canceled the federal debt, the big losers would be U.S. citizens who have bought the federal debt as part of their investment portfolio.

Impact of the Debt

Although the government deficits and debt have indeed grown in recent years, when correctly measured, they didn't grow to historical highs. Nevertheless, they have grown relative to the size of the economy. Is this bad? Are government deficits and debt bad for the economy and for consumers? If so, then whatever the relative size of the deficits and debt, as long as they exist, they create problems for the economy.

Most citizens do indeed think that government deficits and debt are bad for the economy, although they may not be able to articulate why. But economists are not united about the dangers of deficits and debt. Some economists agree with the majority of citizens that deficits and debt are bad. But other economists think that deficits and debt, in and of themselves, are not bad and are simply an alternative way of financing government. These economists argue that the focus should be on the size of government spending, not the way the spending is financed.[13]

Let's look at the two views of deficits and debt. The traditional view says that government deficits are bad because they raise interest rates and "crowd out" private spending and investment. Interest rates rise when the government goes to the credit markets and borrows money to fund the deficits. The additional government borrowing will increase the total demand for credit and will thereby raise interest rates. Higher interest rates will discourage some private investments in new plant and equipment, new technology, and worker training, and will therefore cause the economy to grow at slower rates.[14]

The alternative view agrees that deficit spending causes the government to borrow more funds from the credit markets, which causes the total demand for credit to increase. But the alternative view goes further and says that consumers and businesses have enough foresight to know that taxes will have to be raised in the future to pay for the deficits. Therefore, consumers and businesses save more today in order to afford the higher taxes later. The greater private saving counteracts the additional government borrowing and leads to no impact on the interest rate. Therefore, this view says that the important aspect of deficit spending is not the deficits and debt it creates, but the additional government spending it represents. The focus should therefore be on the need for, and efficiency of, government spending and not necessarily on how the government spending is financed (taxes versus borrowing).[15]

Recent research by economists actually provides considerable support for the alternative view that government deficits do *not* lead to higher interest rates.[16] Also, there is no necessary relationship between deficits and inflation. Consistently higher inflation rates result when the Federal Reserve System, the central bank of the United States, increases the growth rate of money and credit relative to the growth rate of goods and services in the economy. The only possible tie between this action and deficits would occur if the Federal Reserve created more money and credit in order to purchase the government debt caused by deficit spending. In recent years, this link has not occurred.

One other aspect of the deficit's and debt's impacts that should be mentioned concerns social security's funding of the debt. Some people have argued that surpluses which have been accumulated in the social security trust fund for future retirees are being squandered because they have been spent to partially fund the deficits and debt.

What's really going on is simply this. If the social security system accumulates surpluses, which it has recently done, we certainly would want those surpluses invested so that interest can be earned. The question is: Where do we want those surpluses invested? Since social security surpluses represent our future retirement income, we probably don't want the surpluses invested in risky ventures. In fact, the law which set up the social security system recognizes this desire and says that any social security surpluses must be invested in the safest investment available. What is the safest investment? Any investment advisor will tell you that the safest investment in terms of protection of the original investment is treasury securities issued by the federal government! This is because the federal government has a perfect track record for more than 200 years in never missing an interest payment or principal payoff. So by law, social security surpluses must be invested in treasury securities. And, of course, treasury securities are issued by the federal government to raise money to cover the deficit.

Therefore, it is correct to say that social security surpluses are being loaned back to the federal government to partially fund the deficit. But it is wrong to think this means the surpluses are being squandered and will never be repaid. If history is any guide, the loans will be repaid to the social security system with interest.

WHAT CAN BE DONE ABOUT THE SIZE OF GOVERNMENT?

So the verdict is in, and yes indeed, the relative size of government has grown over the past three decades (although not as much as you might have thought), and the relative sizes of the deficits and total debt have grown, particularly since the mid-1970s. If these trends are disturbing to you, then what's a citizen to do? We'll investigate two solutions here, changes in government budgeting procedures and privatization.

Reforming Budgeting Procedures

One approach to controlling the size of government is to reform the process by which government decides how much money to spend, that is, to reform the budgeting process. In discussing these reforms, I'll focus on the largest of our government units, the federal government and the federal budget.

Before discussing how to reform the federal budget process, it's important to understand some aspects of the current process. One of these aspects is the concept of the *baseline budget*. The baseline budget is a projection of what the federal government will spend in the future if no changes are made to federal programs or revenues. In other words, it assumes the federal government will run on "automatic pilot" in the future. This budget is, however, based on given assumptions about how the economy will perform in the future and what the demand will be for various government services.[17]

The baseline budget is important to keep in mind when discussing a *cut* in federal spending. A cut in federal spending can be claimed if a plan results in less spending than under the baseline budget. In fact, a cut in federal spending can be claimed, even if a plan results in more real (inflation-adjusted) spending, as long as the *increase* in spending is *less* than that projected under the baseline budget. This means that, in budget language, an *increase* in future spending can actually be labeled a *cut* in spending.

If you're confused, maybe Figure 4-4 will help. Figure 4-4 shows a baseline budget of increasing federal spending over time (preferably all spending is expressed in real dollars). Figure 4-4 also shows an alternative proposal for federal spending, which has spending increasing at a slower rate than with the baseline budget. The difference in spending between the baseline budget and the proposal would be counted as a cut in federal spending if the proposal

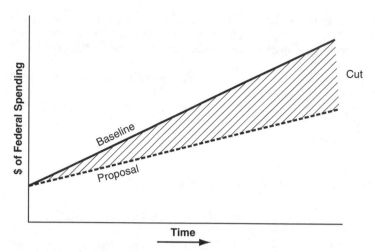

Figure 4-4   Baseline Budgeting and a Cut in Federal Spending

is adopted. Usually a total cut is presented by simply adding the annual cuts over a specified number of years.

So the idea is that a budget proposal can claim a cut in federal spending if federal spending increases less under the proposal than it would under the baseline budget. Likewise, a budget proposal can claim a cut in the deficit if the deficit is less with the proposal than with the baseline budget.

Another important aspect of federal budgeting has to do with budgeting for *entitlement programs*. An entitlement program is a federal program which pays benefits to any citizen who meets the eligibility requirements for the program. Social security, Medicare, Medicaid, farm price support programs, food stamps, and other welfare programs are examples of entitlement programs. Entitlement programs account for slightly over half of total federal spending.

What makes entitlement programs different than other federal programs is that they are treated differently in the budget process. With other federal programs, from spending on defense to spending on office equipment, Congress and the president jointly decide on the precise amount to spend. With entitlement programs, Congress and the president may estimate what will be spent, and this estimate will be in the baseline budget, but in the past they have not limited the amount that will be spent. With entitlement programs, the amount spent is driven by the degree to which citizens use the programs, not by how much Congress and the president decide to spend. With entitlement program spending uncapped, it is no wonder that this spending has exploded in recent years.[18]

With this background, what can be done to the federal budgeting system to control spending? First, you shouldn't necessarily be impressed with budget proposals which claim savings in federal spending and reductions in the deficit when these savings are based on comparisons with the baseline budget. Instead, always look at what will actually be spent in real dollars and as a percent of the economy.

Any serious attempt to control federal spending must address the "open-wallet" system now used with entitlements. Entitlement spending must be capped in some way in the federal budget in order to control the total growth in federal spending. This does not mean "freezing" entitlement spending in nominal dollars. Instead, entitlement program spending can be allowed to increase each year based on inflation and the estimated growth in the eligible population. But such a formula would cap entitlement spending each year and put a hard lid on the federal budget. However, it might also create some pain if federal budget makers underestimated either inflation or growth in the eligible program population.

A more fundamental way to limit the size of government would be to limit the percentage of the total economic pie (national income or GNP) that government can spend in any year. As already shown, this percentage is 35 percent for all government including retirement programs, and around 28 percent for all government excluding retirement programs. Collectively (i.e., through our political representatives), we could decide what this percentage should be and require by law that government spending not exceed this percentage. This would set a total limit on the relative size of government, but would still leave within this limit much discretion (and disagreement) about how to spend public money.

Federal budgeting would take a large step forward if it adopted a simple budgeting technique used by businesses and most states. This technique is to divide spending into two categories, a current account budget and a capital account budget. The current account budget includes spending for current services, primarily salaries of government employees and transfer payments to low-income citizens and other beneficiaries of government programs. The current account budget would be required to be funded by tax revenues; that is, borrowing would not be allowed to fund any of the current account budget.

The capital account budget includes spending for long-lasting government projects, such as roads, bridges, buildings, water and sewer infrastructure, and military hardware. These projects last many years. Therefore, it makes economic sense to borrow the money to build the projects now, and repay the loans over the life of the projects. Businesses do this all the time when they build factories and other long-lasting projects. An added reason for paying for long-lasting government projects with borrowed funds is that future taxpayers will bear some of the repayment burden, which seems fair since future taxpayers will also benefit from the long-lasting projects.

Therefore, if a current account/capital account budget technique was adopted by the federal government, the current account budget would be required to be paid for with current tax revenues with no deficit spending allowed for the current account budget. However, the capital account budget could be funded with borrowed monies with deficit spending allowed for the capital account budget. Again, this would put the federal government on the same logical footing with businesses and most state and local governments.

What should we do about the deficits and debt? First, we shouldn't lose our heads. As I've already shown, the deficits and debt have increased relative to the size of our economy in recent years, but they haven't reached historical highs. There are two ways to reduce the relative sizes of the deficit. The plan recommended by most politicians and the media is to reduce the deficit either by increasing taxes or cutting spending. Of course, almost every politician and citizen has his or her list of wasteful programs that could be cut or eliminated, but there's obviously no agreement on the lists. However, the deficit could be gradually cut by using a simple rule: Don't raise taxes, but limit the increase in government spending each year to the rate of inflation plus a factor to allow for population growth. This would maintain the real (inflation-adjusted) level of government spending per person. However, because government revenues tend to grow faster than inflation and population growth (since revenues follow the growth of the real economy per person), this rule would slowly reduce the deficit.

The other way to reduce the deficit and debt is to increase the rate of economic growth (i.e., make the economic pie grow faster). This is the plan emphasized by many so-called supply-side economists. These economists state that the important relationship to watch is the rate of growth of the debt compared to the rate of growth of the economy. If the economic growth rate exceeds the debt growth rate, then the relative size and importance of the debt decline. Therefore, following this approach, the important focus is on economic growth. We talked about possible ways to increase the long-run economic growth rate in Chapter 2.

Should our goal be no deficit spending and no national debt? Not necessarily. Borrowing, which creates debt, is a way of transferring future resources to the present. As stressed repeatedly in this chapter, businesses and households are constantly borrowing, and most businesses and households carry some debt. The focus should not be on achieving no deficit spending and a zero national debt, but instead should be on the productivity of government spending compared to the productivity of that spending if left in private hands. For example, if it is determined that a government-financed road provides a very productive return for the money invested compared to other public and private projects, then the road should be built. If government borrowing is necessary to build the road, then so be it; the borrowing shouldn't stand in the way of building the road. Of course, calculating the rate of return from a public project like a road is not easy to do. The point is that more attention should be placed on the productivity of government spending, and less attention should be placed on whether that spending is financed by taxes or borrowing.

Privatization

A second way to arrest the growth of government is to *privatize* some government activities. Privatizing government activities means turning those activities over to the private (nongovernment) sector. There are three ways to do this: selling government assets, contracting out government activities to private firms, and providing vouchers to consumers for purchase of goods and services from private providers.[19]

Selling government assets means selling government operations to private concerns and letting the private buyer run the government as he or she sees fit. After the sale, the operation would no longer receive government funding or direction. Examples would be selling the U.S. Postal Service to private investors and severing all ties to the federal government, and doing likewise with the federally subsidized passenger train service, Amtrak.

Contracting out government activities means the government hires private firms to perform the activity rather than have the government perform the activity using government employees. However, the government still sets requirements and standards for the activity and is able to terminate the contract with the private firms at designated times and hire other firms. Examples are cities contracting out the collection of garbage to private firms rather than the city using city employees and trucks to collect the garbage, and states hiring private firms to run prisons rather than using state employees to operate them.

With vouchers, the government transfers purchasing power to citizens it wishes to help, but lets those citizens directly purchase goods and services from private firms. This is instead of the government directly providing those goods and services to the intended citizens. For example, instead of directly providing food to needy families, the government provides purchasing power via food stamps and lets the families purchase food from supermarkets. In the 1980s, the federal government moved away from building public housing for needy families, and instead provided housing vouchers which the families could use to rent privately constructed housing. An issue of current controversy is education vouchers. Under this system, government would provide education vouchers (or education "stamps") to parents, and in turn, the parents would use the vouchers to purchase education for their children at any publicly run or privately run school.

How can privatization save money? Isn't privatization just shifting around who spends the money and won't the same amount of money be spent? Privatization should save money because it harnesses the forces of the competitive market and avoids the inefficiencies associated with a government monopoly. The beauty of the private competitive market is that, with no direction from government or any other body, private firms are motivated to use resources in the most efficient manner in order to provide the services and products that consumers want and are willing to pay for at the lowest possible price.

This result is created by the profit motive. Although profit is a "dirty" word to some, it provides a valuable function in the competitive economic system. It motivates private companies to get the most out of their labor and nonlabor resources so they can increase the difference between their revenues and costs to make a profit. But what prevents profits from being abnormally high? Here's where competition comes in. If a firm or group of firms is making profits higher than necessary to stay in business, then other firms will enter the market and drive the price down to where profits are only high enough to provide a normal rate of return to the firms' owners.[20]

Why can't government operations give us these results? The reasons are simple—government doesn't operate on the profit motive, and government can make it tough for competitors to enter the market. Anyone who has worked in government knows that it doesn't operate on the profit motive.

Most government agencies don't directly receive revenues from taxpayers; instead, government agencies receive a budget allocated from the elected government officials. Government agencies are not motivated to maximize the difference between their allocated budget (revenues) and their costs. Indeed, most government agencies are motivated to always spend all of their budget for fear that if they don't, they'll receive less budget next year.[21] Therefore, government managers don't have the same drive to most efficiently use resources and keep costs down.

Government usually doesn't have competitors waiting around the corner to take away business if government doesn't provide the service or product in the best and cheapest way to the consumer. Either government legally prohibits competitors, or it makes it very expensive for the citizen to use competitors. An example of the latter is the fact that citizens must frequently pay for government services through taxes whether they use the government service or not. For example, you could hire a private firm to pick up your garbage, but in most cities you would still be required to pay for the city-provided garbage service, even though you didn't use it. Similarly, many parents are deterred from sending their children to private schools because, if they do so, they still pay for public schools through their property taxes; that is, they would pay for schooling twice.

Now that I have established, in theory, that privately provided services should be less costly than the same governmently provided services, what's the evidence that this is actually the case? The evidence comes from a number of sources and comparisons. Studies have been made of garbage collection, fire protection, health care (e.g., Veterans Administration hospitals versus private hospitals), education, jails, and airlines, showing private provision is cheaper than government provision.[22] For example, Savas found that contracting out garbage collection reduced costs by 29 to 37 percent.[23] Studies also show that housing vouchers have been a more effective way than public housing of providing shelter to needy families.[24] How can this be if private firms must make a profit? The answer is that private firms more than compensate for their profit requirement by their more efficient use of resources. Also, since profit-maximizing, competitive firms can lose customers to competitors, they have a strong incentive to listen to customers and cater to their desires.

Of course, not all government services can be privatized. Privatization works best for those government services which are individually consumed by families and for which it is easy to measure the consumption and assess a fee.

Before leaving this section, let me address one other privatization proposal which is very controversial, and this is the privatization of social security.

As discussed earlier, social security taxes have been the fastest-growing federal tax during the past three decades. Social security is the federally mandated retirement savings program, in which citizens contribute to the social security fund while they're working, and in exchange they receive a social security pension when they retire. However, social security doesn't operate like a typical savings plan, where the saver gets back everything he or she has saved plus interest. Instead, in social security there is considerable redistribution from high-income workers to low-income workers. Low-income workers get back much more than the investment value of what they contributed; high-income workers get back much less.[25]

Since social security is a politically run program, it is also subject to the whims of Congress for changing tax rates and benefit levels. This creates uncertainty among citizens, who are never quite sure what they will pay in social security taxes or get back in benefits.

An alternative to social security would be a mandated, privatized retirement system. Under this system, workers would be required to place a minimum percentage of their earnings in a retirement savings account.[26] The retirement savings accounts would be administered privately under the direction of the worker. The worker would be assured that this money is his or her money, and it will not be redistributed to other workers upon retirement. The value of benefits received in retirement from the savings account would depend on how much the worker contributed and how well the savings account was invested (i.e., what rate of return it earned). The value of benefits would not be determined by Congress and the president, and would not be subject to political considerations.

But what about low-income workers who don't earn enough to be able to save the mandated percentage? Would these citizens be left out in the cold at retirement under a privatized social security system? No. There would continue to be a "safety net" retirement income level provided to low-income retirees who couldn't afford to save enough for their retirement. This "safety net" would be funded out of general federal tax revenues, just as income-support programs for the nonretired poor citizens are currently funded.

One final comment should be made about the size of government and government spending before concluding this chapter. As I have discussed, the size of government is most commonly measured by its real (inflation-adjusted) dollar spending, or its spending as a percent of our total economic pie. But government can have influences beyond its direct spending. One of these indirect influences is through regulations. Government can impose costs on the economy without spending a penny by passing laws and enacting regulations which require businesses and consumers to spend money in a certain way. These regulatory costs are tough to estimate, but they have been pegged as high as $400 billion to $600 billion annually (in 1988 dollars).[27] We should be watchful of these regulatory costs, and like direct government spending, should constantly evaluate their costs in comparison to their estimated benefits.

NOTES

1. An alternative measure of the total size of the economy is gross domestic product, which is the standard now used by the government. Gross national product and gross domestic product are very close in size. Because most historical statistics are still quoted in terms of gross national product, gross national product will be used here.

2. Higher levels of government spending can be obtained if quasi-public enterprises, such as the Postal Service and state-regulated liquor stores, are included. Adding

this spending increases government spending as a percent of GNP to 29 percent in 1960 to 38 percent in 1989 (The Tax Foundation, *Facts and Figures on Government Finance*, Washington, DC, 1992).

3. Government spending in the United States as a percent of the total economy is less than in most European countries but is more than in many of the developing (and rapidly growing) countries of East Asia, such as South Korea, Taiwan, and Singapore.

4. The government interest number needed here is net interest, instead of gross interest. Gross interest payments include all interest payments paid to all holders of federal debt. However, some federal debt is held by agencies of the federal government, such as the social security system and federal and military retirement systems. These interest payments never leave the government; they are expenditures to one agency (the U.S. Treasury) and are revenues to another agency. Net interest payments only include those payments made to holders of the debt outside of the federal government (*Congressional Budget Outlook: Fiscal Years 1992–1996*, Washington, DC, Superintendent of Documents, 1991).

5. There are important differences in the growth of various components of federal poverty programs, which we will return to in the chapter on poverty.

6. There's been no lack of newsprint and book print on the dangers of the budget deficits and national debt. For "doomsday" views of the debt, see Harry Figgie and Gerald Swanson, *Bankruptcy 1995* (Boston: Little, Brown and Co., 1992); and Larry Burkett, *The Coming Economic Earthquake* (Chicago: Moody Press, 1991). For more analytical yet negative views of the deficits and debt, see David P. Calleo, *The Bankrupting of America* (N.Y. Wm. Morrow and Co., 1992), and Peter G. Peterson, *Facing Up* (New York: Simon and Schuster, 1993). For alternative views of the deficits and debt, see Robert Eisner, *How Real Is the Federal Deficit?* (New York: The Free Press, 1986); and Robert Ortner, *Voodoo Deficits* (New York: Dow-Jones Irwin, 1990).

7. For more discussion of this point, see Robert Eisner, "Deficits: Which, How Much, and So What?" *American Economic Review*, 82, no. 2 (May 1992), 295–298.

8. Federal capital expenditures are taken from the U.S. Office of Management and Budget, Budget of the U.S. Government, fiscal year 1993, historical tables; state and local government budget surpluses are taken from the U.S. Dept. of Commerce, Survey of Current Business.

9. Deficits and national debt are not only an American phenomenon. In fact, during the late 1980s and early 1990s, many European countries had deficits and national debt as a larger percentage of their national economy than in the United States. For example, of the 19 major industrial countries, nine had a larger budget deficit as a percent of their economy than the United States in 1993 (*The Economist*, January 23, 1993, p. 103).

10. See Dean Croushore, "How Big Is Your Share of Governmental Debt?" *Business Review*, Federal Reserve Bank of Philadelphia (November/December 1990), pp. 3–12.

11. In an exhaustive study, Lawrence Kotlikoff also found that fiscal policy in the 1980s *decreased* the unfunded tax burden on future generations due to the 1983 reforms in social security; see Lawrence J. Kotlikoff, *Generational Accounting*, (New York: The Free Press, 1992).

12. Data are from the Federal Reserve Bank of St. Louis, National Economic Trends.

13. This argument is presented very clearly in Allan Meltzer, "The Deficit: A Monetarist's Perspective," *Choices* (1st Quarter 1993), pp. 7–9.

14. For more details on the traditional view of the effects of deficits, see Robert Gordon, *Macroeconomics*, 4th ed. (Boston: Little, Brown and Co., 1987), pp. 131–133.

15. For details on the alternative view of the effects of deficits, see Robert Barro, *Macroeconomics*, 4th ed. (New York: Wiley, 1993), pp. 361–388.

16. See Paul Evans, "Interest Rates and Expected Future Budget Deficits in the United States," *Journal of Political Economy*, 95 (February 1987), 34–58; Paul Evans, "Do Budget Deficits Raise Nominal Interest Rates? Evidence from Six Countries," *Journal of Monetary Economics*, 20 (September 1987), 281–300; Paul Evans, "Is Ricardian Equivalence a Good Approximation?" *Economic Inquiry*, 29 (October 1991), 626–644; Robert Barro, "The Ricardian Approach to Budget Deficits," *Journal of Economic Perspectives*, 3 (Spring 1989), 37–54; and Roger Kormendi, "Government Debt, Government Spending, and Private Sector Behavior," *American Economic Review*, 73 (December 1983), 994–1010.

17. See Stanley Collender, *The Guide to the Federal Budget*, 10th ed. (Washington, DC: The Urban Institute Press, 1991).

18. For example, from 1985 to 1993 total federal entitlement spending increased from 46 percent of federal spending to 52 percent of federal spending; see David Wessel, "Entitlement-Cap Proposals Resurface Ahead of Vote on Deficit Reduction," *The Wall Street Journal*, May 24, 1993, p. A12.

19. Mark Karscig, "Tracing the Privatization Movement in the UK and US: An Attempt to Address the Question of Industry Productivity," *Eastern Economic Journal*, 16, no. 4 (October–December 1990), 355–368.

20. This is why it is important to keep entry to markets open and to prevent existing firms from using political pressure and power to erect barriers to entry. *Normal* rate of return is defined as the rate of return that company owners could earn in the investment market for the same amount of risk.

21. See William Niskanen, Jr., *Bureaucracy and Representative Government* (Chicago: Aldine and Atherton, 1971).

22. See E. S. Savas, "Public vs. Private Refuse Collection: A Critical Review of the Evidence," *Journal of Urban Analysis*, 6, no. 1 (1979), 1–13; Roger Ahlbrandt, *Municipal Fire Protection Services: Comparison of Alternative Organizational Forms* (Beverly Hills, CA: Sage Publications, 1973); Cotton Lindsay, *Veterans Administration Hospitals* (Washington, DC: American Enterprise Institute, 1975); Office of the Comptroller of New York City, *Policy Analysis of the Cost and Financing of Special Education to Handicapped Children in New York City*, May 1978; Randy Fitzgerald, "Free-Enterprise Jails: Key to Our Prison Dilemma?" *Readers Digest* (March 1986); Anthony Boardman and Ardan Vining, "Ownership and Performance in Competitive Environments: A Comparison of the Performance of Private, Mixed, and State-Owned Enterprises," *Journal of Law and Economics*, 32, no. 1 (April 1989), 1–33; Robert Poole, Jr., "Privatization: Policy Alternatives for a New Era," *Heritage Today*, no. 1 (January/February 1982), 4; and R. M. Spann, "Public vs. Private Provision of Government Services," in T. E. Borcherding, ed., *Budgets and Bureaucrats: The Sources of Government Growth* (Durham, NC: Duke University Press, 1977).

23. Savas, "Public vs. Private Refuse Collection."

24. Arthur Solomon and Chester Fenton, "The Nation's First Experience with Housing Allowances," *Land Economics*, 1, no. 3 (August 1974), 213–223.

25. Laurence Kotlikoff, *Generational Accounting* (New York: The Free Press, 1992), pp. 110–111.

26. Chile has a privatized retirement system. Its system lets workers contribute to a government-run social security system, or to opt out of the system and contribute a minimum required amount to their own private investment account (Robert Genetski, "Private Social Security," *The Wall Street Journal*, May 21, 1993, p. A10).

27. Thomas Hopkins, *Cost of Regulation*, Rochester Institute of Technology, RIT Public Policy Working Paper (November 1991); and Melinda Warren and James Lis, *Regulatory Standstill: Analysis of the 1993 Federal Budget*, Center for the Study of American Business, Washington University, St. Louis, Occasional Paper 105, (June 1992); Robert Genetski, "The True Cost of Government," *The Wall Street Journal*, February 19, 1992.

5

Who pays the tax bill?

Next to government spending, probably no topic is the subject of discussion for Americans more than taxes. Many people think they pay too much in taxes and that many others (particularly the rich) don't pay enough. Many think that their taxes could be cut if the taxes on the rich were increased.

The debate over taxes has increased in recent years as a result of the massive changes made to the federal income tax system in the 1980s. Tax rates were cut and many deductions and exemptions were eliminated. Supporters of the changes say the reduction in tax rates was exactly what was needed to stimulate the economy. Critics of the changes say the rate cuts primarily benefitted the rich and led to the massive budget deficits.[1] A great deal of the presidential election of 1992 was fought over who gained and who lost from the tax changes of the 1980s.

Many citizens believe the tax system is entirely too complicated. The *flat tax*, in which every citizen pays a certain percentage of their income in taxes, is frequently championed as the best alternative to the current system of rates, credits, deductions, and exemptions. Is the flat tax the "way to go" in tax reform? Would everyone gain from a flat tax, or would there be winners and losers?

How big is the tax burden, and who pays it? Do the rich pay their "fair share" of the tax burden? Who benefitted from the tax changes of the 1980s, and did these changes create the budget deficits? Can cutting tax rates actually result in more tax revenues for the government? What is the "best" tax system? These questions and others are addressed in this chapter.

HOW MUCH DO WE PAY IN TAXES?

How much do you think the average American pays in taxes of all kinds,—10 percent, 20 percent, 40 percent, 50 percent, or more? Although this may seem like a straightforward question that should have a straightforward answer, it does have complications. For example, should social security taxes be included, since, presumably, these taxes are later returned in the form of retirement benefits? Also, should taxes that businesses pay be counted as taxes for the average consumer? The argument in favor of including business taxes in the consumer's tax burden is that businesses treat taxes as a cost and pass those tax costs on to consumers in the form of higher prices.

A common way used by economists to measure the tax burden is to calculate the percentage of the annual national economic pie (gross national product), which is paid in taxes of all kinds, including federal, state, and local taxes. These calculations for 1950 to 1990 are shown in Figure 5-1. As can be seen, by this measure the tax burden has risen by over one-third during this period, from 24 percent in 1950 to 33 percent in 1990. In other words, in 1950 government at all levels took about one-fourth of the private economy's resources in taxes; by 1990, government at all levels was taking one-third of the private economy's resources in taxes.

The preceding tax percentages include social security taxes. Since social security is a self-financing program clearly separate from other government programs, and since the taxes collected for social security are ultimately returned to taxpayers in retirement and medical benefits, shouldn't the tax burden be considered without social security taxes? Well, let's see how much difference social security taxes make to the tax burden. In Figure 5-1, I have calculated the tax burden as a percent of gross national product without including social security taxes. This measure of the tax burden shows a sur-

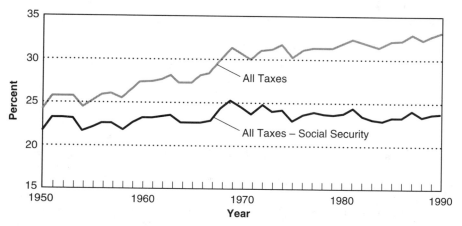

Source: *Economic Report of the President*, U.S. Gov't Printing Office, February 1992.

Figure 5-1   The Total Tax Burden (Taxes as a Percent of GNP)

prising degree of stability from 1950 to 1990, varying only between 21.5 percent and 25 percent (with the high of 25 percent set in 1969). Clearly, then, the large majority of the increase in the relative tax burden has been due to the increase in social security taxes.

A slightly different way of measuring the average tax burden has been developed by the Tax Foundation. The Tax Foundation measures the percentage of income paid in taxes by the average two-earner income family. The Tax Foundation includes all direct federal, state, and local taxes paid by families plus indirect taxes paid by businesses but likely passed on to families in the form of higher prices or lower wages.[2] In 1992, this measure of the tax burden found that the average two-earner income family paid 39.7 percent of their income in taxes.[3] This measure of the tax burden actually declined slightly in the 1980s, from 41.4 percent in 1980. Without social security taxes (both those paid directly by the family and by business), the tax burden was 24.5 percent in 1992.

Finally, a new method of measuring the tax burden has been developed to show the average net tax rate paid, where the net tax rate accounts for taxes paid at all governmental levels minus benefits received (such as social security benefits, Medicare, and food stamps). This methodology shows that the net tax rate has almost doubled in this century, from 17.8 percent for a citizen born in 1900 to 33.9 percent for a citizen born in 1991. Interestingly, this analysis shows that if the current level of government transfers are to be maintained in the future, the net tax rate will have to double for future generations.[4]

The discussion thus far has referred to some average tax burden. But how does the tax burden vary by income level? The evidence here is clear from a number of sources. The tax burden does increase with income. The Consumer Expenditure Survey, the most comprehensive survey of how consumers spend their money, shows that the poorest 20 percent of households spent 4.6 percent of their income on taxes in 1989; the second 20 percent spent 8.9 percent; the third 20 percent spent 14 percent; the fourth 20 percent spent 17.3 percent; and the richest 20 percent spent 19.6 percent of their income on taxes.[5] Using a different methodology, the Congressional Budget Office found the same trend for 1991: The poorest households paid the lowest percentage of their income in taxes, and the percentage gradually increased with income of the household.[6] Furthermore, a comparison of the Consumer Expenditure Survey of 1973 with the survey from 1989 shows that the tax burden (measured as the percentage of income paid in taxes) fell or remained constant for all household income groups except the very richest group.[7]

These statistics indicate that the percentage of total taxes that is paid by the rich has increased in recent years. For example, in 1972, the richest 20 percent of households paid 51 percent of all taxes at all levels of government (including social security). In 1989 this share was up to 55 percent.[8] Also, in 1980 the richest 10 percent of households paid 49 percent of all federal income taxes; in 1990 this share was up to 54 percent.[9]

What about the idea of reducing taxes on the lower and middle classes by raising taxes on the rich? Would this provide enough new revenue to cut

Table 5-1   Income and Federal Income Taxes Paid

SIZE OF INCOME (ADJUSTED GROSS INCOME)^	NUMBER OF RETURNS	TOTAL FEDERAL INCOME TAX PAID ($ MILLION)	PERCENT OF TOTAL FEDERAL INCOME TAX PAID
All Returns, Total	112,136,000	$432,940	100.00%
Under $10,000	32,599,000	4,251	0.98
$10,000–$19,999	26,041,000	24,619	5.69
$20,000–$29,999	16,947,000	38,920	8.99
$30,000–$39,999	12,100,000	45,598	10.53
$40,000–$49,999	8,590,000	44,034	10.17
$50,000–$59,999	5,506,000	38,673	8.93
$60,000–$69,999	3,284,000	30,192	6.97
$70,000–$79,999	2,042,000	23,276	5.38
$80,000–$89,999	1,277,000	17,542	4.05
$90,000–$99,999	872,000	14,240	3.29
$100,000–$124,999	1,057,000	21,526	4.97
$125,000–$149,999	512,000	13,769	3.18
$150,000–$174,999	312,000	10,600	2.45
$175,000–$199,999	210,000	8,576	1.98
$200,000–$299,999	384,000	21,152	4.89
$300,000–$399,999	152,000	12,284	2.84
$400,000–$499,999	77,000	8,196	1.89
$500,000–$999,999	116,000	18,883	4.36
$1,000,000 or more	58,000	36,610	8.46

^Total income after deductions for IRA and Keogh plans, alimony paid to a spouse, and interest penalties.

Source: Internal Revenue Service, *Statistics of Income, 1989 Individual Income Tax Returns*, Publication 1304, Washington, DC, 1992.

the federal budget deficit? Let's see. Table 5-1 shows the detailed breakdown of payment of the federal income tax by income of the taxpayer. The numbers in this table can be used to make some simple calculations about changes in tax revenues resulting from changes in taxation. Suppose, for example, that the federal government wants to increase federal income tax revenue by $100 billion. If tax payments were *doubled*, the higher payments would have to apply to taxpayers with incomes of $200,000 and above. If tax payments were increased 50 percent, the higher payments would have to apply to taxpayers with incomes of $80,000 and above.

Finally, if tax payments were increased 25 percent, the higher payments would have to apply to taxpayers with incomes of $20,000 and above! These estimates are certainly optimistic because they don't account for the reduced work effort and reduced income, and hence reduced tax payments, that higher tax rates would cause (more on this later!). Nevertheless, these numbers do indicate that unless the rates are raised to confiscatory levels, tax rates must be raised on both upper-income and middle-income taxpayers to raise any substantial new revenue.

WHO BENEFITTED FROM THE TAX CHANGES OF THE 1980S?

The American tax system, primarily at the federal level, underwent massive changes in the 1980s, and the merits of these changes are still being debated. There were four main components to the changes: (1) individual income tax rates were lowered, (2) individual income tax rates were indexed to inflation, (3) the income base to which tax rates are applied was expanded by the elimination or curtailment of tax deductions and exemptions, and (4) social security taxes were increased.

There were three main reasons for these changes in the federal tax system. First, many economists and others had become convinced that the complicated federal income tax system, with its seemingly endless set of special deductions, exemptions, and credits, had overtaken economic considerations in many consumer and business decisions.[10] That is, in considering an investment, a business-person might first consider the tax implications (e.g., a possible reduction in the business-person's taxes) before considering whether the investment was sound on economic grounds. Economists worried that such thinking would increase the number of "bad" investments in the economy, which would adversely affect the productivity and growth of the economy.

Second, many economists had become convinced that high tax rates, especially on the richest taxpayers, were counterproductive to the economy because the high rates discouraged investment and work activity.[11] As the decade of the 1980s began, stimulating economic growth was of prime importance because the economy was in the worst of all worlds with high inflation rates and an economywide recession in existence. The economists pushing lower tax rates believed that the lower rates would stimulate a boom of new spending and investment, which would lift the economy out of recession and would reduce inflation rates.

Third, the aging of the population and the longer lives of the retired had put the social security system in trouble; in short, the system was running out of money![12] To keep the system self-financing, higher social security tax rates were needed.

One of the tax changes clearly benefitted all taxpayers, and this was the indexing of federal income tax rates. The federal income tax system divides a taxpayer's income into segments and taxes each segment at a different rate. Also, in general, higher income segments are taxed at higher rates. For example, in 1993 the first $36,040 of a married couple's taxable income was taxed at a 15 percent rate, the next $51,039 of taxable income was taxed at a 28 percent rate, and any additional taxable income was taxed at a 31 percent rate.[13] Before the tax changes of 1986, there were 12 income segments and associated tax rates.

If the income segments to which each tax rate applied never changed, then inflation can push taxpayers into higher tax rates even if their real income didn't change. For example, suppose Jane and John Doe had exactly $36,040 of taxable income in 1993. They would have paid exactly 15 percent of their taxable income in federal taxes. Now suppose that between 1993 and 1994 a 10 percent inflation rate occurs, meaning that average consumer prices rise by

10 percent. Also suppose that Jane and John Doe receive 10 percent more in taxable income, meaning their taxable income rises by $3,604. Notice that Jane and John are not richer in real terms because the increase in their taxable income is just enough to keep up with the increase in prices. But the federal income tax system would consider them to be richer because the additional $3,604 in taxable income would be taxed at the higher tax rate of 28 percent. Most people, except maybe the IRS, would consider this to be unfair.

The indexing of the income segments in the federal income tax, one of the changes made in the 1980s, prevents this kind of unfairness. What this means is that each year the income ranges of each income segment are increased by the previous year's inflation rate. This means that, in our preceding example, the 1994 income segment to which the 15 percent rate applied would have increased by $3,604, meaning the 15 percent income segment would include taxable incomes up to $39,644. Therefore, Jane and John Doe would not be penalized by the tax system when their taxable income merely increased by the same rate as the inflation rate. All of their taxable income would be taxed at the 15 percent rate. Under this indexing of the income segments, taxpayers can have higher tax rates apply only if their taxable income rises faster than the inflation rate.

The other changes in the federal tax system in the 1980s have not been so universally applauded. The most controversial of the changes was the reduction in the tax rates applied to different income segments, and particularly the reduction in the highest tax rate applied to the very richest taxpayers. In 1980, this top tax rate was 70 percent, meaning that the richest taxpayers paid 70 percent of the income in their top-income segment in federal income taxes. This top tax rate was reduced twice in the 1980s, first to 50 percent and then to 28 percent, before being raised to 31 percent in 1990. The reduction in the top tax rate could be interpreted that tax policy in the 1980s benefitted primarily the rich. For example, it could be claimed that the rich saw their federal income taxes fall by 56 percent! This number is obtained by calculating the percentage change in the top tax rate cut from 70 percent to 31 percent.

Such an interpretation is misleading for three reasons. First, the reduction in the top tax rate from 70 percent to 31 percent for the richest taxpayers doesn't apply to the *entirety* of a rich taxpayer's income, but only applies to the highest segment of a rich taxpayer's income. Second, the interpretation ignores the fact that the tax changes in the 1980s doubled the sizes of the personal exemption and the standard deduction and, additionally, indexed both of these to inflation. The personal exemption is the amount of money each family is allowed to reduce their taxable income for each member in the family. The standard deduction is the amount of money a family without sufficient other deductions (such as the deduction for mortgage interest and property taxes paid by a homeowner) is allowed to reduce their taxable income. Both the personal exemption and the standard deduction affect lower-income taxpayers more than higher-income taxpayers. It's estimated that 5 million low-income taxpayers actually had their federal income taxes reduced to zero because of the changes in the personal exemption and standard deduction.[14]

Third, and perhaps most importantly, focusing only on the reduction in the tax rates ignores the fact that included in the tax changes was a broadening of the base of income which could be taxed. Here it's important to consider a concept called the *effective tax rate*. The effective tax rate takes account of both the tax rate and the income base to which the rate is applied. The following example will explain the idea. Take a taxpayer who has $100,000 in income. One tax system has an official tax rate of 50 percent, but first allows the taxpayer to exclude $60,000 of his or her income from taxation due to deductions and exemptions. This means the $100,000 taxpayer is taxed on only $40,000 of his or her income, and the tax paid is 0.50 * $40,000, or $20,000. The effective tax rate is ($20,000/$100,000) or 20 percent.

The alternative tax system has an official tax rate of only 25 percent, but the taxpayer can only exclude $10,000 of his or her income from taxation due to deductions and exemptions. The taxpayer is thus taxed on $90,000 of income. The taxpayer pays 0.25 * $90,000, or $22,500, in taxes. The effective tax rate is ($22,500/$100,000) or 22.5 percent. Thus, even though the tax rate is lower in the alternative system, since more income is taxed, the effective tax rate is higher.

The preceding example appears to illustrate actually what happened to the effective tax rates paid by the rich as a result of the federal tax changes made in the 1980s. These tax changes (especially those made in 1986) expanded the income base by eliminating or limiting many deductions, such as deductions for loans, many business deductions, and deductions for various investment losses. Professor James Long has calculated the effective federal income tax rates paid by various income groups, being careful to take account of changes in deductions, exemptions, and other factors affecting the income base. The results of Long's calculations are seen in Table 5-2. As the table shows, effective tax rates fell between 1981 and 1988 for all but the very richest taxpayers. Also, effective tax rates fell a greater percentage amount for lower-income taxpayers than for middle- or higher-income taxpayers.

This means the federal income tax system actually became more progressive in the 1980s. A progressive tax system is one in which richer taxpayers not only pay more taxes than poorer taxpayers, but the rich also pay a higher percentage of their income in taxes. For example, Long calculates that in 1981 a $250,000-income taxpayer paid an effective rate 85 percent higher than a $25,000-income taxpayer; by 1988, the $250,000-income taxpayer paid an effective rate 123 percent higher than the $25,000-income taxpayer.[15]

How could effective federal income tax rates on the very rich rise in the 1980s when the top tax rate was being cut from 70 percent to 28 percent? Long clearly gives the answer: The rich were taxed on a substantially higher percentage of their income after the tax changes of the 1980s. For example, Long calculates that taxpayers with over $1 million of income were taxed on 75 percent of that income in 1988, whereas they were only taxed on 34 percent of their income in 1981. In contrast, lower-income taxpayers (those with incomes under $50,000) had a smaller percentage of their incomes taxed as a result of the tax changes of the 1980s.

Other studies that examined the impact of federal income tax changes during the entire decade of the 1980s are consistent with the Long study. The

Table 5-2   Effective Federal Income Tax Rates

INCOME[a]	1981	1988	PERCENT CHANGE
Under $10,000	2.24%	1.46%	-34.8%
$10,000–$20,000	9.81%	5.68%	-43.3%
$20,000–$30,000	12.81%	8.98%	-29.9%
$30,000–$40,000	14.97%	10.32%	-31.1%
$40,000–$50,000	17.01%	11.14%	-34.5%
$50,000–70,000	18.63%	12.96%	-30.4%
$70,000–$90,000	20.18%	14.68%	-27.3%
$90,000–$115,000	21.39%	15.87%	-25.8%
$115,000–$150,000	22.56%	17.11%	-24.2%
$150,000–$200,000	23.35%	18.88%	-19.1%
$200,000–$300,000	23.66%	20.05%	-15.3%
$300,000–$400,000	23.32%	20.37%	-12.7%
$400,000–$500,000	24.41%	20.85%	-14.6%
$500,000–$1,000,000	22.32%	20.87%	-6.5%
Over $1,000,000	20.29%	21.11%	+4.0%

[a]Income is gross income, including contributions to individual retirement accounts, all capital gains and dividends, and unemployment compensation.

Source: James E. Long, "Does the Tax Structure Favor the Rich? A Case Study of Federal Income Tax Progressivity Before and After Tax Reform in the 1980's," *Backgrounder*, no. 7 (1993), The James Madison Institute, Tallahassee, FL, p. 4. All rights reserved; used with permission.

IRS calculated effective tax rates by income group through 1989 and found results almost identical to Long's. Pechman, Robbins/Robbins, and Gwartney found that the tax changes *reduced* federal income taxes in percentage terms the most for low-income taxpayers, reduced federal income taxes more modestly for middle-income taxpayers, and either reduced federal income taxes the least or increased federal income taxes for the richest taxpayers. Fullerton and Rogers found that the 1986 tax act benefitted the poor at the expense of the rich.[16]

Corporations also saw their effective tax rate rise in the 1980s. A General Accounting Office report shows that the effective corporate income tax rate doubled from 16.5 percent to 33 percent in the 1980s.[17] Furthermore, careful analysis of who pays the corporate income tax finds that it's not paid only by rich people. The corporate income tax is considered a cost of production by corporations. Hence, the prices of products and services made by corporations are higher with the corporate income tax than without it. In other words, corporations pass on some of the cost of the corporate income tax to buyers of their products. Because these buyers are consumers of all income levels, economists have found that all consumers indirectly pay about the same percentage of their income in the corporate income tax.[18]

What about the last major tax change of the 1980s, the increase in social security taxes? Social security taxes were significantly increased in the 1980s in order to maintain the self-financing nature of the system. However, since social security tax rates don't increase with income (that is, the tax rate is the same for a $10,000 worker as for a $40,000 worker), and since no social security taxes are paid on incomes above a certain limit ($57,600 in 1993), it is claimed that social security taxes are regressive. A regressive tax is one that hits the poor relatively harder than the rich, resulting in the poor paying a higher percentage of their income in the tax than the rich. Therefore, critics of the tax changes of the 1980s say that the increases in social security taxes were particularly damaging to the poor.[19]

It is true that when social security tax changes are considered along with federal income tax changes, the benefits received by the poor from the tax changes of the 1980s are reduced. In fact, Robbins and Robbins find that when federal income tax changes *and* social security tax changes are considered together, the tax reductions received by the poorest taxpayers were cut by one-third to one-half (although Robbins and Robbins still show tax reductions for the poor and middle class). Also, when federal income tax changes and social security tax changes are taken together, Robbins and Robbins find that the greatest percentage tax reductions were received by the richest taxpayers.[20]

However, social security taxes are only regressive if one ignores how social security benefits are paid to retirees. Social security benefits are not returned to all retirees dollar for dollar with what the retiree paid into the system. In fact, there is considerable redistribution from high-income workers to low-income workers within social security. This is clearly seen from the formula for calculating social security benefits. For example, in 1990, social security paid to retirees 90 cents for every dollar of the retiree's average indexed monthly earnings under $365, but paid only 32 cents for every dollar of the retiree's average indexed monthly earnings between $365 and $2,145.[21] Kotlikoff argues that when the redistribution of income from the rich to the poor in the calculation of social security benefits is accounted for, social security is not a regressive system, but in fact is a progressive system (meaning higher tax rates are paid by the rich).[22] Therefore, putting social security on sound footing by raising tax rates in the 1980s actually benefitted most the poor in the long run.

Therefore, the evidence indicates that the federal tax changes in the 1980s did not benefit only high-income taxpayers. In fact, much of the evidence suggests that the rich paid more as a result of the changes. This brings up a debate which has been ongoing for at least 15 years—what is the relationship between tax rates and tax revenues? I turn to this debate next.

DO HIGHER TAX RATES INCREASE OR DECREASE TAX REVENUE?

The notion that tax rates influence economic behavior is not a new idea in economics. In fact, the idea of such a relationship can be found in economic thinking as far back as 200 years ago.[23] The relationship between tax rates and economic behavior is really very simple. It starts with the idea that people will do more of something if the rewards for doing it increase. That is, people will work more if the reward from working (the wage rate) increases, and people will invest more if the reward from investing (the interest rate or rate of return) increases. Conversely, people will do less of something if the reward for doing it decreases. Therefore, we expect that people will be motivated to work less if the wage rate decreases, and people will invest less if the investment rate of return decreases.

How do tax rates enter into these relationships? Tax rates on wages and on investment returns obviously reduce the benefits from both working and investing. So, if tax rates on wages and investment returns are increased, we can expect the amount of working and the amount of investing to decline. On the other hand, if tax rates on wages and investment returns are decreased, we can expect the amount of working and the amount of investing to increase.

These ideas aren't really controversial, and there's much economic evidence to support them.[24] What's controversial is the further link that's sometimes made to tax revenues. That is, if tax rates on work and investing are cut, then since the amounts of work and investing increase, tax revenues won't decrease as much as might be expected because the lower rates are being applied to a larger economic base. This is not controversial because most economists will concede that lower tax rates will stimulate economic activity. What is controversial is whether lower tax rates will stimulate *enough* new economic activity and will increase the economic base so much so that tax revenues actually *increase*! That is, can we really have the best of both worlds—lower tax rates and more tax revenue?

The proposition that lower tax rates could actually result in greater tax revenues for the government was popularized by the economist Arthur Laffer with his so-called Laffer curve (Figure 5-2). The Laffer curve simply relates tax revenues and tax rates. Laffer argues that over a range of lower tax rates (from 0% to M% in Figure 5-2), increasing tax rates does increase tax revenues. However, beyond some critical point (M%), increasing tax rates actually decreases tax revenues.

Does the Laffer curve exist, and in particular, does that part of the curve exist where higher tax rates are associated with lower tax revenues? The answer is a qualified yes. Economists who have studied the possibility of a Laffer curve have found that it can exist under certain conditions. In particular, studies have found that the existence of the Laffer curve depends on how much workers respond to changes in wage rates, how much companies' de-

Figure 5-2 The Laffer Curve

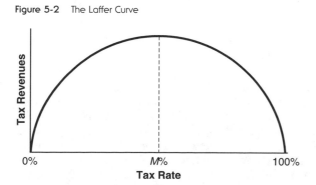

mands for labor respond to changes in wage rates, and how real (inflation-adjusted) interest rates change in response to changes in tax rates. Nevertheless, with reasonable estimates for these factors, studies agree that certainly tax rates above 75 percent are counterproductive (meaning tax revenues actually fall as the tax rate is increased), and some studies find that rates above 50 percent are counterproductive.[25] Therefore, the conclusion from the tax rate cuts of the 1980s is that they resulted in more tax revenue from the rich but probably lost tax revenue from everyone else.[26]

But remember that although federal income tax rates were cut in the 1980s, the tax base was broadened through the elimination or restriction of tax deductions and tax shelters. What was the result for federal income tax revenues? Tax revenues from the federal personal income tax actually increased in the 1980s. At the end of the 1980s' economic expansion in 1990, federal personal income tax revenues were $92 billion higher in real terms (1991 dollars) than at the beginning of the expansion in 1983.[27]

Why then did the federal budget deficit increase in the 1980s if federal tax revenues actually increased? The answer is clearly shown in Figure 5-3. As a percent of the annual economic pie, total federal revenues remained remarkably stable at 19 percent during the 1980s. (And, in fact, this percentage was slightly higher than the 18.5 percent average during the 1970s). So revenues weren't the problem. Instead, federal spending as a percent of the annual economic pie *rose* in the 1980s to an average of 23.1 percent, up from an average of 20.7 percent in the 1970s. Even excluding interest payments on the debt, federal spending as a percent of the annual economic pie rose from an average of 19 percent in the 1970s to over 20 percent in the 1980s. A close look at the spending trends in the 1980s shows that both defense and nondefense spending were responsible for the relative rise in federal spending.[28]

What can we conclude from this discussion of tax rates and tax revenues? Will tax revenues always rise when tax rates are cut? Of course not.

Figure 5-3   Federal Spending and Federal Revenues as a Percent of the National Economy

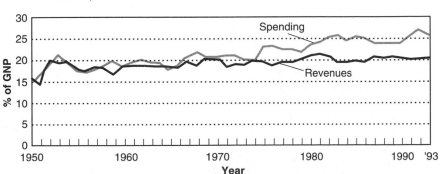

Source: U.S. Office of Management and Budget, *Budget of the U.S. Government, FY 1993*, Supplement, U.S. Government Printing Office, February 1992.

However, current research does indicate that tax rates certainly above 75 percent, and maybe above 50 percent, can be counterproductive, and cutting tax rates at that level can often result in greater tax revenues.

Should politicians and government officials strive to set the tax rate at that level which maximizes tax revenues? (That is, should we strive for the tax rate $M\%$ in Figure 5-2 at the top of the Laffer curve?) Not necessarily. Collectively, we should set the tax rate at that level which provides the revenues needed to do what government can most productively do. This suggests that government projects and programs should all be evaluated on a cost-benefit basis. However, included in the costs should be an accounting of the decline in economic activity or income which occurs if the tax rate must be increased to fund the government project or program, assuming the tax rate before the increase is below the tax revenue-maximizing rate. That is, government should not just consider its financial balance sheet when judging tax policy, but should also consider the financial balance sheet of the entire economy.

An example may help in understanding this point. Suppose the U.S. economy generates $6 trillion of activity annually. Suppose that an effective tax rate of 25 percent generates $1.5 trillion of revenue. Suppose that if the effective tax rate were increased to 30 percent, the economy would shrink by 10 percent ($600 billion) to $5.4 trillion. At a 30 percent effective tax rate and a $5.4 trillion base, tax revenues to the government would be $1.62 trillion, meaning an increase in revenues of $120 billion with the higher tax rate. The question is, however, is it worth losing $600 billion in private economic activity in order to generate $120 billion more in tax revenues? It is this kind of trade-off that policymakers and politicians should recognize.

WHAT'S THE "BEST" TAX SYSTEM?

I should qualify the title to this section by first saying, "Assuming we need to raise tax revenues for government activities, what's the best tax system?" If I don't qualify the question, some of you may say that "no taxes" is the best tax system!

There are three hotly debated topics surrounding the "best" tax system. The first debate is over the pluses and minuses of so-called *consumption taxes* versus income taxes. The second debate involves the relative merits of *user taxes* compared to general taxes such as income or consumption taxes. The third debate asks whether a much simplified income tax system, the so-called *flat tax*, would be preferable to the current system of deductions, exemptions, credits, and different tax rates.

Consumption versus Income Taxes

Consumption taxes are taxes which are paid when you purchase something. For example, if you buy a $50 coat and the consumption tax is 5 percent, then you'll pay $2.50 in taxes. Consumption taxes are more commonly called sales taxes. We've already talked about income taxes, which are simply the taxes paid on the income you earn.

Our tax system has both income taxes and consumption taxes. The income tax is the major revenue producer for the federal government. Most states and some localities also have an income tax, but it is much less than the federal income tax. The general consumption or sales tax is a major revenue producer for the states. The federal government has some sales taxes on specific items, such as alcohol, tobacco products, and gasoline, but the federal government does not have a general sales tax on all products.

So what's the issue? The issue is primarily at the federal level, and it is simply this: Should the federal government replace the income tax with a general federal consumption tax? Think of it. If there were no federal income tax, there would be no federal income tax withholding from your paycheck, and no worries about paying the federal government on April 15. Also, with a federal consumption tax, you only pay tax if you buy something. Savings would not be taxed. Savings would only be taxed when you took the money out of savings accounts and spent it! A federal sales tax of 12 percent would replace the revenue produced by the federal personal income tax, and a federal sales tax of 14 percent would replace the revenue produced by both the federal personal and corporate income taxes.[29]

Many economists recommend a movement to a federal consumption tax and away from the federal income tax because such a change would motivate more saving. Since both the money put into a savings account and the interest which that money earns would not be taxed under a federal consumption tax system until it was used to buy something, all of us would be additionally motivated to save more and consume less today. This is considered a plus by those economists who worry that Americans are not saving enough (see Chapter 3).

But wouldn't the consumption tax and the corresponding increase in saving cause such a big reduction in spending that the economy would fall into a recession (or worse yet, a depression)? Not so, say economists who have carefully analyzed the change.[30] The increase in saving would provide more funds for businesses to invest in new equipment and technology. These investments would make the economy more efficient and productive, which would cause real wages and real incomes to increase at faster rates than they would under the income tax. The increased real income would actually create more spending in the economy in the long run.

Actually, the bigger concern expressed about replacement of the federal income tax with a federal consumption tax has to do with its impact on consumers with different incomes. The conventional wisdom is that a consumption tax is regressive, meaning it hits the poor relatively harder than the rich.[31] This would occur if the poor spent a higher percentage of their income than the rich. This would result in the consumption tax (one with a flat rate which doesn't vary with the income of the consumer) taking a higher percentage of a poor person's income than it takes of a rich person's income. In contrast, the federal income tax, with its personal exemption and rates which rise with income, is a progressive tax. This means the rich pay a higher percentage of their income to the income tax than do the poor. So many think that replacement of the federal income tax with a federal consumption tax would hurt the poor and help the rich.

The preceding analysis was considered to be accurate up until a few years ago. However, there's new thinking to suggest that a consumption tax isn't nearly as regressive as once thought. First, it can be made not to be regressive. A consumption tax can be made progressive by adding a tax-refund feature to it. Under this system, taxpayers would annually file a form with the federal government. The form would show their income and the amount of consumption tax paid. The federal government would refund some of the consumption tax to the taxpayer. The percentage of the refund would depend on the income of the taxpayer; a higher percentage would be refunded to the very poorest taxpayers, and the percentage would decline as the taxpayer's income increased. In this way, the federal government could make the consumption tax as progressive as it desired.[32]

A more fundamental challenge to the conventional wisdom about the regressivity of the consumption tax comes from economists who have studied the lifetime burden of taxes. The traditional way of studying the impact of taxes on taxpayers was to take a sample of taxpayers in a single year and measure the percentage of income paid in taxes by taxpayers of different incomes. This analysis typically showed that low-income taxpayers paid a higher percentage of their income in consumption taxes than did high-income taxpayers.

The problem with this type of analysis is that it takes a snapshot of taxpayers at a particular point in time and doesn't consider taxpayer behavior and patterns over their lifetime. For example, a 40-year-old "rich" taxpayer may indeed save a large percentage of his or her income, but much of these savings will be spent by the rich taxpayer later in life during retirement. Therefore, when lifetime behavior is considered, the percentage of lifetime income consumed by rich taxpayers will be much closer to the percentage of lifetime income consumed by poor taxpayers.[33] This means that the percentage of income paid in consumption taxes, when measured over the lifetime, will be much closer for rich and poor taxpayers than when measured on only an annual "snapshot" basis. In fact, some economists have found just the opposite of the conventional wisdom—they have found that general consumption taxes are progressive over the lifetime of income.[34]

Clearly, there are good reasons to consider replacement of the federal income tax with a federal consumption tax. It could promote saving and long-run increases in real income, and it could be made as progressive as the current federal income tax.

User Taxes

User taxes are taxes on particular products or activities with the tax revenues earmarked for government projects which serve that product or activity. A good example is the gasoline tax paid by drivers, where the revenues are used to build and maintain roads and related transportation facilities.

Are user taxes better than general taxes, such as economywide income or consumption taxes? Obviously roads could be financed out of general income and sales taxes. User taxes are a preferable way of financing certain public projects as long as a clear link can be made between the financing and the project. In this case user taxes have two advantages. First, those citizens who use the user-financed project or activity pay for it, so there is an element of fairness in the user tax. Second, because the users pay the bill for the project or activity, they will take account of this cost when deciding how much to use the project or activity.

A major complaint against user taxes is that they hurt the poor. However, this complaint ignores a fundamental difference between income support and efficient use of resources. Our economy operates best when consumers face the full cost of the resources they use. When this happens, consumers will frugally use resources without overuse or waste. This goal applies to all consumers, rich and poor alike. The poor can face and pay user fees and not be disadvantaged as long as they have adequate income support. Income support for the poor is part of the larger issue of poverty.

The Flat Tax

Finally, there's no lack of complaining about the income tax system, particularly at the federal level. Many citizens say the system is still too complicated with too many deductions, exemptions, credits, and other special treatments of income, despite the changes made in the 1980s. Because of this perceived complexity, many citizens think the federal income tax system must favor the rich, who presumably have the power and money to use the tax system to their advantage.

A long proposed alternative and simplification to the federal income tax system is the flat rate tax. Under a pure flat rate tax, all tax deductions, tax credits, and tax exemptions (except maybe an exemption per person in the family) would be eliminated. Furthermore, all dollars of income would be taxed at the same rate, regardless of how rich or poor the taxpayer is. Of course, since rich taxpayers earn more income, they would still pay more in taxes. To protect very poor taxpayers, there could be some limited amount of income which would go untaxed. Designers of a flat income tax calculate that a flat rate of 19 percent could raise as much revenue as the current system.[35]

There are two big advantages to the flat tax. First, it is simple. Filing a tax form could take only minutes. Under one proposal, the individual income tax form would be reduced to 12 lines. Second, the flat tax would separate the tax system from individual decisions. Under the current tax system, certain expenditures are favored over others. The best example is the mortgage interest deduction for homeowners. This deduction substantially reduces the net cost of owning a home and encourages homeownership. Renters, however, receive no similar tax break. There are numerous other examples like this for consumers and businesses alike in which the federal government uses the tax code to encourage or discourage certain activities.

An argument against the flat tax is that it is not progressive. As stated earlier, a progressive tax system is one in which richer taxpayers pay not only more taxes (because they have more income), but they also pay a higher percentage of their income in taxes. The theory as to why they should according to supporters of a progressive tax system is that the value of a dollar to a rich person is less than the value of a dollar to a poor person. Therefore, to make the "pain" of paying taxes the same for both rich and poor taxpayers, rich taxpayers must have a higher percentage of their income taken away in taxes.

Whether you accept this notion or not, the flat tax could be made progressive in two ways. First, it could be made progressive by not taxing a certain amount of income for poor taxpayers. For example, Hauser shows that with a $16,000 standard deduction, a 20 percent flat tax system would result in an effective tax rate of 4 percent for taxpayers with $20,000 of income, 14 percent for taxpayers with $50,000 of income, 17 percent for taxpayers with $100,000 of income, and 19 percent for taxpayers with $500,000 of income.[36] Second, the flat tax could be made progressive by having a slight variation on the flat tax rate, in which slightly higher tax rates would apply to higher levels of income.[37]

It is unlikely that a pure flat tax system will ever occur because there is widespread support for influencing behavior through the tax code, and because industries which are favored by the tax code will argue for keeping their deductions, exemptions, or credits. Nonetheless, the flat tax can be used as the standard by which to judge other changes to the income tax system.

NOTES

1. For a positive view of the tax cuts, see Robert Bartley, *The Seven Fat Years* (New York: The Free Press, 1992), pp. 163–176; for a negative view of the tax cuts, see Robert McIntyre, *Inequality and the Federal Budget Deficit* (Washington, DC: Citizens for Tax Justice, September 1991).

2. If businesses consider taxes as another cost, then product prices to consumers will rise, but depending on the responsiveness of consumer demand to price, product prices may not rise by 100 percent of the taxes. Similarly, if payroll taxes, such as social security, are considered a cost of labor by businesses, then wage rates will be lower than they would be without the tax, although, again, not necessarily by the full amount of the tax.

3. Tax Foundation, *Tax Features*, 36, no. 9 (October 1992). The Tax Foundation measure is higher than the percent of GNP measure due to the phaseout of social security taxes at a certain level of income ($55,500 in 1992). Since the average two-earner family income was $53,984 in 1992, all of this income would be subject to the social security tax, whereas not all of GNP would be subject to the social security tax.

4. The net tax rates cited are for males. The net tax rates are slightly lower for females (32.8 percent for a citizen in 1991). The net tax rates are also average lifetime rates, which account for the lifetime of taxes paid and transfers received. See Alan Auerbach, Jagadeesh Gokhale, and Laurence Kotlikoff, "Generational Accounts and Lifetime Tax Rates, 1900–1991," *Economic Review*, Federal Reserve Bank of Cleveland, 29, no. 1 (1993), 2–13.

5. U.S. Bureau of Labor Statistics, Consumer Expenditure Survey, 1988–89, Bulletin 2383, Washington, DC (August 1991).

6. Congressional Budget Office, *The Economic and Budget Outlook: Fiscal Years 1992–96* (Washington, DC: U.S. Government Printing Office, 1991), p. 124.

7. U.S. Bureau of Labor Statistics, Consumer Expenditure Survey, 1972–73, Bulletin 1992, Washington, DC, 1978; and Bulletin 2383, August 1991.

8. Ibid.

9. Tax Foundation, *Tax Features*, 36, no. 8 (September 1992).

10. See Jeffrey Birnbaum and Alan Murray, *Showdown at Gucci Gulch* (New York: Random House, 1987), esp. pp. 23–64.

11. See Lawrence Lindsey, *The Growth Experiment* (New York: Basic Books, 1990), pp. 15–52.

12. Robert Myers, *Within the System, My Half Century in Social Security* (Winsted, CT: ACTEX Publications, 1992), pp. 1–30. Myers estimates that in 1983 the social security system was losing $47 million daily.

13. Taxable income is a taxpayer's gross income minus adjustments, exemptions, and deductions taken by the taxpayer.

14. Eytan Sheshinski, "Treatment of Capital Income in Recent Tax Reforms and the Cost of Capital in Industrialized Countries," in *Tax Policy and the Economy*, Vol. 4, National Bureau of Economic Research (Cambridge, MA: MIT Press), pp. 25–42.

15. Long finds the same results for income groups defined by real income.

16. See Internal Revenue Service, *Individual Income Tax Returns, Statistics of Income 1989*, Publication 1304, Washington, DC, 1992; Joseph Pechman, *Tax Reform, The Rich and the Poor*, 2nd ed. (Washington, DC: The Brookings Institution, 1989), p. 85; Gary Robbins and Aldana Robbins, *Tax Fairness: Myths and Reality* (Dallas, TX: National Center for Policy Analysis, Policy Report No. 90, March 1991); James Gwartney, "Taxes in the 1980s and the Clinton Plan," Madison Op-Ed Series (Tallahassee, FL: The James Madison Institute for Public Policy Studies, May 1993); and Don Fullerton and Diane Lim Rogers, *Who Bears the Lifetime Tax Burden?* (Washington, DC: The Brookings Institution, 1993), p. 221.

17. U.S. General Accounting Office, *Tax Policy: 1988 and 1989 Company Effective Tax Rates Higher Than in Prior Years*, Washington, DC (August 1992).

18. Fullerton and Rogers, *Who Bears the Lifetime Tax Burden?*, p. 180. Fullerton and Rogers found some evidence that the corporate income tax hits low-income consumers relatively harder than it hits middle-income consumers. The reason for this is that poorer consumers spend large fractions of their incomes on goods produced by the corporate sector, particularly gasoline, tobacco products, and alcohol products.

19. "Understanding the Tax Decade," the Urban Institute, Policy and Research Report (Winter/Spring), 1992, 1–4.

20. Robbins and Robbins, *Tax Fairness: Myths and Reality*.

21. American Association of Individual Investors, *Social Security's Role in a Retirement Program* (Chicago: American Association of Individual Investors).

22. Laurence Kotlikoff, *Generational Accounting* (New York: The Free Press, 1992), pp. 110–111.

23. See Adam Smith, *The Wealth of Nations* (London: Dent & Sons Ltd.), reprinted 1975, Book V, Chapter II.

24. For the impact of taxes on work, see Jerry Hausman, "Taxes and Labor Supply," in Alan Auerbach and Martin Feldstein, eds., *Handbook of Public Economics*, vol. 1 (Amsterdam: North-Holland Publishing, 1985). For the impact of taxes on saving and investing, see Michael Boskin, "Taxation, Savings, and the Rate of Interest," *Journal of Political Economy*, 86, no. 2, part 2 (April 1978), S3–S27; Owens Evans, "Tax Policy, the Interest Elasticity of Savings and Capital Accumulation: Numerical Analysis of Theoretical Models," *American Economic Review*, 73, no. 3 (June 1983), 398–410; and Alan Auerbach, "Taxation, Corporate Financial Policy, and the Cost of Capital," *Journal of Economic Literature*, 21, no. 3 (September 1983), 905–940. Research

also suggests that higher tax rates can reduce investment in personal education and training (so-called *human capital*); see Philip Trostel, "The Effect of Taxation on Human Capital," *Journal of Political Economy*, 101, no. 2 (April 1993), 327–350.

25. See Don Fullerton, "On the Possibility of an Inverse Relationship Between Tax Rates and Government Revenues," *Journal of Public Economics*, 19 (October 1982), 3–22; and Lindsey, *The Growth Experiment*, pp. 81–92. Fullerton gives a range of estimates, but his most likely estimate is nearer the 75 percent tax rate point. Lindsey's model yields the 50 percent counterproductive tax rate point. Canto, Joines, and Webb find that the Kennedy income tax cuts in the mid-1960s, which cut the top income tax rate from 90 percent to 70 percent, didn't result in lower tax revenues; (see Victor Canto, Douglas Joines, and Robert Webb, "The Revenue Effects of the Kennedy and Reagan Tax Cuts: Some Time Series Estimates," *Journal of Business and Economic Statistics*, 4, no. 3 (July 1986), 281–287. The maximum tax rate point on the Laffer curve ($M\%$ in Figure 3-2) may occur at much lower rates for localities, where individuals and businesses find it easier to move from high-tax jurisdictions to low-tax jurisdictions; see Robert Inman, "Can Philadelphia Escape Its Fiscal Crisis With Another Tax Increase?" *Business Review*, Federal Reserve Bank of Philadelphia (September/October 1992), pp. 5–20.

26. For estimates on the additional tax revenue from the rich, see Daniel Feenberg and James Poterba, *Income Inequality and the Incomes of Very High Income Taxpayers: Evidence from Tax Returns*, working paper No. 4229, Cambridge, MA, National Bureau of Economic Research (December 1992).

27. In 1991 dollars, federal personal income tax receipts increased from $395 billion in 1983 to $487 billion in 1990. As a percent of gross national product, federal income tax revenue rose from an annual average of 7.9 percent in the 1970s to 8.6 percent in the 1980s (*Economic Report of the President*).

28. Lindsey estimates that between 1980 and 1987, 66 percent of the increase in the national debt was due to defense spending increases, 13 percent was due to nondefense spending increases, and 21 percent was due to tax reductions (Lindsey, *The Growth Experiment*, pp. 96–97).

29. Sales tax rates are based on 1991 data in the *Economic Report of the President*.

30. Laurence Kotlikoff, "The Economic Impact of Replacing Federal Income Taxes With a Sales Tax," *Policy Analysis*, no. 193, Washington, DC, Cato Institute (April 1993).

31. Pechman, *Tax Reform, The Rich and the Poor*, pp. 111–116.

32. The same effect could be accomplished with a refund based on family size (see Kotlikoff, Cato Institute, p. 3).

33. James Poterba, "Lifetime Incidence and the Distributional Burden of Excise Taxes," *American Economic Review*, 79, no. 2 (May 1989), 325–330.

34. G. E. Metcalf, "The Lifetime Incidence of State and Local Taxes: Measuring Changes During the 1980s," Cambridge, MA, National Bureau of Economic Research Working Paper No. 4252 (January 1993). Fullerton and Rogers still find the country's existing sales taxes to be repressive. However, this is due to the larger proportion of income which the poor spend on goods that have very high sales tax rates, such as gasoline, alcohol, and tobacco products (Fullerton and Rogers, *Who Bears the Lifetime Tax Burden?*, pp. 174–176).

35. Robert Hall and Alvin Rabushka, *The Flat Tax* (Stanford, CA: Hoover Institution Press, 1985).

36. W. Kurt Hauser, "Try the Flat Tax," *The Wall Street Journal*, May 14, 1993, p. A10.

37. Ibid., pp. 67–68.

III. BUSINESS, JOBS, AND OUR COMPETITIVE POSITION

In some ways, this is the most important part of our excursion into economic issues. This section deals with issues which determine our country's ability to produce income and a good standard of living for its citizens: the success of business, the creation of jobs, and our ability to compete with foreign companies and countries.

There's been no lack of concern about these issues. Some observers long ago pronounced the death of U.S. industry and manufacturing. There have also been questions raised about the ability of U.S. workers to compete with lower-paid foreign workers. Many citizens yearn for the "good old days" of the 1950s and 1960s when, they perceive, U.S. industry and products dominated the world. Some also say that industrial development can no longer be left to the market system, that the government must establish an active industrial policy. Would this be a good idea? These issues are wrestled with in Chapter 6.

Jobs, jobs, jobs! Nothing really matters, economically speaking, unless you have a job. But where are the jobs today? Are they all going to Mexico? Almost everyday newspapers and news programs carry stories of large corporations cutting jobs. Furthermore, many argue that the jobs being cut are high-paying manufacturing jobs, and the jobs being created are low-paying service jobs. What's really going on here? Has the great American jobs machine ground to a halt? Are we facing a jobless economic expansion, or are there jobs and opportunities being created which don't make the headlines? These issues are examined in Chapter 7.

Finally, many Americans measure America's economic success or failure by the country's ability to go "head to head" with foreign companies and countries in international trade. Using this standard, many observers interpret recent evidence as not being good for the United States. For the better part of two decades, the United States has run a trade deficit, meaning the country has imported more goods and services than it has exported. Also, it is alleged that the United States is now a *debtor nation*, meaning the country owes more money to foreign countries than those countries owe to us. And everyone knows that foreign ownership in the United States has been on the rise. So on the surface, the numbers don't look good. Have we really lost our edge in international trade? Have we become a second-rate economic power? Will free-trade agreements like NAFTA (North American Free Trade Agreement) increase or decrease these problems? The answers are all in Chapter 8.

6

The rise (not the fall)
of American industry

The news has not been good about American industry in recent years. U.S. manufacturing jobs are down and imports of foreign manufactured products are up. American factory workers are now competing with workers in Mexico, Europe, and the Far East. The American industrial plant is old, but the factories of South Korea and Japan are new. Has the twilight of the American industrial engine arrived?

Maybe not. In this chapter you'll learn the economic way of measuring the size of an industry. You'll also learn about the importance of worker productivity and how high wages don't necessarily imply uncompetitive workers. Finally, we'll examine the evidence on American business investments for the future.

MEASURING U.S. MANUFACTURING

Although manufacturing employment in America rose from 15 million workers after World War II to 19 million workers in 1990, U.S. manufacturing employment declined by over 1 million workers in the 1980s. Furthermore, as a percentage of all U.S. workers, manufacturing's share fell from 35 percent in 1946 to 22 percent in 1980 to 17 percent in 1990.[1] Isn't this strong evidence that manufacturing is on the decline in America?

No. The employment shares just cited are one way of measuring the relative importance of an industry, but they're not the best way. Employment is an input, which along with other inputs of machinery, land, and management, is used to produce the output of manufactured products. Our focus here is on the relative importance of the output, manufactured products, in the economy. Therefore, to gauge this, we should use some measure of the output (manufactured products) rather than a measure of one of the inputs (employment). This is not to say that employment in manufacturing in not an important issue—it is, but it's a different issue than the relative importance of manufactured products in the economy.

So how do we measure the relative importance of manufacturing output in our economy? There are two ways. One way is to measure the dollar value of manufactured products, being careful to eliminate the impact of increases on prices of manufactured products over time. In essence, this measure is a proxy for the total quantity of manufactured products. If we didn't eliminate the impact of price increases, then the measure of manufactured output could increase simply because prices increased, not because the quantity of output increased.

The second measure of the relative importance of manufacturing output answers the following question: Of the total value of goods and services produced in the economy in a given year (gross national product), what percent is manufactured products? This measure truly puts the volume of manufactured output in the perspective of the entire economy and is similar to our earlier measures of the relative sizes of private and public debt.

Both measures are shown in Figure 6-1 for the post-World War II period. In terms of the real (inflation-adjusted) dollar value of manufactured products, this value has steadily increased from $226 billion in 1947 to $963 billion in 1990 (all in 1982 dollars), a fourfold increase. In terms of its percentage of total output of the economy, manufacturing's share has fluctuated between 19 percent and 24 percent since World War II, and the share in 1990 was over 20 percent.[2] So rather than declining, manufacturing is just as important today as at any time in the past 40 years.[3]

Figure 6-1   Relative Size of U.S. Manufacturing

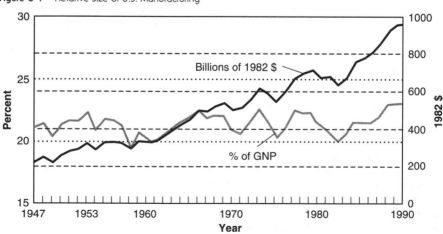

Source: *Economic Report of the President*, U.S. Government Printing Office, February 1992; Michelle Clark, "The Pitfalls of Industrial Policy," *The Regional Economist*, Federal Reserve Bank of St. Louis, April 1993, p. 11.

There' more. Most people probably think that the U.S. share of total world manufacturing output has fallen in recent decades. Not so. As Table 6-1 shows, the U.S. share of world manufacturing output actually increased between 1975 and 1988. Among the major producers of world manufactured products, only Japan and Italy also experienced share increases.

Although I have not favored using employment to measure the importance of manufacturing, it's still interesting to look at worldwide trends in manufacturing employment. It is true that the U.S. share of total *world* manufacturing employment fell in the 1980s, from 8.8 percent in the early 1980s to 7.8 percent in the late 1980s.[4] But among the *major industrialized* countries in the world, the U.S. share of total manufacturing employment has held steady at 27 percent between 1980 and 1988, while the U.S. share of total industrial employment (employment in manufacturing, mining, construction, and utilities) among industrialized countries has actually increased over the past three decades, from 25 percent in 1965 to 28 percent in 1980 to 29 percent in 1988.[5] These statistics mean that the United States is moving out of industrial employment and into service employment *no faster* than other industrialized countries. In fact, among the major industrialized countries, only New Zealand has had a slower growth in its service employment relative to its industrial employment.[6]

Although these statistics show a stronger U.S. manufacturing than is commonly thought, there could still be problems within specific manufacturing industries. One manufacturing industry which has received much attention is the U.S. high-tech industry. High-technology industries include companies which develop cutting-edge products and technology. Typically these companies do substantial research and product development. Much attention is devoted to high-tech companies because research and development in new technology and products is considered to be crucial to keeping a coun-

Table 6-1   Share of World Manufactured Output[a]

	1975		1988
United States	25.5%		27.0%
Germany, Federal Republic	12.0		9.5
Japan	11.5		17.5
France	7.5		5.5
United Kingdom	7.0		4.8
Italy	4.5		4.9
Spain	3.0		2.0
Brazil	2.5		2.5
Canada	2.3		2.3
Argentina	2.0	India	2.0
Other Countries	22.5		23.0

[a]Country's share of world (excluding centrally planned economies) manufacturing value-added at constant 1980 prices.

Source: United Nations Industrial Development Organization, *Handbook of Industrial Statistics, 1990,* Vienna (1990), pp. 67–68.

try competitive in international trade. The high-tech industry includes companies in aerospace, computers and office machines, electronics, drugs, instruments, and electrical machinery.

Has the U.S. high-tech industry been shrinking, and has it been losing ground to high-tech industries in countries like Japan and Germany? Let's look at the evidence. First, by every measure, the relative size of the U.S. high-tech industry has been increasing in recent years, not decreasing. High-tech manufacturing output increased from 20 percent of total U.S. manufacturing output in 1980 to 30 percent in 1990. Real business expenditure on research and development almost doubled between 1970 and 1990, rising from $43 billion in 1970 to $79 billion in 1990 (all in 1982 dollars). Real business expenditures on research and development as a percent of the total economy also increased from 1.7 percent in the late 1970s to 2 percent in the late 1980s.[7]

It is true that two of our major competitors, Japan and Germany, have caught up to the United States in the relative size of their high-tech spending. Of course, because the U.S. economy is so much bigger than the economies of Japan and Germany, the absolute size of research and development spending in 1990 was over twice as big in the United States compared to Japan, and was over five times as big in the United States compared to Germany. But as a percentage of their economies, the United States, Japan, and Germany in 1990 spent about 2 percent of their annual national incomes on business research and development. In contrast, in the late 1960s, the United States spent twice as much of its annual national income on business research and development as did Japan and Germany.[8]

Should this be a concern for us? Not necessarily. Much of the increase in relative spending on business research and development in Japan and Germany is probably due to the *war recovery effect*. By this I mean the recovery from the devastation of World War II in both Japan and Germany. With the U.S. economy relatively untouched by the war, it shouldn't be surprising that the United States dominated the world economy in almost every area in the 1950s and 1960s. However, as time has passed, both Japan and Germany have been able to rebuild and to regain the competitive positions they held before the war.

Many who worry about the Japanese and Germans catching up to us in high-tech industries and in the relative amount of research and development spending say that we need government intervention to help us regain the dominance we held in the 1950s and 1960s; that is, we need an *industrial policy*. I'll address this issue in the last part of this chapter. But our next stop is the worker in terms of effectiveness and efficiency. This is the topic of labor productivity.

LABOR PRODUCTIVITY

The American workers' efficiency and productivity have been called into question. Furthermore, with the high wages paid to American workers compared to many foreign workers, many wonder how the American worker can expect to compete in the future world of more open trade. Are the days of the American worker, especially in manufacturing, limited?

Before answering this question, let me address why you should be interested in this discussion at all. There are two reasons. Obviously, more productive workers are more competitive workers in the worldwide economic race. Everything else equal, countries which can get more output from each worker will be viewed by businesses as better places to locate factories and offices. Thus, countries with more productive workers are more likely to get the jobs.

The second reason you should be interested in worker productivity is even more personal. More productive workers will usually be paid more. More productive workers produce more output per hour for their company. This means the company will have more output to sell per hour of work, and will thus receive more revenues per hour of work from more productive workers. The company will therefore be able to pay more productive workers a higher wage per hour.[9]

With your interest now sufficiently piqued, where does the United States stand on worker productivity? The answer is that the United States is still the world leader in worker productivity. As measured by total economic output per full-time employed person, in 1988 U.S. workers were 10 percent more productive than French workers, 16 percent more productive than German workers, 30 percent more productive than British workers, and 39 percent more productive than Japanese workers.[10] Furthermore, U.S. workers beat most of their foreign counterparts in productivity within specific industries. U.S. workers are 25 percent more productive than both Japanese and German workers in manufacturing, 10 percent more productive than Europeans in airline travel, 47 percent more productive than the Germans in retail banking, 127 percent more productive than the Japanese in merchandise retailing, and 3 percent more productive than the Japanese in telecommunications.[11]

How can these numbers be correct? How can U.S. manufacturing workers be 25 percent more productive than Japanese manufacturing workers when there are many stories of how much more efficient Japanese manufacturing is than U.S. manufacturing? The answer is that productivity varies widely among manufacturing firms, and a relatively small number of Japanese firms with very high productivity rates have received much of the attention. For example, worker productivity in the Japanese machinery, electrical engineering, and transport equipment firms is 17 percent higher than worker productivity in the same U.S. firms, yet those firms account for only 36 percent of all hours worked in Japanese manufacturing.[12] In the other Japanese manufacturing firms, worker productivity is lower than that in the United States, and in some cases by very wide margins. (For example, Japanese worker productivity in textiles and apparel is 41 percent lower than in the United States, and is 60 percent lower in food product manufacturing.)[13]

Even though we currently lead the world in worker productivity, are other countries gaining on us? Before I answer this, what has been the trend in worker productivity in the United States? Worker productivity is most easily and reliably measured over time in manufacturing primarily because output in manufacturing is fairly easily measured (e.g., number of cars produced per worker, number of refrigerators produced per worker). Figure 6-2 shows trends in U.S. worker productivity in manufacturing from 1960 to 1991. The graph shows that productivity gains in manufacturing were actually greatest in the 1980s. Manufacturing productivity increased 32 percent in the 1960s, 22 percent in the 1970s, and 35 percent in the 1980s. The slower rate of productivity growth in the 1970s is largely attributable to the two energy crises in that decade.[14]

It is true that these productivity gains, especially those in the 1980s, are less impressive if productivity in the service sector is included. However, this may not be because productivity gains are necessarily lower in services, but simply because productivity is harder to measure in the service sector. For example, how are the outputs of the insurance industry or the legal industry measured? In some service industries, the government actually uses inputs as proxies for measures of output. Some economists think this measurement automatically results in service productivity being lower. When alternative measures of service productivity are used, much better results are found. For example, Schmidt found that service productivity was as high as manufacturing productivity over the period from 1963 to 1986.[15]

What about the productivity race? Are other countries catching up? The focus of the race has been on three countries, the United States, Japan, and Germany, since these three countries account for 54 percent of manufacturing output in noncommunist (and former communist) countries. Figure 6-3 shows there has been some convergence in manufacturing productivity among the three countries since 1973. In part, this is because Japan and Germany started from such low levels of productivity after the devastation they suffered in World War II. However, the gains in productivity which Japan and Germany have made against the United States slowed considerably in the 1980s. From

Figure 6-2   Index of U.S. Manufacturing Labor Productivity (1982 = 100)

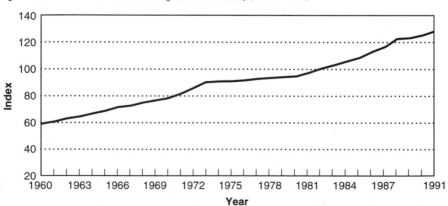

Year

Source: *Economic Report of the President*, U.S. Government Printing Office, February 1992; Bureau of Labor Statistics, *Monthly Labor Review*, various issues.

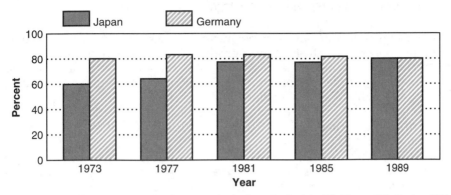

Source: Raw data from McKinsey Global Institute, *Service Sector Productivity*, Washington DC, October 1992, Exhibit 1–12.

Figure 6-3   Japanese and German Manufacturing Productivity as a Percent of U.S. Manufacturing Productivity

1950 to 1973, annual Japanese productivity growth rates in manufacturing were three times higher, and German rates were two times higher as in the United States. From 1973 to 1979, annual Japanese productivity growth rates in manufacturing were five times higher, and German rates were three times higher, as in the United States. But from 1979 to 1989, annual U.S. productivity growth rates in manufacturing were over three times *higher* than German rates, and annual U.S. rates were only 31 percent lower than Japanese rates.[16] So U.S. manufacturing firms have closed the lead held by Japanese and German firms in the productivity race.

There's one other issue to address before leaving our look at productivity. Many citizens are confused as to how U.S. companies can hope to compete with foreign companies when many foreign companies pay their workers wages so much lower than U.S. wages. This concern is particularly an issue when comparing U.S. companies and wages to companies and wages in developing (or Third World) countries.

The answer, in a word, is productivity. U.S. companies can compete with low-wage foreign companies as long as U.S. workers have productivity rates sufficiently higher than the foreign workers. An example reported in *The Wall Street Journal* will clearly illustrate this. The South Korean steel industry has wage rates which are less than half of those paid by Birmingham Steel Corporation, a U.S. steel firm. Yet labor costs per ton of steel produced by the South Korean steel industry are over 30 percent more than labor costs per ton of steel produced by Birmingham Steel Corporation. How can this be? Simply, labor productivity at Birmingham Steel is over three times better than labor productivity in the South Korean steel industry. That is, it takes over three times more hours of labor to make a ton of steel in South Korea than it does at the Birmingham Steel Corporation in the United States.[17] If U.S. workers are sufficiently more productive than their foreign counterparts, they can effectively compete even with higher wage rates.

ARE U.S. BUSINESSES INVESTING IN THE FUTURE?

It's been argued by some that U.S. businesses are lacking in foresight, that they are only concerned with short-term profits, and that, as a consequence, they are no longer investing in the equipment, structures, and technology needed for America's long-term economic health. These concerns aren't to be taken lightly. As we discussed in Chapter 2, the long-run economic growth rate of a nation is related in part to the rate at which businesses invest in new plants, equipment, and technology. Are our business leaders forsaking the future for the "quick buck" of the present?

The statistics that critics of U.S. business investment activity point to are those for *net fixed nonresidential investment*, which is really a simple concept. The *fixed nonresidential investment* refers to business investment in structures and equipment. *Net* indicates that an estimate of depreciation of existing business equipment and structures has been subtracted from what businesses actually invest. This is done because depreciation accounts for the "wearing out" of equipment and structures. Therefore, new investment that simply replaces this "wearing out" of existing equipment and structures is not counted as net new investment. Only new investments above and beyond the depreciation of existing investments are counted as net fixed nonresidential investment.

What do the statistics show? Measured in real (1982) dollars, average annual net fixed nonresidential investment increased from $44.6 billion in the 1950s to $72.7 billion in the 1960s to $91.8 billion in the 1970s. But in the 1980s, average annual net fixed nonresidential investment didn't increase, and was stuck at $91.6 billion. Furthermore, as a percent of the total economy (GNP), average annual net fixed nonresidential investment went from 3.1 percent in the 1950s to 3.5 percent in the 1960s to 3.3 percent in the 1970s, and fell to only 2.6 percent in the 1980s.[18] Isn't this strong evidence that U.S. businesses aren't thinking of tomorrow?

Well, maybe not. There's more to this story, and it has to do with the accounting for depreciation of existing business equipment and structures. In recent years businesses have invested relatively more in computers and other equipment with short usable lives, and they have invested relatively less in structures with long usable lives. This has resulted in higher annual depreciation amounts for existing investments simply due to the type of investment.

An example will clarify this. If $100 billion is invested in existing equipment with a ten-year average life, this will result in $10 billion of depreciation annually. However, if the $100 billion is invested in buildings with a 30-year average life, this will result in $3.3 billion of depreciation annually. So greater existing investment in short-lived equipment will result in more annual depreciation and lower net investments.

For this reason, many economists have chosen to look at gross (before depreciation is subtracted) business investment, with the idea that net (after depreciation) investment is distorted by the shift in business capital stock from structures to equipment. Statistics on gross business investment present a much more optimistic and positive picture of business farsightedness. Gross business investment in equipment and structures as a percent of the economy has risen from 9.5 percent in the 1960s to 10.6 percent in the 1970s to 11.4 percent in the 1980s.[19] Within this investment, investment in information processing and related equipment has increased at almost breakneck speed. For example, investment in this equipment accounted for only 11 percent of total gross business investment; by the late 1980s, investment in this equipment accounted for over one-third of total gross business investment.[20] This shift to information processing investment by business makes sense in light of the revolution in computer science and the application of computers to worker productivity.

There's an issue related to investment in the future by businesses, and that is investment in the future by government. Just as business invests in plant, equipment, and technology, which contribute to long-run economic growth, so too does government. The government investment is called *infrastructure*, and it includes investment in roads, bridges, water and sewer systems, and public buildings.

The issues are whether government has been doing enough infrastructure investing and the consequences if this is not the case. Indeed, the data show that government infrastructure investment has not kept up with the size of the economy. The top line of Figure 6-4 shows government spending on new highways and water and sewer facilities as a percentage of the total economy (GNP). The trend was down in the late 1960s and 1970s, but the rate of new infrastructure spending actually increased in the 1980s.[21]

However, these numbers are distorted somewhat by spending on the federal interstate highway system, which was building at full steam in the 1950s and 1960s. If only relative spending on sewers and water facilities is examined (bottom line in Figure 6-4), then no noticeable trend, up or down, is seen in the past three decades.

Some say this isn't enough. They argue that the United States is suffering from an infrastructure deficit, and that a big spurt in infrastructure spending would go far in stimulating long-run economic growth in the coun-

Figure 6-4   Public New Construction as a Percent of GNP

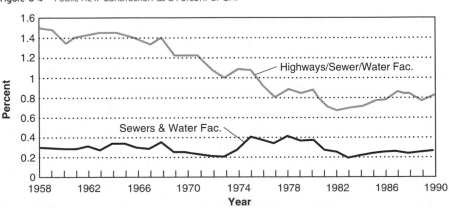

Source: U.S. Bureau of the Census, *Construction Reports*, "Value of New Construction Put in Place," 1992.

try.[22] Unfortunately, there is no settled agreement among economists about the rate of return from public infrastructure investments. Some studies find double-digit rates of return from infrastructure investments, whereas other equally competent studies find low, zero, or even negative rates of return from infrastructure spending.[23] So what's an average citizen to think?

Although economists disagree on the impact of infrastructure investments, many do agree that the method of financing infrastructure projects, particularly highways, is very inefficient and, in fact, has contributed to overuse of public infrastructure. Highway construction and maintenance are currently financed by gasoline taxes. The amount of gasoline taxes a driver or trucker pays is thus directly related to the number of miles driven. Sounds fair, right? Not really. Basing gasoline taxes on miles driven assumes that the amount of use, or damage, a driver or trucker does to highways is only related to miles driven. This may be close for automobile drivers, but it is way off the mark for truckers. For truckers, highway damage rises exponentially with axle weight.[24] Ignoring this relationship by not charging truckers with greater axle weight a higher per mile gasoline tax encourages such truckers to overuse highways, causing the roads to deteriorate at faster rates.

Professor Clifford Winston, an expert on highway economics, has recommended altering the gasoline tax for truckers to account for axle weight. Certainly this would lead to more gasoline tax revenues paid by truckers, which in turn would be passed on to consumers in the form of higher product prices, but Winston's analysis shows that these higher costs would be more than offset by savings in road maintenance costs due to more efficient use of highways. In fact, Winston finds that the savings would be almost twice as great as the added transportation and consumer product costs.[25]

The current system of charging automobile drivers a gasoline tax to fund highways is also not without fault. The reason is that it doesn't take into account congestion costs imposed by drivers on other drivers. When a driver enters a highway that is lightly traveled, the driver uses his or her time and money, but doesn't slow down anyone else. But when a driver enters a crowded highway, he or she imposes additional time costs on other drivers by slowing them down. Our current system of gasoline taxes doesn't take this into account; therefore, drivers only recognize their own costs (time and money) when deciding to use a busy highway. This is inefficient and it motivates overuse of busy highways. It is inefficient because a guiding principle in economics is that people best use resources when they pay for all the resources they use. In the case of crowded highways, drivers aren't paying for the added driving time they impose on other drivers.

A longstanding solution to this problem is a congestion fee.[26] Drivers would pay a congestion fee based on how crowded the highway is they are using. For a lightly used highway at off-peak times, the congestion fee would be small or zero. But for a crowded highway at rush hour, the congestion fee would be larger. The congestion fee would be a signal to the driver that he or she is imposing additional time costs on other drivers by using the crowded highway. A congestion fee would motivate some drivers to use less crowded routes, and would motivate other drivers to travel at off-peak times. A congestion fee would thus reduce the load on popular highways at rush-hour times, which in turn would reduce the damage to such roads and reduce the need to add more and more lanes to these roads.

Now you may be thinking that a congestion fee sounds good in theory, but how could it be implemented in practice? It already has been implemented in such diverse locations as Hong Kong, Dallas, and New Orleans. Congestion fees are implemented using sensors implanted at entrances to roads. The sensors identify and record a vehicle identification number on the bottom of autos entering the highway along with the time the vehicle enters. The time is important because the congestion fee will be altered with the time of day and traffic on the road. Vehicle owners are sent a monthly bill for the congestion fees their autos have accumulated during the month.

The point of this discussion about both truckers and auto drivers is that the need for more public infrastructure can't really be evaluated until reforms are made to how the infrastructure, particularly highways, is paid for. Our guiding light here should be the principle that users of the infrastructure pay for the use, or damage, they cause.

DO WE NEED A NATIONAL INDUSTRIAL POLICY?

The culmination of all the issues discussed in this chapter, from the alleged decline in U.S. manufacturing to the state of U.S. worker productivity to concerns about business and public investment, can be summarized in the debate over *industrial policy*. What does this term mean, and do we need it and want it?

A national industrial policy is one of those concepts that means different things to different people, but all versions of its definition have two common elements. First, a national industrial policy means a set of national policies to promote certain industries, presumably those industries in which the nation can best compete in international trade. Second, a national industrial policy inevitably means that government will interfere with the market by propping up some industries and giving them special favors at the expense of other industries.[27]

The call for a national industrial policy is based on two assumptions. First, it assumes that the U.S. economy has suffered a decline in the importance of the manufacturing sector. Second, the pushers of a national industrial policy assume that such a policy has worked in other countries, particularly in Japan.[28]

Both assumptions are contrary to the evidence. We've already discussed the issue of the relative importance of manufacturing. To summarize, although manufacturing employment has declined in both absolute and relative terms, the absolute and relative value of manufactured output has not declined. The relative importance of manufactured output has held its own, even with fewer employees, due to the increased productivity of manufacturing workers.

The assumption that industrial policy has worked in Japan is based on the alleged success of Japan's Ministry of International Trade and Industry (MITI). MITI is a government agency which directs public investment and assistance to certain industries and companies.[29] Supporters of a national industrial policy argue that Japan's postwar economic success is due, in part, to MITI's actions.

But a closer look at MITI reveals a less than shining record. Admirers forget that MITI bureaucrats tried to prevent the development of the transistor in Japan in the 1950s and opposed the country's auto companies moving into the export market. MITI also discouraged Sony from getting into the consumer electronics business, and MITI's support of the Japanese steel and oil industries has been judged to be a failure.[30]

The latest failure of Japanese industrial policy is in the competition for development of high-definition television (HDTV). Both Japan and the European Community funneled large amounts of public money into development of HDTV in the late 1980s and early 1990s. Meanwhile, the U.S. government refused to assist U.S. firms in the race. So who won the race, the Japanese, the EC? No, the United States won, with its hands-off government policy. The high-definition TV developed by private U.S. firms is expected to become the world standard and to be adopted by both Japan and the European Community.[31]

Rather than pointing to MITI and Japanese industrial policy as the reason for Japan's economic success, better candidates are the industriousness of the Japanese people and the stable economic environment created by the Japanese government and central bank.

There's a larger issue in the debate over a national industrial policy, and this is whether government can replace private individuals and companies in making investment decisions. This is doubtful. Picking economic winners is not easy. There's no magic formula that tells someone which companies will succeed and which will fail in the future. Successfully investing in new or expanding companies requires much information gathering, and requires constant nurturing and monitoring. It also requires a willingness to cut losses and end the investment when the company isn't succeeding. Private investors and entrepreneurs know that it's not wise to continue investing in a failing company when those funds could be put to better use and earn a higher return somewhere else.

Government is not well suited to following any of these principles of successful private investing. Political pressures make it difficult for government to cut off funding and destroy jobs in unsuccessful ventures. Instead, because government is by nature a political body, it should be expected that political considerations would be a part of government's investment decisions. That is, unlike private investors, who are guided only by financial and economic considerations in their decisions, government decisions would be equally (if not overwhelmingly) guided by political power and promises. In short, it would be very easy for national industrial policy to become "pork barrel" policy.

Supporters of a national industrial policy overlook the fact that there's no lack of funds to invest in new or start-up projects and companies. These funds are called venture capital. In the 1980s, real (inflation-adjusted) managed venture capital rose over 450 percent.[32] Funding is available for new ideas which are well conceived and which have a potential for success. But these new ideas must stand the test of hard-nosed analysis.

Rather than pursuing a national industrial policy of attempting to pick economic winners and losers, an alternative government policy is supporting an economic environment in which this selection can occur by private investors.

NOTES

1. Data are from *Economic Report of the President*, U.S. Government Printing Office, February 1992.
2. Durable manufactured products, which are longlasting are manufactured products like autos, refrigerators, furniture, and machinery, are responsible for most of the increased importance of manufacturing in the postwar period. For example, as a share of total output of the economy, durable goods manufacturing increased from 13 percent in the late 1940s to 14.5 percent in the late 1980s. Also, the U.S. Department of Commerce recently revised its estimation of manufacturing's contribution to the U.S. economy. The revisions, only available from 1977 to 1991, reduced manufacturing's contribution, but still showed it accounting for 19 to 20 percent of the economy over the period. (U.S. Dept. of Commerce, *Survey of Current Business*, November 1993).
3. This is not to say that all U.S. manufacturing industries and firms have prospered in the postwar period. In particular, the U.S. steel and auto industries have suffered. See Michael Dertouzos, Richard Lester, and Robert Solow, *Made in America* (New York: Harper Perennial, 1989).
4. Based on data from The World Bank, *World Tables 1991*, and country reports of *The Economist* Intelligence Unit.
5. Organization for Economic Cooperation and Development, *Labour Force Statistics, 1968–1988*, Paris, France, 1990. The major industrialized countries are the United States, Japan, Australia, New Zealand, Austria, Belgium, Denmark, Finland, France, Germany, Greece, Iceland, Ireland, Italy, Luxembourg, the Netherlands, Norway, Portugal, Spain, Sweden, Switzerland, Turkey, and the United Kingdom.
6. William Baumol, "U.S. Industry's Lead Gets Bigger," *The Wall Street Journal*, March 21, 1990.
7. Alison Butler, "Is the United States Losing Its Dominance in High-Technology Industries?" *Review*, The Federal Reserve Bank of St. Louis, 74, no. 6 (November/December 1992), 19–34.
8. Ibid.
9. For empirical support for this argument, see Michael L. Walden, "Trends in Productivity and Real Wages in North Carolina Industries," ARE Report No. 3, North Carolina State University (November 1992).
10. Mckinsey Global Institute, *Service Sector Productivity*, Washington, DC (October 1992), Exhibit 1–6. Other measures of productivity, such as productivity per person or productivity per hour worked, show different differentials between the countries, but generally show the United States as the world leader.
11. Ibid., Exhibit 1–11, Exhibit 2A–4, Exhibit 2B–10, Exhibit 2D–3, Exhibit 2E–11.
12. Ibid., Exhibit 1–14, Exhibit 1–10B.
13. Ibid., Exhibit 1–14.
14. For an analysis of the impacts of the energy crises on U.S. worker productivity, see Dale Jorgenson, "Productivity and Postwar U.S. Economic Growth," *Journal of Economic Perspectives*, 2, no. 4 (Fall 1988), 23–41.

15. Ronald Schmidt, "Services: A Future of Low Productivity Growth?" *Federal Reserve Bank of San Francisco Weekly Letter*, No. 92-07, February 14, 1992.

16. McKinsey Global Institute, *Service Sector Productivity*, Exhibit 1–13.

17. Dana Milbank, "U.S. Productivity Gains Cut Costs, Close Gap with Low-Wage Overseas Firms," *The Wall Street Journal*, December 23, 1992, p. A2.

18. *Economic Report of the President*, U.S. Government Printing Office, February 1992.

19. Richard Kopche, "The Determinants of Business Investment: Has Capital Spending Been Surprisingly Low?" *New England Economic Review*, Federal Reserve Bank of Boston (January/February 1993), pp. 3–31, Table 1.

20. Ibid., Table 2.

21. The numbers in Figure 6-3 are gross investment spending, that is, not accounting for depreciation of existing public investment. However, estimates of net (after depreciation) public investment show the same trends, with a decline in net public investment as a percent of GNP from the mid-1960s to the mid-1980s, and an increase since the mid-1980s; see David Alan Aschauer, "Infrastructure: America's Third Deficit," *Challenge*, 34, no. 2 (March/April 1991), 39–45.

22. Ibid.

23. For large rates of return from infrastructure spending, see David Aschauer, "Is Public Expenditure Productive?" *Journal of Monetary Economics*, 23 (March 1989), 177–200; for small rates of return from infrastructure spending, see Dale Jorgenson, "Fragile Statistical Foundations: The Macroeconomics of Public Infrastructure Investment," paper presented at American Enterprise Institute Conference on Infrastructure Needs and Policy Options for the 1990s, Washington, DC, February 4, 1991.

24. Kenneth Small and Clifford Winston, "Efficient Pricing and Investment Solutions to Highway Infrastructure Needs," *American Economic Review*, 76, no. 2 (May 1986), 165–169.

25. Ibid.

26. Clifford Winston, "Efficient Transportation Infrastructure Policy," *Journal of Economic Perspectives*, 5, no. 1 (Winter 1991), 113–127.

27. Some argue that federal tax policies which favor certain industries or spending constitute a de facto national industrial policy; see Peter Fisher, "Corporate Tax Incentives: The American Version of Industrial Policy," *Journal of Economic Issues*, 19, no. 1 (March 1985), 1–20.

28. Michelle Clark, "The Pitfalls of Industrial Policy," *The Regional Economist*, The Federal Reserve Bank of St. Louis (April 1993), pp. 10–11.

29. For a description of MITI's activities, see Thomas Pugal, "Japan's Industrial Policy: Instruments, Trends and Effects," *Journal of Comparative Economics*, 8, no. 4 (December 1984), 420–435.

30. Don Lavoie, "Two Varieties of Industrial Policy: A Critique," *The Cato Journal*, 4, no. 2 (Fall 1984), 437–484.

31. "Do Not Adjust Your Set," *The Economist*, February 27, 1993, pp. 65–66.

32. Allan Meltzer, "Why Governments Make Bad Venture Capitalists," *The Wall Street Journal*, May 5, 1993, p. A22.

7

Where are the jobs?

As the decade of the 1990s began, there was much pessimism about jobs. The recession of the early 1990s destroyed many jobs, and as we've already seen, businesses were slow to replace them even when the economy recovered. Big businesses seemed to be slashing jobs with little concern for the consequences, and a college education no longer appeared to be the ticket to a good job.

These trends in the 1990s were in sharp contrast to what happened in the 1980s. From 1980 to 1989, employment rose by over 17 million jobs, and the American economy was referred to as the "great jobs machine." But there's been wide disagreement over the quality of jobs created in the 1980s. Some analysts claim that these jobs and the jobs continuing to be created today are primarily low-paying service jobs. Furthermore, the argument continues, these "poor" service jobs are replacing high-paying manufacturing jobs. However, other economists reach different conclusions when the occupations of new jobs are examined. The quality of new jobs is an issue we will examine in depth.

There are other important job-related issues. Fringe benefits as a percentage of total compensation paid to employees have trended upward over time. Is this good, or is it creating problems and unforeseen impacts in the economy? At the same time, there's concern that many jobs don't have fringe benefits, like company-provided health care, leave, and retirement plans. Is mandating these benefits through law the solution to this concern, or would this do more harm than good?

Part-time jobs as a percentage of all jobs have risen since the late 1970s. This fact would not sound any alarm bells if the increase was due to workers voluntarily choosing to work part-time. But as we will see, most of the increase in part-time work is from people involuntarily working part-time; that is, they want to work full-time but can only find part-time work. Why? Are companies preferring to hire part-time workers over full-time workers? If so, what implications does this have for worker well-being?

Finally, workers are increasingly worried that jobs are leaving the United States and going to low-wage countries like Mexico. To what extent is this happening, and what are the implications? If you want a manufacturing job in the future, will you have to go to Mexico, Japan, Korea, or Taiwan?

JOB GROWTH

The first fact to recognize about job growth in the U.S. economy is the tremendous number of job changes which are continuously ongoing. For example, between 1980 and 1986 the U.S. economy had a net gain of 10.5 million jobs. But this gain did not come from simply adding 10.5 million jobs on top of the jobs existing in 1980. Instead, it resulted from the difference between the creation of 44.5 million new jobs and the destruction of 34 million existing jobs, for a net gain of 10.5 million jobs.[1] So job change is the rule rather than the exception. You should not necessarily become upset upon hearing of the loss of x number of jobs at company ABC because, more than likely, y number of new jobs will be created at another company.

The second fact to recognize about job growth in the United States is that it is occurring. At the end of 1992 there were 118 million jobs in the American economy, up from 99 million in 1980 and 79 million in 1970. Also, the percentage of the noninstitutional population over 16 years of age who have jobs has risen from 56 percent in 1950 to 57 percent in 1970 to 61 percent in 1990.[2] Of course, much of this increase is due to the increase in females holding jobs in the economy.

But what kind of jobs have we been adding? Are they "good-paying" jobs or "bad-paying" jobs? There has been avid controversy about this question. On one side are economists who point to the rising share of jobs in the so-called service sector as reason for concern because, they argue, service jobs generally pay less than manufacturing jobs.[3] Indeed, service-sector jobs increased by over 20 million between 1980 and 1990, and service-sector jobs as a percentage of all jobs increased from 71 percent in 1980 to 77 percent in 1990. Meanwhile, the nation lost over 1 million manufacturing jobs in the decade of the 1980s, and manufacturing jobs as a percentage of all jobs decreased from 22 percent in 1980 to 17 percent in 1990.[4] These changes create the image of well-paid steel and auto workers losing their jobs and becoming minimum-wage hamburger flippers and dry cleaners.

But if jobs in the service sector are rising and jobs in manufacturing are falling, does this necessarily mean that we are trading high-paying jobs for low-paying jobs? Not necessarily. The service job versus manufacturing job classification is not very helpful because it tells us nothing about the occupation of the job. All service-industry jobs are not hamburger flippers and floor sweepers; there are managers, accountants, executives, and other professionals working in the service sector. And a manager in a service company could be paid the same as the manager in a manufacturing company. In fact, the average hourly wage of service jobs is 91 percent of the average hourly wage of manufacturing jobs,[5] and 44 percent of the service jobs have hourly wages above the average wage for all of private industry.[6]

A more useful way of looking at job changes is to look at changes in occupations, regardless of where those occupations occurred. Table 7-1 shows the changes in occupations in the 1980s, along with their average weekly pay, for full-time wage and salary workers (that is, part-time and self-employed workers are excluded).[7] Most of the occupations should be self-explanatory, but a few need further discussion. Craft and kindred workers are workers who use a trade skill, such as mechanics, repairers, construction trades (carpenters, brick masons, electricians, and so on), machinists, woodworkers, and food production occupations (butchers, bakers). Operatives are workers operating a machine of any kind, such as printing press operators, molding and casting machine operators, and furnace and kiln operators. The service occupation is somewhat of a "catchall" category, and includes child care workers, cleaners, janitors, police officers and firefighters, cooks, waiters and waitresses, hairdressers, dental assistants, and orderlies.

Picking through the details of Table 7-1 reveals some interesting trends. Net job losses occurred in three occupational categories: clerical workers, operatives, and nonfarm laborers. All of these occupations had weekly

Table 7-1 Job Gains and Losses by Occupation and Earnings, 1981–1990, Full-Time Wage and Salary Workers

| | 1981 | | 1990 | | |
OCCUPATION	NUMBER	REAL MEDIAN WEEKLY EARNINGS[a] (1990 $)	NUMBER	REAL MEDIAN WEEKLY EARNINGS (1990 $)	CHANGE IN NUMBER
Professional and technical	12,592,000	$536	14,911,000	$580	+2,319,000
Managers and administrators	7,934,000	$587	11,165,000	$604	+3,231,000
Sales workers	3,633,000	$418	8,197,000	$401	+4,564,000
Clerical workers	14,475,000	$333	14,384,000	$350	−91,000
Craft and kindred workers	10,819,000	$509	11,062,000	$477	+243,000
Operatives, except transportation	9,660,000	$343	7,350,000	$325	−2,610,000
Transportation equipment operatives	2,905,000	$438	3,948,000	$413	+1,043,000
Nonfarm laborers	3,636,000	$334	3,635,000	$298	−1,000
Service workers	7,534,000	$270	9,007,000	$268	+1,473,000
Farm workers	927,000	$247	1,423,000	$257	+496,000
Total	74,415,000	$422	85,082,000	$415	+10,667,000

[a]Using the CPI-U X1 index.

Source: Bureau of Labor Statistics, *Earnings and Employment*, January 1982; January 1991.

earnings below the average for all occupations. Therefore, 100 percent of the job losses occurred in occupations with below-average pay. In contrast, about half (51 percent) of the net job gains in the 1980s occurred in occupations with above-average weekly earnings (professional and technical, managers and administrators, craft, and transportation equipment operatives), and about half (49 percent) of the net job gains occurred in occupations with below-average weekly earnings (sales, service, and farm workers). So, if "good" jobs are defined as those with above-average pay, and "bad" jobs are defined as those with below-average pay, then in the 1980s there was a shift out of "bad" jobs into 50 percent "good" jobs and 50 percent other "bad" jobs.[8]

But this is old news. Where will the new jobs be in the future? Table 7-2 gives the answers. Between 1990 and 2005, it's estimated the economy will create 24.6 million jobs. Interestingly, 59 percent of these jobs are projected to be in occupations paying salaries higher than the annual average (executives, administrators, managers; professional specialty; technicians; marketing and sales; precision products, craft, and repair). Also, three of these occupations (executives, administrators, managers; professional specialty; technicians), accounting for 41 percent of the total increase in jobs, require the highest levels of education. Thus, the emphasis on education in the economy will continue, and acquiring an education will continue to be the surest ticket to a high-paying job.[9]

Now you know what kinds of jobs have been created and where they will be created in the near future. But in what kinds of companies will these new jobs be found? Many of you probably think the new jobs will be in large companies, since large companies always receive the greatest amount of attention. But the share of jobs in large companies has actually been declining

Table 7-2   Where the New Jobs Will Be, 1990–2005

OCCUPATION	MEDIAN ANNUAL EARNINGS (1987)	NUMBER
Total, all occupations	$21,543	+24,600,000
Executives, administrators, and managers	$30,264	+3,400,000
Professional specialty	$30,116	+5,100,000
Technicians	$24,489	+1,600,000
Marketing and sales	$22,220	+3,400,000
Clerical and administrative support	$17,120	+2,800,000
Service	$13,443	+5,600,000
Precision products, craft, and repair	$24,856	+1,100,000
Operators, fabricators, and laborers	$18,132	+1,400,000
Agriculture, forestry, fisheries, and related	$11,781	+200,000

Source: George Silvestri and John Lukasiewicz "Occupational Employment Projections," *Monthly Labor Review*, 114, no. 11 (November 1991), 64–94; U.S. Bureau of Labor Statistics, *Occupational Outlook Handbook*, 1992–93 ed., Bulletin 2400 (May 1992).

since 1970. For example, in 1970 the 500 largest U.S. companies (the so-called *Fortune* 500 companies) held 20.6 percent of nonfarm jobs. Since 1970, this share has steadily declined, and in 1991 the *Fortune* 500 companies held only 10.9 percent of nonfarm jobs.[10] Between 1980 and 1987, the *Fortune* 500 companies laid off 3.1 million people, while the rest of the economy was adding 14 million jobs.[11]

Instead most of the new jobs will be in small and medium companies, just as it has been in the past. David L. Birch, a professor at the Massachusetts Institute of Technology, has been a pioneer in the study of the life cycle of businesses and their impacts on regional economies. As long ago as 1976, Birch's research found that two-thirds of all net, new jobs were created by companies with 20 or fewer employees, and 80 percent were created by companies with 100 or fewer employees.[12] More recently (1980–86), 39 percent of net, new jobs were created in firms with 20 or fewer employees, and 53 percent were created in companies with 100 or fewer employees.[13]

In fact, recent technological changes have probably increased the competitiveness of small companies relative to big companies. Before the development of low-cost computers and sophisticated software, only large firms could afford to employ fancy, yet effective, customer forecasting, inventory control, and account management models. Now any firm, even one-person companies, can employ these models. Also, the gradual reduction of trade barriers between nations has opened up market niches to small companies that can move fast to take advantage of new opportunities.

There's one other somewhat troubling aspect of the job outlook, and this has to do with part-time work. Since the early 1970s there has been an upward trend in the percentage of persons who are working part-time involuntarily. These are persons who would prefer to work full-time but can only find part-time work. This percentage usually rises during recessions, but the upward trend in involuntary part-time work has proceeded beyond recessions. For example, looking at the last year of recent economic expansions, in 1973 the percentage of working people who were working part-time involuntarily was 3 percent; in 1980 it was 3.7 percent; and in 1989 it was 4.3 percent.[14] Is this a troubling trend, and if so, what's the reason for it?

It is a troubling trend for the simple reason that if a person desires to work full-time but can only find part-time work, then labor resources will be underutilized and individuals will not find their optimal mix of work time and leisure.

So why has involuntary part-time work increased? The best answer seems to be one of simple dollars and cents, which is that part-time workers have become relatively cheaper to employers compared to full-time workers. Researchers have found that even after adjusting for differences in education, experience, skill, and training, part-time workers are less costly to employers than full-time workers.[15] Part-time workers with the same education, experience, and personal characteristics as full-time workers are paid lower wage rates. Also, part-time workers are less likely to be covered by employer-provided fringe benefits, such as health insurance and pension plans.[16] It makes sense, therefore, that as fringe benefits have become a bigger part of total employee costs to companies, companies have shifted to hiring relatively more part-time workers.[17]

This observation leads to a very important job-related issue. As a compassionate society, we want to make the work environment as pleasant as possible for as many workers as possible. This has led many politicians to consider, and in some cases to impose, job-related requirements or mandates on companies. Is this a good idea, or could the costs of such mandates outweigh the benefits? This is the issue we take up next.

JOBS, BENEFITS, AND MANDATES

There's renewed interest in making the workplace more appealing to workers. In 1993 the Family Leave Act was passed, which requires companies with 50 or more employees to provide up to 12 weeks of unpaid leave to workers for certain family emergencies. Mandatory provision of health insurance by employers is considered by many as a key "right" of workers. A number of groups are pushing for a significant increase in the minimum wage, arguing that the current minimum wage doesn't guarantee a decent living. Finally, in response to a concern with the competitive position of U.S. workers in today's global marketplace, there's support for mandatory training programs for workers, with payment of the training funded by a tax on company payrolls.

What's wrong with these ideas and programs? After all, if all companies won't provide a decent work environment and decent pay for workers, isn't it the government's obligation to require companies to do so? Unfortunately, I can't give a direct answer to this question now (no, I'm not avoiding the question). First, we must take a detour into the economics of fringe benefits.

Fringe benefits are a catchall term for all nonwage and nonsalary benefits provided to workers by a company. Examples of fringe benefits are holiday leave, sick leave, vacation leave, family leave, retirement (or pension) plans, health insurance, life insurance, and company-provided training. Some of these fringe benefits are quite common with most jobs, and others are rare. For example, in 1990 90 percent of private-sector firms provided paid holiday leave and 93 percent provided paid vacation leave, but only 13 percent provided unpaid paternity leave (prior to the Family Leave Act).[18]

On the surface, having the government mandate that firms provide certain fringe benefits looks like an effective and compassionate way of improving the life of workers. But this viewpoint ignores the issue of who actually pays for the fringe benefits. Most people think companies pay for fringe benefits provided to workers. Although the company signs the check paid to workers during their paid vacation leave and pays the premium for the company-provided health insurance, the money actually comes out of workers' pockets. How so? What is overlooked is that fringe benefits are considered a cost of labor by companies. That is, when a company is evaluating hiring a worker, it looks not only at the wage or salary paid to the worker, but also at the cost of the fringe benefits provided to the workers. So, for example, if a company will pay a worker $20,000 in salary annually, and if that worker will cost the company $5,000 in fringe benefits, then the total cost of the worker to the company will be $25,000. If the company did not provide $5,000 of fringe benefits to the worker, it would be willing to pay the worker $25,000 in annual salary rather than $20,000.

If this is true, then why do we see workers willingly taking jobs with lower salaries and with fringe benefits, when they could have had a job with a higher salary but no fringe benefits? Doesn't each of us want as much salary as possible now and do without the fringe benefits? The answer is simple. The fact that we do see jobs with fringe benefits and salaries lower than they would be without the fringes means that some workers value the fringes enough that they're willing to accept lower pay in return. For example, a worker may find that health insurance provided through an employer costs less in lost salary than the cost of buying comparable health insurance as an individual.[19] In other words, many workers find that their company can provide health insurance more cheaply than the workers could purchase it on their own. Also, there are some fringe benefits, such as sick leave and vacation leave, that only companies can provide; these fringes can't be "purchased" by the worker elsewhere.

So the point is this. In a freely functioning market without government mandates, companies will provide the fringe benefits that workers are willing to pay for through lower pay. The fact that workers are willing to accept the lower pay must mean the value of the fringes to them is greater than the loss in pay.[20]

Our excursion into the economics of fringe benefits is now complete. How can we apply what we've learned to the issue of mandated benefits? I think you can anticipate the answer. If the government mandates a fringe benefit which is not currently provided by a company, then workers, and not the company, will pay the cost of this benefit through lower wages and salaries.[21] But so what? Won't the workers receive the advantages of the new mandated benefit, so even though they've paid for it through lower pay, they're not any worse off? Well, here's the clincher: The workers will be *worse off* with the mandated benefit! The reason is that if workers valued the fringe benefit more than the income they would lose to have the fringe benefit, then companies would already be providing the fringe benefit voluntarily. The fact that the fringe benefit must be mandated by government must mean that, to the average worker, the value of the fringe benefit is less than its cost. So mandated fringe benefits reduce worker welfare.

There are more implications of mandated fringe benefits. Mandated fringe benefits are often promoted as a way to help workers at the bottom of the economic ladder—workers with low skills earning low pay. But workers at this level have little to give up to pay for the mandated fringe benefits because their pay is so low. Reducing wages is often not feasible because the required minimum wage will be bumped against. So the alternative is to lay off low-wage workers in response to the new mandated benefits. Thus, an unintended consequence of mandated fringe benefits is to reduce the employment of low-wage workers.

Now let's turn to one of the longest standing of government mandated worker benefits, the minimum wage. You may think it odd that I call the minimum wage a mandated benefit. However, it is a mandated benefit in that it guarantees that any worker will be paid some minimum wage rate, despite the worker's skills and despite what companies would want to pay the worker.

The impacts of the minimum wage on workers, especially on low-wage workers, is one of the few areas in economics where there is almost unanimous agreement. The reasoning is very simple. If a minimum wage raises the wage rate which a company must pay a worker above that wage which represents the value of the worker to the company, then what will the company do? That's right, the company won't keep the worker. Private-sector companies aren't in the business of paying workers more than they are worth to the company. If they are forced to, then they won't use the workers. Instead, they'll substitute more highly productive and more highly paid workers for the low-skilled and low-paid workers, or they'll substitute machines for those workers who would have their wages raised by the minimum wage.[22] Notice that the workers who are hurt are precisely those directly affected by the minimum—workers with few skills and, therefore, with low wages.

The evidence on this is overwhelming. Numerous empirical studies have found that a higher minimum wage reduces employment among the low skilled and unskilled, and particularly among teenagers. Higher minimum wages reduce both full-time and part-time work. There's even empirical evidence suggesting that higher minimum wages reduce on-the-job training for those low-skilled workers who keep their jobs as a way of compensating for their increased cost to the company.[23]

If the minimum wage isn't the answer to ensuring that all workers earn a decent living, then what is? Well, first is an educational system which enables students to acquire skills to allow them to earn a decent living. Second is a social support system (social safety net) which assists or supplements workers whose skill levels aren't sufficient to command a wage producing a decent living. Both of these elements are topics of later chapters. But for now, the answer is clearly *not* to force companies to pay workers more than they're worth; such a mandate, as we've seen, backfires.

One other job-related mandate which deserves discussion here is unemployment insurance. I'm not going to advocate elimination of unemployment insurance, but I am going to point out some problems in the current system and suggest some changes.

Unemployment insurance is a government mandated program which requires that employers contribute funds to a common pool, and in turn, those funds are paid out to unemployed workers for a specified number of weeks. The program is run by each state, and 26 weeks is typically the maximum length of time that an unemployed worker can receive unemployment benefits (although the federal government can step in during special times, such as recessions, and provide money for extensions beyond the 26 weeks).

What's wrong with unemployment insurance is that the system as currently constructed encourages persons to remain unemployed for a longer period of time. Although unemployment benefits are generally only half of what a person earns when employed, if that person values free time, the gap between the employed wage and the implied unemployment benefit wage won't be nearly as great. In addition, social security taxes aren't paid on unemployment benefits. The point is that because more unemployment benefits are paid the longer a person remains unemployed (until the limit is hit), unemployed persons will be motivated to take more leisure time or search for jobs longer under the current unemployment compensation system.

Indeed, economic researchers have found a positive link between unemployment insurance and longer periods of unemployment. Meyer and Katz found that a 13-week extension of unemployment benefits increased the average duration of unemployment for someone receiving benefits by 2.2 weeks.[24]

Should we get rid of the unemployment compensation system? No, but the current system could be replaced by a new system which still assists unemployed workers but doesn't motivate longer periods of unemployment. The new system would give unemployed workers a lump-sum benefit at the time of their unemployment instead of a weekly benefit for as long as they are unemployed (up to the limit). With the single lump-sum benefit, there would be no motivation to remain unemployed for a longer period of time. The unemployed worker could use the lump-sum benefit for financial support or for retraining for a new job.

THE MEXICAN CONNECTION

Some of you may be puzzled as to why I have focused on job growth in the United States, since you hear so much about U.S. jobs going to other countries, especially low-wage countries. With these trends, will there be any good jobs left in the United States?

Much of this concern has been directed at Mexico. During the debate about the North American Free Trade Agreement, newspapers were filled with stories of U.S. manufacturing companies taking jobs to Mexico. And why not? Aren't the wages of Mexican workers 75 percent less than the wages of American workers?

Wages of Mexican workers are less than wages of American workers, but in Chapter 6 I showed you that wages aren't only what matters. The productivity of workers also matters, and indeed, a high-wage worker can still be cheaper than a low-wage worker if the high-wage worker's productivity is sufficiently higher.

This doesn't indicate whether U.S. companies have been moving jobs to Mexico. The answer is in Figure 7-1. U.S. companies have increased their jobs in Mexico by a significant amount (left scale of Figure 7-1). In fact, employment of U.S. nonbank affiliates in Mexico increased by 39 percent from 1977 to 1989 at the same time that total employment of U.S. foreign affiliates in all countries decreased 8 percent, or over 500,000 workers, during the same period (right scale of Figure 7-1). Furthermore, much of the employment growth of U.S. companies in Mexico has been in the transportation and electronics industries.

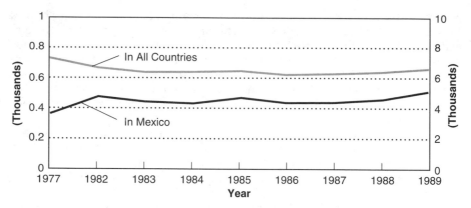

Source: Raw data from Linda Aguilar, "The North American Free Trade Agreement: The Ties That Bind,"
Chicago Fed letter, No. 61, Federal Reserve Banks of Chicago, September 1992.

Figure 7-1   Employment of U.S. Nonbank Foreign Affiliates

Why has Mexico suddenly become attractive to U.S. companies? The answer is that the "rules of the game" of trade between Mexico and the United States changed in a significant way in the 1960s. In the 1960s the *maquiladora* program was established between the United States and Mexico. This program allowed U.S. companies to ship materials to Mexico without paying any Mexican import tariffs or fees as long as the materials were manufactured into products which in turn were shipped back to the United States. When the finished products were shipped back to the United States, only the increase in value of the finished product above the values of the raw materials were subject to U.S. import tariffs and fees.

For example, the maquiladora program allowed U.S. auto companies to ship automotive component parts to Mexico, not pay Mexican import fees (which were significant before NAFTA) on the parts, assemble the parts into automobiles, ship the finished autos back to the United States, and only pay U.S. import fees on the difference between the value of the finished autos and the value of the component parts. As a result, all along the Mexican-U.S. border there sprung up scores of maquiladora plants manufacturing autos and consumer electronic products for shipment back to the United States.

So the maquiladora program was an example of one-sided free trade because the Mexican import fees were removed on the imported component parts. (The maquiladora program will effectively end when NAFTA eliminates nearly all tariffs and fees on trade between Mexico and the United States). Is not, therefore, the maquiladora program ammunition for those who say that further free trade will destroy the American economy because all the jobs (or at least all the good jobs) will migrate to low-wage countries? Can the American worker and the American economy compete "head to head" with foreign workers and countries, or does America need high tariff "walls" to protect itself from low-cost foreign competitors? To get the answers, you'll have to read on to Chapter 8!

NOTES

1. Thomas A. Gray, "Let Small Business Do What It Does Best—Create Jobs," *Journal of Labor Research*, 10, no. 1 (Winter 1989), 73–81.

2. *Economic Report of the President*, 1992.

3. See Barry Bluestone and Bennett Harrison, *The Deindustrialization of America* (New York: Basic Books, 1982); Barry Bluestone and Bennett Harrison, "The Great American Jobs Machine: The Proliferation of Low-Wage Employment in the U.S. Economy," report prepared for the U.S. Congressional Joint Economic Committee (December 1986); and Lester Thurow, "A Surge in Inequality," *Scientific American* 256, no. 5 (1987), 30–37.

4. *Economic Report of the President*, 1992.

5. U.S. Bureau of Labor Statistics, *Monthly Labor Review*, (July 1992), Table 15.

6. Herbert Stein and Murray Foss, *An Illustrated Guide to the American Economy* (Washington, DC: The American Enterprise Institute Press, 1992) p. 39.

7. The occupation changes are measured from the peak of the business cycle in 1981 (that is, right before the 1981–82 recession) to the peak of the next business cycle in 1990 (before the 1990–91 recession).

8. Kosters reaches a similar conclusion by finding that "high earnings" and "middle earnings" jobs increased their shares of all jobs from 1980 to 1986; Marvin Kosters, "The Changing Quality of American Jobs," *Journal of Labor Research*, 10, no. 1 (Winter 1989), 23–31.

9. However, the Bureau of Labor Statistics projects that the supply of college graduates will more than keep up with demand for them, resulting in stiff competition for college-level jobs; see Kristina Shelley, "The Future of Jobs for College Graduates," *Monthly Labor Review*, 115, no. 7 (July 1992), 13–21.

10. M. Hale, "For New Jobs, Help Small Business," *The Wall Street Journal*, August 10, 1992.

11. David L. Birch, "Change, Innovation, and Job Generation," *Journal of Labor Research*, 10, no. 1 (Winter 1989), 33–38.

12. Ibid.

13. Gray, "Let Small Business Do What It Does Best—Create Jobs."

14. U.S. Bureau of Labor Statistics, *Employment and Earnings*, various issues.

15. Ronald Ehrenberg, Ramada Rosenberg, and Jeanne Li, "Part-Time Employment in the United States," in Robert Hart, ed., *Employment, Unemployment, and Labor Utilization* (Boston: Unwin Hyman, 1988), pp. 256–287.

16. Ibid. Ehrenberg, Rosenberg, and Li find that part-time workers are one-third less likely to be covered by employer-provided health insurance and are one-fourth less likely to be covered by a pension plan.

17. Fringe benefits rose from 10 percent of total employee compensation in 1970 to 17 percent in 1990; see Stein and Foss, *An Illustrated Guide to the American Economy*, p. 49.

18. G. M. Grossman, "U.S. Workers Receive a Wide Range of Employee Benefits," *Monthly Labor Review*, 115, no. 9 (September 1992), 36–38.

19. The tax system also enters into these calculations. Currently (1993) companies aren't taxed on the value of fringe benefits, such as health insurance, provided to employees. This means, for example, that a $1 of health care benefits provided by a company would cost the company $1.43 in additional salary to the employee if the company paid the employee extra cash rather than health insurance, and if the employee's tax rate is 30 percent [$1.43 – ($1.43 ¥ .30) = $1.00].

20. An excellent elaboration of this and earlier points is in Dwight Lee, *The Misguided Policy of Mandated Benefits*, Contemporary Issues Series 58 (April 1993), Center for the Study of American Business, Washington University, St. Louis.

21. Empirical evidence for this with respect to mandated health benefits is found in Jonathan Gruber, *The Efficiency of a Group-Specific Mandated Benefit: Evidence from Health Insurance Benefits for Maternity*, NBER Working paper No. 4157, 1992, Cambridge, MA: National Bureau of Economic Research.

22. Not all such workers will lose their jobs; indeed, those low-wage workers who keep their job and who see an increase in their wage due to the minimum wage obviously benefit from the minimum wage. But this is at the expense of those workers who do lose their jobs.

23. For the impact of the minimum wage on on-the-job training, see Masanori Hashimoto, "Minimum Wage Effects on Training on the Job," *American Economic Review*, 72, no. 5 (December 1982), 1070–1087. For other impacts of the minimum wage, see the collection of papers in Simon Rottenberg, ed., *The Economics of Legal Minimum Wages* (Washington, DC: American Enterprise Institute for Public Policy Research, 1981). For example, in this volume see James Ragan, Jr., "The Effect of a Legal Minimum Wage on the Pay and Employment of Teenage Students and Nonstudents," pp. 11–41, and J. Peter Mattila, "The Impact of Minimum Wages on Teenage Schooling and on the Part-Time/Full-Time Employment of Youths," pp. 61–87 for measures of the reduction in teenage employment caused by the minimum wage; for impacts on part-time employment see James Cunningham, "The Impact of Minimum Wages on Youth Employment, Hours of Work, and School Attendance: Cross-Sectional Evidence from the 1960 and 1970 Censuses," pp. 88–123; for more impacts on on-the-job training, see Linda Leighton and Jacob Mincer, "The Effects of Minimum Wages on Human Capital Formation," pp. 155–173; for impacts on reducing farm labor employment, see Bruce Gardner, "What Have Minimum Wages Done in Agriculture," pp. 210–232, and John Trapani and J. R. Moroney, "The Impact of Federal Minimum Wage Laws on Employment of Seasonal Cotton Farm Workers," pp. 233–246.

24. Lawrence Katz and Bruce Meyer, "The Impact of the Potential Duration of Unemployment Benefits on the Duration of Unemployment," *Journal of Public Economics*, 41, no. 1 (1990), 45–72.

8

Have we lost our edge in international trade?

American companies and business-people seemingly ruled the world in the 1950s and 1960s. American-made products were everywhere, providing both necessities and luxuries to a world recovering from war. Foreign-made products in the United States were a curiosity with dubious quality. Jokes were made about German Volkswagens ("beetles") and Japanese transistor radios.

Times have changed. Far from a curiosity, foreign-made products in the United States now dominate some markets (for example, consumer electronic products), and Japan and Germany, once devastated war enemies, are now economic superpowers. It seems as if American companies are on the run even in their own country. A U.S. trade deficit (imports exceeding exports) has become commonplace. What happened? Are U.S. companies "on the ropes" in international trade? Are we being outcompeted and outproduced by foreign companies? What does this mean for the future of American jobs and the American economy? What actions, if any, should American policymakers take? Should we throw up barriers and keep out foreign products, or does free international trade benefit all of us, even if it means a trade deficit?

At the same time that America's trade position has apparently declined, foreign ownership of America has apparently increased. If this has occurred, how much has foreign ownership increased, and what does it mean? Is it bad that foreign ownership of American assets and companies has increased? Also, it is claimed that America is now a debtor nation, meaning that we owe more to foreigners than they owe to us. Is this true, and if so, what does it mean? Chapter 8 deals with all of these international questions about our economy.

WHAT TRADE DEFICIT?

Much has been written and discussed in recent years about the U.S. trade deficit. As you probably know, a trade deficit occurs when a country imports more goods and services from other countries than it exports to them. In contrast, a trade surplus occurs when a country exports more goods and services to other countries than it imports from them.

There are many issues related to a trade deficit or surplus, so let's get to them. First of all, how do we measure whether a country has a trade deficit or surplus? There are two ways. One way is to measure the difference between a country's exports and imports in monetary terms, being careful to adjust for inflation in prices between years so that dollar amounts in different years can be compared. For U.S. international trade, the measurement is made in inflation-adjusted dollars, and the result is called the real trade deficit or surplus. By correcting for price changes, this measure is essentially measuring the volume of a trade deficit or surplus.

The second measurement calculates the dollar amount of the trade deficit or surplus as a percentage of the entire economy, or gross national product (GNP). This measure tells us the size of the trade deficit or surplus relative to the size of the economy.

If we use these measures to examine the U.S. trade position in recent years since World War II, what do they show? The answers are in Figures 8-1 and 8-2. The figures reveal a number of important points. First, trade deficits (negative numbers in both figures) aren't new in recent U.S. history. In fact, in the 46 years from 1947 to 1992, trade deficits have occurred in 29 of the years.[1]

Second, the figures show that in both dollar value and as a percent of GNP, the U.S. trade deficit did reach record post-World War II levels in the mid-1980s. But equally important, the figures also show that the trade deficit narrowed considerably in the late 1980s and early 1990s. In fact, *by the early*

Figure 8-1   U.S. Trade Balance in Goods and Services

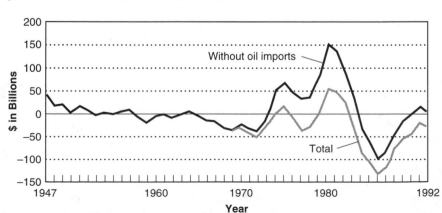

Source: *Economic Report of the President*, U.S. Government Printing Office, February 1992.

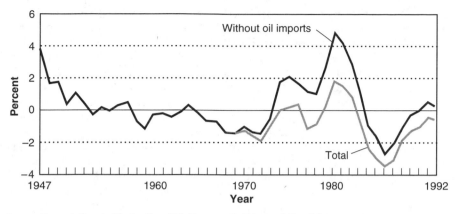

Source: *Economic Report of the President*, U.S. Government Printing Office, February 1992.

Figure 8-2   U.S. Trade Balance as a Percent of GNP

1990s, the trade deficit had been virtually eliminated. By 1992, the trade deficit had been reduced to less than 1 percent of GNP (0.7 percent), down from a high of 3.5 percent of GNP in 1986.

An even better picture is painted if oil imports are taken out of the trade picture. Both Figures 8-1 and 8-2 show the U.S. trade position without oil imports. Both figures show considerably lower trade deficits in the 1980s when oil imports are excluded. Also, without oil imports, the U.S. trade position actually turned to a surplus in the early 1990s.

Some skeptics may reply that the U.S. trade deficit improved in the early 1990s only because the 1990–91 recession dampened American consumers' appetites for foreign imports. But the figures clearly show a steady improvement in the trade deficit beginning in the mid-1980s, well before the recession of the early 1990s.

Figures 8-1 and 8-2 aren't like the figures usually seen printed in newspapers or shown on news programs. The trade deficit figures in newspapers and on news programs only show the position in merchandise or goods trade. (They also don't adjust for inflation or show the deficit as a percent of GNP.) That is, the typical trade figures don't include trade in services. But what is trade in services? Well, if a U.S. firm provides architectural plans to a Japanese builder in Japan, or if U.S. lawyers do legal work for a German company, then these are "exports" of U.S. services. Also, if foreign visitors come to the United States for a vacation and spend money on rooms and meals, this is counted as an "export" of entertainment services to foreign countries. Trade in services has become an increasing part of the total trade picture. For example, service exports as a percentage of total U.S. exports increased from 22 percent in 1980 to 27 percent in 1991.[2] In 1992, the U.S. actually ran a services *surplus* with Japan of $14 billion.[3] Since the income earned from selling services is just as good as the income earned from selling goods, failure to consider international trade in services is missing an important component of the total trade picture.

Is the improvement in our trade picture since the mid-1980s only due to our services exports? Are we still being beaten in trade in goods? Not at all. Table 8-1 reveals the explosion in U.S. export trade since the mid-1980s. In the five years between 1987 and 1992, our exports of services increased 63 percent and imports increased 18 percent. But exports of durable goods increased 97 percent, while imports increased 34 percent. Also, exports of nonfood consumer goods increased 110 percent, with imports increasing only 20 percent, and U.S. exports of automotive vehicles, engines, and parts increased 50 percent while imports actually decreased 10 percent.

The picture is just as impressive when trade with specific countries is examined (also in Table 8-1). Between 1987 and 1992, our exports of goods to Japan increased 70 percent, while our imports of goods from Japan increased only 15 percent. This caused a 33 percent reduction in our trade deficit in goods with Japan. Equally impressive improvements in our trade position with other countries also occurred in the late 1980s and early 1990s. In fact, the U.S. share of world manufactured goods exports increased from 14 percent in 1987 to 18 percent in 1990. This put the 1990 U.S. share ahead of its 1980 share and ahead of Japan's 1990 share of 15 percent.[4]

So the U.S. trade position went through a roller coaster in the 1980s, moving from surplus to deficit and then back near a surplus position. What was going on in the 1980s to cause this volatility? Did U.S. workers and companies all of a sudden become lazy, inefficient, and uncompetitive, and then suddenly return to being hard-working, efficient, and competitive?

Table 8-1   Changes in the Real (Inflation-Adjusted) Value of Trade Category, 1987–1992

Broad Categories	Exports	Imports
All goods and services	+75%	+24%
Durable goods	+97%	+34%
Nondurable goods	+50%	+29%
Services	+63%	+18%
Specific Categories		
Nonfood consumer goods, except autos	+90%	+78%
Foods, feed, and beverages	+40%	+5%
Automotive vehicles, engines, and parts	+50%	−10%
Industrial supplies and materials, excluding petroleum	+50%	+12%
Petroleum	—	−3%
With Specific Countries (goods only)		
Mexico	+180%	+76%
Canada	+45%	+38%
Central and South America	+120%	+47%
Hong Kong, Korea, Singapore, Taiwan	+105%	+8%
Western Europe	+70%	+15%
Japan	+70%	+15%

Source: U.S. Dept. of Commerce, *Survey of Current Business*, Vol. 75, no. 12, December 1993.

The roller coaster of our trade position in the 1980s was largely the result of a factor having a profound effect on our economy, that is, the international exchange rate of the U.S. dollar. The exchange rate of the dollar gives
the rate at which it can be traded for currencies of other countries. For example, if the exchange rate between Japanese yen and the U.S. dollar is 100, then
currency traders are willing to trade 100 yen for one dollar. Similarly, if the exchange rate between German marks and the U.S. dollar is 1.7, then currency
traders are willing to trade 1.7 marks per one U.S. dollar.

Changes in the dollar exchange rate profoundly affect the competitive position of U.S. international trade. If the dollar exchange rate rises, then
it takes more yen and more marks to equal one dollar. This means that the relative cost of U.S. goods and services, which are priced in dollars, rises for
Japanese and German buyers. In other words, U.S. exports to foreign buyers
become more expensive. In contrast, a higher exchange rate for the dollar
means that it takes fewer dollars to equal one yen or one mark. This means
the relative cost of Japanese and German goods and services, which are priced
in yen and marks, falls for American buyers. That is, imports to American buyers become less expensive. So a rising exchange rate for the dollar, which makes
the dollar more "expensive" to foreigners, contributes to falling U.S. exports
and rising U.S. imports, moving the United States toward a trade deficit.

The opposite impacts result from a falling dollar exchange rate. A
lower exchange rate for the dollar makes the dollar "cheaper" for foreigners
and makes foreign currencies more expensive for Americans. Therefore, a
falling exchange rate for the dollar causes a rise in U.S. exports, a fall in U.S.
imports, and moves the United States toward a trade surplus.

How far can this information go toward explaining the fluctuation in
the U.S. trade position during the 1980s? Actually, quite a way. Figure 8-3 shows
the relationship between the dollar exchange rate (a weighted average of the

Figure 8-3   Relationship of Dollar's International Value and U.S. Trade Balance

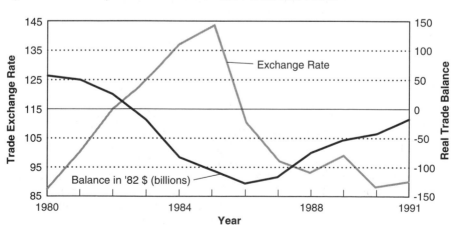

Source: *Economic Report of the President*, U.S. Government Printing Office, February 1992; Federal Reserve of St.
Louis, International Economic Conditions, February 1988 and February 1994.

exchange rates with the major trading partners of the United States) and the U.S. international trade position during the 1980s and early 1990s. In the early 1980s the dollar's exchange rate almost doubled, thereby doubling the relative "price" of dollars to foreigners. Although many Americans may have taken pride in this change (a stronger, or more expensive dollar, must be "good"), the higher-valued dollar was devastating to U.S. exports. U.S. exports became more expensive to foreigners and therefore dropped, while foreign imports to the United States became less expensive to Americans and therefore rose. These two effects pushed the United States to a large trade deficit.

In the late 1980s the dollar's exchange rate dropped and returned to its 1980 level. Consequently, the U.S. trade position moved toward a surplus and almost reached a trade surplus in the early 1990s. Also, as we have already seen, this movement was driven by rising U.S. exports and slow growth in imports to the United States.

Now you know the relationship between the exchange rate of the dollar and the U.S. trade position, and you know that the exchange rate is the "dog" wagging the trade position "tail." But have we reached the "head" of the dog; that is, what causes the dollar's exchange rate to move?

The best way to understand changes in the dollar's exchange rate is to think of the U.S. dollar and other currencies as investments. International investors, like the rest of us, want to pick investments with the highest real (after inflation) rate of return. To do this, international investors compare investments from around the world. Of course, each country's investments are denominated in that country's currency. If something happens to increase the real rate of return of a particular country's investments, then international investors will flock to that investment. This increase in demand means more investors want the currency of the country with the attractive investments. From elementary economics, we know that when more people want something, the price of that something rises. The same thing happens here. In this case, the "price" that rises is the exchange rate of the currency of the attractive investment.

What happened in the early 1980s which would increase the real rate of return on U.S. investments and cause foreign investors to bid up the value of the U.S. dollar? What force in the United States is powerful enough to influence investment returns in a short period of time? The answer is the Federal Reserve System (the Fed). The Fed, which is the central bank of the United States, can influence real interest rates through its use of monetary policy. Simply stated, monetary policy is the Fed's policy of increasing the money supply, that is, the supply of dollars in the economy.[5] If the Fed dramatically changes its policy and reduces the volume of dollars it is supplying to the economy (a "tight" monetary policy), then dollars and dollar-denominated investments become scarcer, and the real interest rate on investments rises.

This is exactly what the Fed did in the early 1980s. In an effort to slow the economy and reduce the double-digit inflation rate, the Fed tightened monetary policy and sent U.S. real interest rates higher than real interest rates in other countries. Consequently, foreign investors flocked to U.S. investments, such as treasury securities, and drove up the foreign exchange rate of U.S. dollars. In essence, the Fed's tight monetary policy increased the value of the dollar relative to other currencies.[6]

The Fed's tight monetary policy of the early 1980s worked, but at a cost. The inflation rate fell dramatically, but the economy suffered through the 1981–82 recession as a result. Also, U.S. exporters suffered from the high-valued dollar. However, once the tight monetary policy was ended, the spike in the U.S. dollar's value ended and U.S. international competitiveness returned.

So the deterioration and then improvement in the U.S. trade position in the 1980s and early 1990s can largely be related to the fluctuating foreign exchange value of the U.S. dollar. But a question may be bothering you. If the dollar's exchange value in the early 1990s returned to its level of 1980, then why didn't the U.S. run a trade surplus in the early 1990s of the same magnitude as in 1980?

There are at least three possible answers. One answer is that many U.S. companies are no longer competitive with foreign companies.[7] Of course, this flies in the face of the tremendous strides made by U.S. companies in the export market since the mid-1980s. Yet economists who support this view use it to argue for special governmental help for export companies—in other words, a form of export industrial policy.[8] We'll put this discussion aside for now and return to it in future sections.

Another answer is that there are considerable lags between changes in the dollar's exchange value and changes in a country's trade position. It takes time for trade patterns to change, and it may take up to two years for a change in the dollar's exchange value to have its full impact on exports and imports.[9] This means that the U.S. trade position may continue to improve in the 1990s in reaction to the dollar's lower exchange value reached in the early 1990s.

A third potential reason why the United States continues to run a trade deficit may be that the structure of trade has changed. Professor Richard Baldwin hypothesizes that the "beachhead effect" has permanently changed the structure of U.S. international trade.[10] Baldwin says that when the dollar's exchange value rose dramatically in the early 1980s, it became profitable for many new foreign firms to pay the fixed costs of entering the U.S. market in order to sell their goods. This gave them a "beachhead" in the U.S. market. When the exchange value of the U.S. dollar fell, foreign firms found it less profitable to sell goods in America, but they didn't totally dismantle their beachhead. They continued to sell some goods because they had already paid the fixed costs of establishing their presence in the U.S. market.

In closing this section, let's address a basic question which I could have posed at the beginning of this chapter: Who cares if the country runs a trade deficit; what difference does it make? Many of you probably think that a trade deficit matters very much because if cars are bought from Japan rather than from a U.S. company, then those auto jobs go to Japan rather than remain here in the United States. So is the issue jobs? Is it important for a country to run a trade surplus in order to keep and create jobs?[11]

There's no question that domestic jobs can be adversely affected by international trade. There is ample evidence that jobs in selected industries, such as the auto industry, were lost as foreign auto companies made inroads in the U.S. market in the 1980s.[12] But what is ignored is the fact that the lost jobs are compensated for in two ways. First, if U.S. consumers save money by buying the foreign products rather than American-made products, then that saved money can be spent on other U.S. products, which in turn creates jobs in those industries. For example, it's likely that U.S. consumers saved money in the early 1980s by buying high-quality, fuel-efficient foreign automobiles rather than gas-guzzling domestic cars. Consumers then used some of this saved money to buy other American-made products and services.

The "lost-jobs" argument of the trade deficit also ignores what happens to the dollars earned by foreign producers when they sell products to American consumers. As will be explained in more detail later, these foreign-owned dollars eventually come back to the United States in the form of investments in our country, which also create jobs in the United States. In this way jobs lost by U.S. companies to foreign trade are, in part, replaced by other jobs created by foreign investors.[13]

So trade deficits aren't all bad, and they aren't the "job-draining" processes that they have been claimed to be.[14] Furthermore, if we look at a country-by-country basis, we should expect the United States to chronically run a trade deficit with some countries. Japan is a good example. Japan is a country with few natural resources. To prosper economically, Japan must import raw materials and export finished products. Therefore, we should expect Japan to run a trade deficit with countries that supply them with natural resources and to run a trade surplus with countries that import finished products. In fact, even when the United States had an overall trade surplus, it still ran a trade deficit with Japan. Also, the United States has twice the population of Japan. It makes sense that Japan exports more to the United States than vice versa because the United States is a bigger market than Japan. Actually, on a per-person basis, U.S. exports to Japan and Japanese exports to the United States are remarkably similar. For example, in 1992, U.S. exports to Japan were $378 per Japanese citizen, and Japanese exports to the United States were $383 per American citizen.[15]

IS THE UNITED STATES COMPETITIVE?

At the crux of the issues of international trade is the issue of competitiveness. Is the United States still competitive against foreign countries? The image that many Americans have is of U.S. companies with highly paid work forces that can't compete with the more efficient Japanese and Germans and the low-paid Mexicans and Koreans. Is this image accurate?

Although this image may have been accurate at one time, it is no longer accurate in the early 1990s. In 1993 the World Economic Forum ranked the United States second only to Japan in competitiveness among the major industrialized countries.[16] The forum's rankings are based on both statistical data and opinions of worldwide business executives. The forum shows the United States rising in competitiveness from the mid-1980s to the early 1990s.

A second way of examining competitiveness is to compare unit labor costs between countries. Unit labor costs are the labor cost of producing a unit of output (say, a ton of steel) in different countries. The costs are expressed in a common currency (e.g., U.S. dollars), so they account not only for productivity and pay differences but also exchange rates between currencies. In essence, investors and entrepreneurs can look at unit labor costs and determine where it is cheapest, in terms of labor, to operate in the world.

Figure 8-4 shows unit labor costs in manufacturing for selected countries.[17] Notice that unit labor costs in the United States were higher in the early and mid-1980s than in other countries. This occurred despite strong productivity growth in U.S. manufacturing in the early and mid-1980s. For example, between 1980 and 1985, manufacturing output per worker grew 4 percent annually in the United States, compared to 4 percent in Japan, and 2.7 percent in Germany.[18]

Instead, the rise in unit labor costs in the United States in the first half of the 1980s occurred as a result of the appreciation of the dollar, which, as we have already discussed, was a direct result of the anti-inflation policy of the Federal Reserve. Once the spike in the dollar's value disappeared by the early 1990s, U.S. unit labor costs returned to competitive levels. In fact, in 1990, U.S. unit labor costs in manufacturing were only 54 percent of those in Germany, 90 percent of those in Japan, and 74 percent of those in France. U.S. unit labor costs were estimated to be greater than those in Korea, but the gap between U.S. and Korean unit labor costs was cut by 74 percent between 1986 and 1990.

Of course, labor costs aren't the only factor that determines the relative competitiveness of a country. (This is why not all businesses are moving to Korea!) The quality of management and finance costs are also important. But the evidence on unit labor costs indicates that the United States is definitely "in" the world competition for markets and customers.

Figure 8-4   Unit Labor Costs in Manufacturing

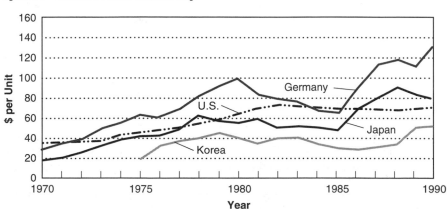

Sources: Peter Hooper and Kathryn Larin, "International Comparisons of Labor Costs in Manufacturing," *Review of Income and Wealth*, series 35, no. 4, December 1989, pp. 335–356; U.S. Bureau of Labor Statistics, *Monthly Labor Review*, vol. 115, no. 6, June 1992.

WHAT SHOULD BE OUR TRADE POLICY?

So we've learned that our trade situation isn't as bleak as you might have thought. The U.S. trade deficit dropped considerably in the second half of the 1980s, and there are logical reasons why the deficit developed in the early 1980s. Also, evidence from several sources indicates that U.S. companies and workers are now competitive with companies and workers in other countries.

So is everything rosy, or soon to become rosy? Does the federal government need to take any action regarding international trade? What should be our national trade policy?

There are three options for a national trade policy. One option is free trade. With this option, our national government works to promote open markets around the world including in the United States by lowering trade barriers. But beyond this, companies are on their own to compete. A national free-trade policy is limited to "leveling the playing field" of trade between nations and then letting companies battle it out for the customer.

As the second possible national trade policy, protectionism is at the opposite end of the spectrum from free trade. At the extreme, protectionism calls for erecting a high trade barrier around the United States to keep out foreign imports. It relies on U.S. consumers being served only by U.S. companies and workers. A milder form of protectionism calls for protecting only certain industries, such as the automobile and steel industries, from foreign competition.

The third national trade policy option is managed trade. Managed trade is best thought of as being a middle ground between free trade and protectionism. Managed traders promote controlled free trade where the federal government has two roles. First, the federal government selects important, or strategic, industries which are viewed as critical to the long-run health of the economy. The federal government helps these strategic industries by giving them subsidies, protecting them from international competition, and promoting their exports. The second role of the federal government in managed trade is to set quantitative goals for imports and exports with countries that have a large trade surplus with the United States. For example, under managed trade, the United States and Japan would agree on quantitative goals for Japanese imports in the United States and for U.S. exports to Japan.[19]

Which policy is the way to go? Let's look at protectionism first. Most countries of the world already practice some form of protectionism in international trade, including the United States. In fact, the United States ranks about in the middle of the pack among countries in terms of barriers to free trade. It's estimated that the United States has trade barriers covering a quarter of all manufactured goods sold in the country. For example, the United States limits free trade by foreign producers for a number of agricultural commodities (including sugar), textile and apparel products, steel, motorcycles, and shoes, to name a few[20] So since the United States is already not a free-trade zone, why not go all the way and close the borders to trade, thereby creating more jobs for Americans?

The simple answer is that protectionist policies which limit foreign imports in the United States don't necessarily save jobs. In fact, there's ample evidence that protectionist policies cost U.S. consumers income and may very well cost jobs. The reason is that protectionist policies raise product prices because they limit competition and keep out lower-priced goods and services. Studies have documented that protectionist policies cost U.S. consumers several billion dollars annually in additional costs for goods and services.[21] In other words, if the trade barriers were removed, consumers would save money. This is money which consumers could then have spent on other goods and services.

Another way of looking at the costs of protectionism is to calculate the costs per job saved by the protectionist policies. Table 8-2 gives this information for the United States, and the evidence is sobering. In most cases, the annual cost per job saved is over $100,000. This means that if the protection-

Table 8-2   Annual Costs per Job Saved of U. S. Protectionist Policies

SECTOR	ANNUAL COST PER JOB
Manufacturing	
Book manufacturing	$100,000
Benzenoid chemicals	over $1 million
Glassware	$200,000
Rubber footwear	$30,000
Ceramic articles	$47,500
Ceramic tiles	$135,000
Orange juice	$240,000
Canned tuna	$76,000
Textiles and apparel	$22,000–$42,000
Carbon steel	$240,000–$750,000
Ball bearings	$90,000
Specialty steel	$1,000,000
Nonrubber footwear	$55,000
Color televisions	$420,000
CB radios	$93,000
Bolts, nuts, large screws	$550,000
Prepared mushrooms	$117,000
Automobiles	$105,000
Motorcycles	$150,000
Services	
Maritime industries	$270,000
Agriculture and Fisheries	
Sugar	$60,000
Dairy products	$220,000
Meat	$160,000
Fish	$21,000
Peanuts	$1,000 per acre
Mining	
Petroleum	$160,000
Lead and Zinc	$30,000

Source: Cletus Coughlin, K. Alec Chrystal, and Geoffrey Woods, "Protectionist Trade Policies: A Survey of Theory, Evidence and Rationale," *Review*, Federal Reserve Bank of St. Louis, Vol. 70, No. 1, January/February 1988, pp. 12–26.

ist policies were ended, then the savings consumers would receive could be used to pay laid-off workers over $100,000 annually. In the vast majority of cases, this would be much more income than received by the trade-sensitive workers in their jobs.

In reality, it is unlikely that the savings received by consumers from the elimination of protectionist policies would all go to displaced workers. Realistically, some of the savings could be taxed and used to retrain the displaced workers for other jobs.

Will there be new jobs for displaced workers if we reduce trade barriers in the United States and move to freer trade? Yes, and there are two reasons why. First, most of the money saved by consumers (as I said earlier, estimated at several billion dollars annually) by eliminating trade barriers will be spent on other goods and services in the economy, and this spending will create new jobs. Second, if the reduction of U.S. trade barriers encourages other countries to reduce their trade barriers, then we would expect U.S. exports to rise, and this too would create new jobs.

So there are substantial costs from a protectionist trade policy. But what about managed trade? Isn't international trade too important to be left completely in the (invisible) hands of the free market? Isn't managed trade a nice compromise between protectionism and free trade? Well, let's see.

Supporters of managed trade say that free trade can't be relied on because some foreign countries, like Japan, won't permit free and open trade in their markets.[22] Although this is disputed by some economists, many studies do indeed show that Japan has serious trade barriers which make it difficult for foreign countries to enter the Japanese market and succeed.[23] Therefore, managed-trade advocates say that export and import goals must be negotiated with Japan and countries like Japan for key industries and products. For example, Japan must be lobbied to agree to importing X percent more American-made autos and computer parts, while at the same time, Japan must agree to limit its exports of key products, like autos and consumer electronic products, to the U.S. market. Managed traders also support management of exchange rates as a way to control the terms of trade between countries.

However, managed trade has the same basic flaws as industrial policy (see Chapter 6). Although managed trade may sound good in theory, in practice it can easily be "hijacked" by political considerations. The concern is that politicians won't ignore politically connected companies in designing the managed-trade goals and passing out the subsidies to key industries. Won't every politician find a key industry in his or her district or state? Managed trade can easily turn into a political "pork barrel" like industrial policy.

There are other disadvantages to managed trade. If a domestic firm is subsidized and assured of a secure market share in a foreign market, then that firm will have less incentive to change and do those things necessary to compete in international trade. In short, managed trade, by sheltering key industries and firms, will reduce the incentives of those firms and industries to innovate and to become more efficient.

The management of currency exchange rates (e.g., the exchange rate between the dollar and yen) is also misguided. Currency exchange rates can't be directly controlled because they result from fundamental economic factors. If, for example, it is desired by the managed traders to reduce the value of the dollar relative to the yen, thereby making U.S. exports cheaper to the Japanese, then real U.S. interest rates will have to fall relative to Japanese real interest rates. The most direct way to do this would be for the U.S. Federal Reserve to create more inflation in the United States by increasing the rate of growth of the money supply. So the trade-off would be more U.S. inflation in exchange for a lower-valued dollar.

So I have cast doubt on both protectionism and managed trade. This leaves free trade as the other national policy option. Indeed, there are a number of reasons to think free trade is the best national trade policy. Free trade allows U.S. and foreign consumers access to the greatest array of products and services. Free trade allows maximum choice for consumers. Free trade also increases competition, thereby forcing companies to be more competitive on price and attentive to consumer desires. If companies don't pay attention to consumer tastes and pocketbooks, they are punished by losing business. The American auto companies are a good example of firms being punished if they don't move rapidly with the market. In the 1970s American auto companies were outcompeted by Japanese auto companies on price, quality, and gas mileage.[24] Consequently, American auto companies lost sales and market share to foreign producers. However, American consumers were the winners because they obviously "voted with their wallets" for what they considered to be superior foreign-made products.

But, you might ask, why can't a single country, like the United States, produce everything it needs at the lowest possible cost without relying on foreign producers and foreign trade? Surely a country as big and well endowed as the United States can produce the major products and services desired by today's consumers. Of course, without foreign trade, some of us would have to go without French wine, German cars, and silk suits from Hong Kong. But there are American-made substitutes for all these products. What do we really gain from foreign trade if we can produce almost everything that foreigners produce?

This question really gets to the heart of the issue of the benefits from trade. This is an age-old yet very important issue. Most people can understand that benefits from trade can occur if each country can produce a particular product more cheaply than any other country. U.S.-Saudi Arabian trade is a good example. Saudi Arabia can produce a barrel of high-grade oil at about one-seventh the cost of production in the United States. On the other hand, the United States can produce agricultural products much more cheaply than such products can be produced in the hot, arid climate of Saudi Arabia. Therefore, it makes sense that the United States and Saudi Arabia trade, and the trade makes both countries better off. The United States sends agricultural products and foodstuffs to Saudi Arabia, and Saudi Arabia exports relatively cheap oil to the United States.

But trade can be mutually beneficial to two countries even if one country can produce all products more cheaply than the other country. I'm sure this assertation is counterintuitive to most of you, but hopefully my logic will convince you of its truth.

Consider the following hypothetical yet realistic example for the United States and Mexico. Figure 8-5 shows that it is cheaper to produce both telephones and shirts in the United States than in Mexico. However, even though this is the case, telephones are still *relatively* cheaper in the United States than in Mexico, and shirts are *relatively* cheaper in Mexico than in the United States. That is, the United States has a comparative advantage in the production of telephones, and Mexico has a comparative advantage in the production of shirts.

Figure 8-5 further shows one hypothetical production point in both the United States and Mexico if no trade occurs (in the United States, 30 telephones and 70 shirts; in Mexico, 10 telephones and 35 shirts). But there's motivation for trade to occur between the countries because telephones and shirts don't trade at the same rate in the United States and Mexico. If, for example, trade between the two countries occurs at the rate of one telephone for seven shirts (implying also that one shirt trades for one-seventh telephone), then the United States will be motivated to trade telephones to Mexico for shirts because the rate of one telephone for seven shirts is better than the internal U.S. rate of one telephone for six shirts. And Mexico will be motivated to trade shirts to the United States for telephones because the rate of one shirt for one-seventh telephone is better than the internal Mexican rate of one shirt for one-ninth telephone. Part C of Figure 8-5 shows how trade can make both countries better off with the same number of telephones but more shirts.[25]

A good example of the benefits of free trade can be seen in the recently approved North American Free Trade Agreement (NAFTA). NAFTA will sig-

---

Figure 8-5   How the United States and Mexico Can Benefit from Trade

A. Labor costs to produce:

	1 Telephone	1 Shirt
U.S.	$12	$2
Mexico	$36	$4

Therefore, in the United States, 1 telephone = 6 shirts, and in Mexico, 1 telephone = 9 shirts, so in the United States telephones are relatively cheaper.

Also, in the United States, 1 shirt = 1/6 telephone, and in Mexico, 1 shirt = 1/9 telephone, so in Mexico shirts are relatively cheaper.

B. If no trade ($500 total resources in each country)

	Number of Telephones	Number of Shirts
U.S.	$360 = 30 telephones	$140 = 70 shirts
Mexico	$360 = 10 telephones	$140 = 35 shirts

C. With trade where 1 telephone = 7 shirts, the United States trades 10 telephones to Mexico for 70 shirts

	Number of Telephones	Number of Shirts
U.S.	$480 = 40 telephones	$20 = 10 shirts
	– 10 telephones to Mexico	+ 70 shirts from Mexico
	30 telephones	80 shirts
Mexico	$0 = 0 telephones	$500 = 125 shirts
	+ 10 telephones from United States	– 70 shirts to United States
	10 telephones	55 shirts

nificantly lower trade barriers between Mexico, the United States, and Canada. Many people and politicians have worried that NAFTA will result in many U.S. jobs, particularly manufacturing jobs, moving to Mexico where wage levels and environmental regulations are significantly lower.

The fears about NAFTA are overblown for three reasons. First, it is already relatively easy and costless for U.S. manufacturing firms to set up shop in Mexico and take advantage of low Mexican wages. (Although remember, these wages aren't as low as they appear because they don't account for productivity differences between U.S. and Mexican workers; indeed, when the higher productivity of U.S. workers is accounted for, U.S. and Mexican unit labor costs are virtually the same.)[26] Indeed, as we have seen in Chapter 6, there has been a significant increase in Mexican employment in U.S. firms during the past 20 years. So U.S. firms who want to take advantage of "cheap" Mexican labor can already do so. In fact, it's estimated that the U.S. auto industry and auto workers will actually benefit from NAFTA. Mexican tariffs on American-made autos and ports are currently much higher than U.S. tariffs on autos and parts imported from Mexico. Therefore, eliminating both countries' tariffs will increase the competitiveness of U.S. auto exports in Mexico much more than the competitiveness of Mexican auto products in the United States.[27]

Second, the fears that weaker environmental regulations in Mexico will cause a wholesale movement of U.S. firms to south of the border are unfounded for a simple reason. The business costs of complying with environmental standards, while significant, are not a major factor in determining business location and the patterns of trade.[28]

Third, the fears about NAFTA ignore the principle of comparative advantage, which we discussed earlier. Mexico does have a comparative advantage in low-cost, unskilled labor, but the United States has a comparative advantage in high-skilled labor and technology. Therefore, we would expect NAFTA to result in Mexico increasing its production of goods and services using low-cost, unskilled labor, while the United States increases its production of goods and services using skilled labor and technology. This specialization will result in increased trade and higher incomes for both nations. Indeed, numerous mathematical models, which attempt to predict economic impacts of policy changes, show Mexico, the United States, and Canada all increasing their incomes and employment as a result of NAFTA.[29]

There will be losers, at least in the short run, as NAFTA is implemented. Although most models show the United States gaining a net 35,000 to 170,000 jobs from the implementation of NAFTA, jobs will be lost. For example, the study showing a net gain of 170,000 jobs derived this figure from a gain of 320,000 jobs and a loss of 150,000 other jobs.[30] Economic transition is not smooth and costless. Unskilled workers cannot be turned into skilled, high-tech workers overnight. Obvious short-run economic losers in the United States will be unskilled workers, who will see more of their jobs go to Mexico, and certain U.S. industries, such as apparel, that will see their production move to rival Mexican firms. Although the benefits from NAFTA will outweigh these losses, the losses do suggest that education and retraining will be important for displaced workers.

FOREIGN OWNERSHIP OF AMERICA

America is an open country. With some exceptions, foreigners are free to buy U.S. assets, such as land, buildings, factories, and companies.

Foreign owners did increase their purchase of U.S. assets in the 1980s, and for a very good reason. The trade deficits which the U.S. ran in that decade put dollars in the hands of foreigners. Foreigners used these dollars to purchase U.S. assets. In essence the goods and services which the United States imported in the 1980s that weren't paid for with exports were paid for with assets.

So are foreigners ready to take over the United States? As Figure 8-6 shows, foreign ownership of U.S. assets did increase substantially in the 1980s, but as a percent of U.S. corporate assets, foreign ownership is still less than 7 percent. Even this percentage overstates foreign ownership, since federal statisticians consider a company to be foreign owned if the foreign stake is 10 percent or more.

Foreign control of U.S. employment is even smaller, standing at 4.4 percent of nonbank U.S. employment in 1990.[31] In 1987, foreigners owned only 1 percent of U.S. land.[32]

Why is there so much discussion concerning foreign ownership? One answer is that Americans, perhaps with World War II on their minds, believe the Japanese are the major movers behind the increase in foreign ownership. The Japanese did substantially increase their ownership of U.S. assets in the 1980s, and so too did the British. Table 8-3 shows that indeed the Japanese are the largest foreign owners in the United States, followed by the British and the Dutch. But in 1992, the Japanese accounted for less than one-fourth of total foreign ownership in the United States.

Figure 8-6   Foreign Ownership as a Percent of The U.S. Economy*

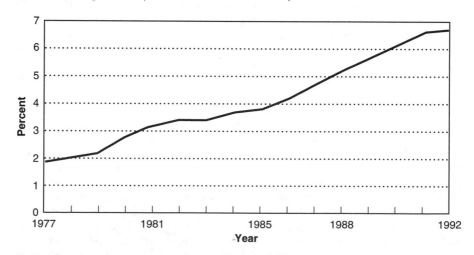

*Foreign direct investment as a percent of U.S. nonfinancial corporate assets.

Source: U.S. Department of Commerce, *Survey of Current Business*, June 1992; Board of Governors of the Federal Reserve System, *Balance Sheets for the U.S. Economy, 1960–1991*, September 1992.

Table 8-3   Ranking of Countries by Foreign Direct Investment Position in the
United States, 1992 (top 6 countries)

COUNTRY	$ MILLIONS	PERCENT OF GRAND TOTAL
Japan	96,743	23.1
United Kingdom	94,718	22.6
Netherlands	61,341	14.6
Germany	29,205	7.0
France	23,808	5.7
Switzerland	19,562	4.7

Source: U.S. Department of Commerce, *Survey of Current Business*, June 1992.

Another reason for concern about foreign ownership is whether foreign owners behave differently than American owners. If foreign owners pay American employees less, or if foreign owners invest less, then these may be legitimate sources of concern about foreign ownership.

The facts don't back up these potential concerns. Foreign owners pay compensation to workers that's very comparable to the compensation paid by U.S. owners. (In 1987, U.S. affiliates of foreign-owned companies paid average compensation per worker of $29,800 compared to $24,200 for all U.S. firms.) Regarding research and development spending, foreign owners in 1988 spent $2,000 in research and development per worker in the United States, almost twice the $1,070 spent per worker by American owners.[33]

IS THE UNITED STATES A DEBTOR NATION?

Perhaps the statement that most convinces people that the American economy has hit the skids is the statement that "America is a debtor nation." But what does this really mean and how important is it?

In simple terms, a nation is a debtor nation if the value of assets it owns in foreign countries is less than the value of assets owned by foreigners in the nation. In making this comparison, it's important to value real assets, such as land, buildings, and factories, at their current market value rather than their value when purchased.

Figure 8-7 shows the international position of the United States from 1977 to 1992. Positive dollar values indicate that the United States is a creditor nation where U.S. citizens own more foreign assets abroad than foreign citizens own in the United States; negative dollar values indicate the United States is a debtor nation. As the figure shows, the United States did indeed become a debtor nation in 1987 and has remained a debtor nation through 1992.[34] However, if American-owned assets abroad are *incorrectly* valued at their original cost rather than at their current value, then the current debtor position of the United States would be approximately $100 billion higher.[35]

Nevertheless, the numbers do show that the United States did move from a creditor-nation status to a debtor-nation status in the 1980s. Why did this occur? The conventional wisdom is that most of the foreign investors bought U.S. government securities (treasury securities), thereby helping to

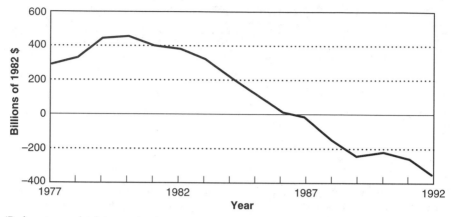

*Real assets are valued at current cost.
Source: U.S. Department of Commerce, *Survey of Current Business*, September 1992 and September 1993.

Figure 8-7   International Investment Position of the United States, Billions of 1982 $*

fund the federal budget deficits. This is incorrect. As Table 8-4 shows, the vast majority (80 percent) of the increase in foreign-owned U.S. assets went to private investments, including bank and nonbank loans, stocks and bonds, and land, buildings, and factories. *In short, foreigners increased their investment in the private U.S. economy during the 1980s to a much greater extent than U.S. citizens invested in foreign economies.* Their investments helped propel the economic growth of that decade.

There's one more worry that many people have about the debtor status of the United States. Is the debt owed to foreigners so great that there's a chance that the U.S. (government and companies) couldn't pay it, thereby allowing them to "foreclose" on America? Is the U.S. debtor status similar to the debtor status of some developing countries (like Brazil) 20 years ago?

Although the United States is, on net, in debt to other nations, there are two reasons not to consider this a "crisis." First, the size of the debt relative to the size of the U.S. economy is still quite small. In 1992, the net debt of the United States as a percent of GNP was 8.7 percent, and as a percent of domestic (U.S.) net worth was 2.8 percent.[36] These percentages are far less than similar indicators of international indebtedness for other countries.[37]

Second, the United States is still earning more in interest and dividends from its assets abroad than foreigners are earning on their assets in the United States. For example, in 1992, income receipts from American-owned assets abroad were $6 billion more than the income earned by foreigners on their American-based assets, and this difference has been positive for the past 30 years.[38] In fact, due to the problems in valuing assets (both U.S. owned and foreign owned), some economists put more weight on comparing the flow of money from assets. Because the net flow is still positive for the United States, these economists express no concern about the alleged net debtor status of the United States.[39]

Table 8-4   Increase in Foreign-Owned U.S. Assets, 1980–1991[a]

TYPE OF ASSET		PERCENT OF TOTAL
Foreign official (government) assets in the United States		
(1) U.S. treasury securities	+$194,552	10.94%
(2) Other assets	+$25,993	1.46%
Foreign private assets in the United States		
(3) U.S. treasury securities	+$138,552	7.79%
(4) Direct investment (land, buildings, factories, etc.)	+$361,078	20.31%
(5) U.S. stocks and bonds	+$485,541	27.31%
(6) Bank and nonbank loans	$572,360	32.19%
Total	+$1,778,076	100.00%
(4) + (5) + (6) as % of total		79.81%

[a]Increase in nominal dollar values.

Source: U.S. Department of Commerce, *Survey of Current Business*, June 1992.

NOTES

1. Trade deficits aren't new in earlier periods of U.S. history. For example, in the 65-year period from 1830 to 1895, trade deficits occurred in 52 years; see K. Alec Chrystal and Geoffrey Wood, "Are Trade Deficits a Problem?" *Review*, Federal Reserve Bank of St. Louis, 70, no. 1 (January/February 1988), 3–11.

2. *Economic Report of the President.*

3. Ralph King, Jr. "U.S. Service Exports Are Growing Rapidly, But Almost Unnoticed," *The Wall Street Journal*, April 21, 1993, p.A1.

4. Reuven Glick, "U.S. International Trade and Competitiveness," Federal Reserve Bank of San Francisco Weekly Letter, No. 92-13, March 27, 1992.

5. The Fed alters the money supply through the buying and selling of treasury securities.

6. Many economists argue that the increase in the federal budget deficits in the early 1980s increased real interest rates and led to the higher-valued dollar. However, a positive link between higher budget deficits and higher real interest rates has not been consistently established (see Chapter 4). Also, Niskanen shows there is no empirical correlation between budget deficits and trade deficits both in the United States over time and across countries; see William Niskanen, "The Uneasy Relation Between the Budget and Trade Deficits," in James Dorn and William Niskanen, eds., *Dollars, Deficits, and Trade*, (Boston: Kluwer Academic, 1989), 305–316.

7. For an expansion on this viewpoint, see Robert Blecker, *Beyond the Twin Deficits* (Armonk, NY: M.E. Sharpe, Inc.), 1992.

8. Ibid., pp. 115–137.

9. Thomas Grennes, *International Economics* (Englewood Cliffs, NJ: Prentice-Hall, 1984), pp. 480–509.

10. Richard Baldwin, "Hysteresis in Import Prices: The Beachhead Effect," *American Economic Review*, 78, no. 4 (September 1988), 773–785.

11. A theory called mercantilism, popular in the sixteenth and seventeenth centuries, said that a country's goal should be to accumulate a trade surplus so that more

gold could be obtained. Adam Smith, author of *The Wealth of Nations*, attacked this doctrine because it favored producers over consumers and created inefficiencies in the economic system; see David Pearce, ed., *The Dictionary of Modern Economics* (Cambridge, MA: The MIT Press 1981), p. 279.

12. Robert Bednarzik, "An Analysis of U.S. Industries Sensitive to Foreign Trade, 1982–87," *Monthly Labor Review*, 116, no. 2 (February 1993), 15–31.

13. For an expansion on this argument, see Richard McKenzie, *The American Job Machine* (New York: Universe Books, 1988), pp. 134–159.

14. Some economists worry about another problem from trade deficits. They worry that trade deficits signify a lack of savings in the country, i.e., investment is greater than savings, and the difference is made up by foreign funds. (See Blecker, *Beyond the Twin Deficits*, pp. 33–56). U.S. savings behavior was discussed in Chapter 3.

15. U.S. Dept. of Commerce, *Survey of Current Business* (March 1993); Organization of Economic and Cooperative Development.

16. *The Economist*, June 26, 1993, p. 111.

17. For unit labor costs for other major industrialized countries, see Peter Hooper and Kathryn Larin, "International Comparisons of Labor Costs in Manufacturing," *Review of Income and Wealth*, series 35, no. 4 (December 1989), pp. 335–356; and U.S. Bureau of Labor Statistics, *Monthly Labor Review*.

18. Glick, "U.S. International Trade and Competitiveness."

19. For an expansion on the managed-trade concept, see Laura D'Andrea Tyson, "Managed Trade: Making the Best of the Second Best," in Robert Lawrence and Charles Schultze, *An American Trade Strategy: Options for the 1990s* (Washington, DC: The Brookings Institution, 1990), pp. 142–194.

20. For an excellent and comprehensive presentation of U.S. restrictions on free trade, see James Bovard, *The Fair Trade Fraud* (New York: St. Martin's Press, 1991).

21. One study "conservatively" estimated that U.S. trade restraints cost U.S. consumers $14 billion in 1984, "The Consumer Cost of U.S. Trade Restraints," *Quarterly Review*, Federal Reserve Bank of New York, 10, no. 2 (Summer 1985), 1–12.

22. See Bob Davis, "Clinton's Get-Tough Stance With Japan Signals Rise of Revisionist Thought," *The Wall Street Journal*, June 14, 1993, p. A11. A key proponent of the "Japan is different view" is Clyde Prestowitz of the Economic Strategy Institute.

23. Japan's barriers are of the nontariff or intangible variety, such as product standards which are different for foreign producers than for domestic Japanese producers. See Dorothy Christelow, "Japan's Intangible Barriers to Trade in Manufacturers," *Quarterly Review*, Federal Reserve Bank of New York, 10, no. 4 (Winter 1985–86), 11–18.

24. Michael Dertouzos, Richard Lester, and Robert Solow, *Made in America: Regaining the Productive Edge* (New York: Harper Perennial, 1989), pp. 171–187; Clifford Winston and Associates, *Blind Intersection? Policy and the Automobile Industry* (Washington, DC: The Brookings Institution, 1987).

25. This is only one example of the results from trade. The final posttrade position depends on the final trading rate between goods (telephones and shirts here) and the amount of resources in each country.

26. Daniel Oks and Sweder van Wijnbergen, "Mexico After the Debt Crisis: Is Growth Sustainable?" Washington, DC, The World Bank (October 1992).

27. Congressional Budget Office, *A Budgetary and Economic Analysis of the North American Free Trade Agreement* (Washington, DC: U.S. Government Printing Office, July 1993), p. 39.

28. James Tobey, "The Effects of Domestic Environmental Policies on Patterns of World Trade: An Empirical Test," *Kyklos*, 43 (1990), 190.

29. Since the U.S. economy is many times larger than both the Canadian and Mexican economies, the impact of NAFTA on the Mexican economy is estimated to be much greater. See Drusilla Brown, "The Impact of a North American Free Trade Area: Applied General Equilibrium Models"; and Raūl Hinojosa-Ojeda and Sherman Robinson, "Labor Issues in a North American Free Trade Area"; both in Nora Lustig, Barry Bosworth, and Robert Lawrence, eds., *North American Free Trade* (Washington, DC: The Brookings Institution, 1992), pp. 26–108.

30. Congressional Budget Office, *A Budgetary and Economic Analysis of the North American Free Trade Agreement* p. 84. For an excellent reply to the critics of NAFTA, see Alan Reynolds, *The Impact of NAFTA on U.S. Jobs and Wages: A Critique of the Critics* (Indianapolis: The Hudson Institute, 1993).

31. U.S. Dept. of Commerce, *Survey of Current Business* (May 1992).

32. Edward Graham and Paul Krugman, *Foreign Direct Investment in the U.S.* (Washington, DC: Institute for International Economics, 1989), p. 24.

33. Cletus Coughlin, "Foreign Owned Companies in the U.S.: Malign or Benign," *Review*, Federal Reserve Bank of St. Louis (May/June 1992), p. 28.

34. The value of U.S. real assets (land, buildings, factories) owned abroad are still greater than the value of foreign-owned real assets in the United States.

35. The majority of American-owned foreign assets were purchased in the 1950s, 1960s, and 1970s, whereas the majority of foreign-owned U.S. assets were purchased in the 1980s. Using historical (original) values ignores appreciation in assets which occurred since they were bought. Since the Americans owned foreign assets were purchased much earlier than foreign-owned U.S. assets, using historical costs hurts the U.S. position much more.

36. U.S. Dept. of Commerce, *Survey of Current Business*; Board of Governors of the Federal Reserve System, *Balance Sheets for the U.S. Economy 1945–92*.

37. Norman Fieleke, "The United States in Debt," *New England Economic Review*, (September/October 1990), pp. 34–54.

38. U.S. Dept. of Commerce, *Survey of Current Business* (June 1993).

39. Thomas Gale Moore, "The Reagan Economic Performance," Amandi Sahu and Ronald Tracy, eds., *The Economic Legacy of the Reagan Years: Euphoria or Chaos?* (New York: Praeger, 1991), pp. 107–113.

IV. DEREGULATION

The decade of the 1980s was the decade of deregulation and, some argue, also a decade of selling out to business at the expense of the consumer. Actually beginning in the late 1970s, a number of major industries had federal regulations on them significantly reduced. Key among these industries were airlines, trucking, and telecommunications.

The reduction in regulations opened up the industries to more competition but also allowed the companies to establish prices and product and service quality as they saw fit. Did this deregulation benefit consumers, or was it a sellout to big business? This is a critical question because deregulation is a test of whether the unbridled market can benefit consumers. Many of you may hold the viewpoint that, if left to their own devices, businesses will "run over" the consumer and set high prices. An analysis of the deregulation of the 1980s found in Chapter 9 will determine if your viewpoint is right or wrong.

Along with the deregulation of major industries in the 1980s came a run of company mergers, with many of them financed by high-risk ("junk") bonds. The public perception, fueled by the trial of junk-bond dealer Michael Milkin, is that such mergers were bad for the economy and for consumers and good only for "greedy" owners, managers, and deal makers. Who does benefit from company mergers? Should they be restricted? Also, are the CEOs (chief executive officers) of large companies, many of whom were active in the deregulation and merger activities of the 1980s, earning exorbitant salaries that are unrelated to their performance? Shouldn't there be restrictions on CEO salaries? We'll also address these issues in Chapter 9.

One other major industry which was deregulated in the 1980s is the savings and loan industry. You might wonder how the deregulation of the savings and loan industry can be regarded as beneficial to anyone but a handful of "crooks." Doesn't the savings and loan debacle prove that major industries must be regulated in order to prevent the wholesale cheating of the consumer? We'll see in Chapter 10.

9

Is unregulated business exploiting the consumer?

Deregulation, job-destroying mergers, and exorbitant executive pay have all been cited as examples of business being allowed to run wild by the laissez-faire attitude of the 1980s. Did all this business freedom and executive perks and privileges come at the expense of the consumer? Can both business and the consumer prosper at the same time? Indeed, reflecting these questions, as the 1980s ended and the 1990s began, there were calls to reregulate and recontrol many of the same industries that had been deregulated in the 1980s.

The deregulation and merger activity set off in the 1980s is really a test of the market system. Can the pursuit of profits by companies in unfettered competition benefit the consumer? If left unregulated, won't companies simply gouge consumers? Isn't government regulation needed to "level the playing field" between business and consumers? We'll try to answer these questions in this chapter.

WHO HAS BENEFITTED FROM DEREGULATION?

Regulating an industry means the government doesn't allow totally free and open competition. Although there are many kinds of government regulation of business, the kind we're concerned with here is regulation of price and/or entry in an industry. Government regulation of price means the government sets or approves of prices in an industry. Government regulation of entry means the government controls which companies can operate in the industry.

At first glance, government regulation of price and entry may seem sensible and beneficial to consumers. Surely the government will set or approve prices that are most affordable to consumers! And certainly the controls on entry will prevent cutthroat competition. So how could price and entry regulation be bad?

Price and entry regulation are bad because they strike at the heart of the benefits of competition. Economists believe that by allowing new firms to enter and compete in an industry, existing firms must constantly work hard to please consumers and keep them buying their product or service. The threat of losing customers to a rival firm is what keeps firms attentive to customer needs and desires. Price competition has the same benefit. The possibility that a rival firm will sell the product or service at a lower price is what motivates a firm to keep its costs low and to price its product or service as close to total costs as possible.[1]

This is theoretical support for open entry and competition in an industry. But can it be proven with actual evidence that price and entry competition benefit the consumer and not just line the pockets of business owners? To see whether these good results come from unregulated competition, we'll look at the empirical evidence from four major industries which have been deregulated over the past two decades: airlines, telecommunications (telephone service), trucking, and cable television.

Airlines

Prior to 1978, the U.S. airline industry operated under stringent federal price and entry regulations. Operators could only enter the industry if they could demonstrate that "their entry was required to benefit the public." Existing airlines had to have new routes approved by federal regulators. Ticket prices also had to be approved by federal bureaucrats, and this meant that price competition between airlines was virtually nonexistent.

With federal legislation passed in 1978 and implemented in the early 1980s, price and entry regulation of the airlines came to an end. Operators are now free to enter and leave specific routes, and are free to enter and leave the entire industry. Operators are also free to set ticket prices at whatever cost they desire.

It's an understatement to say that airline deregulation set off a wave of dramatic changes in the industry. New competitors have entered the industry and many existing (and new) carriers have left the industry. (This is the polite way of saying they have gone bankrupt!) The route system has been radically changed, with most national carriers going to the "hub-and-spoke" system of serving customers. And certainly ticket prices have been affected. There is now intense competition between airlines in ticket prices. Discounts and special prices are now available for an almost astonishing (and confusing) number of situations. It's become a game for some, and a business for others, to find the cheapest fare for any given airline trip.

These changes have not gone without criticism. Some call the current deregulated airline industry a mess.[2] Critics see the price competition spawned by deregulation only as cutthroat competition designed to eliminate weak rivals. They yearn for the big traditional carriers, such as Eastern and Pan-Am, which couldn't make it in the new competitive world and have gone "bankrupt." Such critics call for reregulation of the airline industry to provide order and stability and to clean up the problems created by deregulation.

But are stability, order, and the preservation of traditional carriers the correct criteria by which deregulation should be judged? No! Competition is not always pretty. By its nature, competition creates change and disorder. Also, it certainly shouldn't be surprising that a number of carriers went bankrupt with the advent of deregulation. Regulation of price and entry probably protected many poorly managed and inefficient airlines.

Instead, what matters in judging the merits of deregulation are the impacts on real (inflation-adjusted) prices, on the quantity and quality of service, and on the overall cost of airline service to the economy. On each of these factors, the overwhelming conclusion from the evidence is that airline deregulation has been a soaring success.

Let's first look at price. The price that matters here is the real price (or revenue) per passenger mile. Numerous studies have concluded that real price per passenger mile fell as a result of deregulation.[3] For example, Evans and Kessides estimate that average real price per passenger mile fell 16 percent between 1978 and 1988 as a result of deregulation. Simon calculates that real revenue (price) per passenger mile would have fallen without deregulation due to falling fuel prices. But Simon estimates that real prices fell even more due to deregulation, and in 1988 were about 10 percent lower than they would have been if deregulation had not occurred (see Figure 9-1).

Figure 9-1   Index of Real Revenue per Passenger Mile and Projected Index of Real Revenue per Passenger Mile

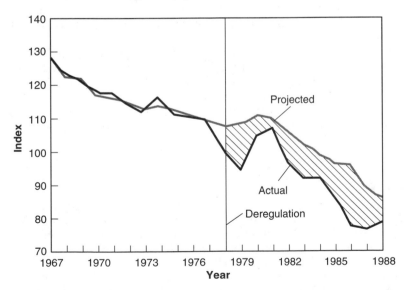

Source: Julian Simon, *Airline Service Improves Under Deregulation,* Center for the Study of American Business, Occasional Paper 114 (October 1992), Figure 4. Reprinted with permission of the Center for the Study of American Business.

There is evidence, however, that not all ticket prices have "fared" equally. Evans and Kessides conclude that low-cost ticket prices (the cheapest 25 percent of ticket prices) declined 25 percent in real terms between 1978 and 1988, while high-cost ticket prices (the most expensive 10 percent of ticket prices) increased by 10 percent.[4] The authors surmise that this most benefitted consumer, or tourist, travelers, who have the flexible schedules to take advantage of discount fares, while less flexible business travelers more often paid the higher fares.

There's also good news for deregulation from the quantity and quality of airline service. Total revenue passenger miles rose 110 percent between 1977 and 1988. It's estimated that most of this increase would have occurred simply due to economic growth, but as much as 12 percent of the increase is attributable to deregulation.[5]

Quality of service also seems to have improved since deregulation. Total passenger complaints per 100,000 passengers have trended downward since 1978, and passenger bumpings per 100,000 passengers, after initially rising, have fallen since 1984.[6] Safety has also improved. Numerous studies have shown that both airline accident rates and fatality rates have declined since deregulation.[7]

The bottom line is that the economy has benefitted from a more efficient and competitive airline industry. One study estimates that the economy is saving over $18 billion (1992 dollars) annually as a result of the greater efficiencies and lower prices in the airline industry.[8]

But there's a lingering issue as to whether these savings will continue. Some airline observers worry that the hub-and-spoke alignment of airline service has resulted in dominant, or near-monopoly, control of travel out of certain airports and markets (for example, Delta out of Atlanta and American out of Raleigh-Durham). They worry that this alignment has resulted in less rather than more competition.

Fortunately, these worries seem to be without foundation. Recent analysis shows that only 4 percent of the 5,000 largest routes, which account for 94 percent of all coach traffic, are monopolized. Also, research shows that it takes only two competitors to hold prices down.[9]

The preponderance of evidence indicates that, at least with respect to airline travel, the ivory-tower theory is correct; that is, deregulation has helped, not harmed, consumers and the economy. Now let's see if the same can be said for other deregulated industries.

Telephone Service

Telephone service was partially deregulated in 1984 with the breakup of AT&T into regional "baby Bells." The breakup followed the entry of effective competition in the provision of long-distance service (e.g., MCI, Sprint). Since the breakup, competition has come to long-distance service (i.e., customers have a choice of long-distance providers), but local service is still under a "baby Bell" monopoly, and local rates are still regulated.[10] The breakup has also forced both local service and long-distance service to "pay their own way." Before the breakup, long-distance service rates were kept artificially high in order to subsidize artificially low local rates. Since the breakup, this subsidization has ended.

Have results been good or bad because of partial deregulation of the telephone industry? The answer again is that results have been good. As with the airlines, deregulation in telephone service has been a success in lowering prices to consumers and increasing efficiency in the industry. Figure 9-2 shows that average real telephone service prices have continued to fall after the AT&T breakup in 1984. Local prices initially rose due to the end of subsidization, but since 1986, they have fallen. Long-distance prices have fallen the most.

Deregulation also appears to have had a positive impact on productivity in the telephone service industry. Crandall reports that total factor productivity in telephone service increased an average annual rate of 3.9 percent from 1984 to 1988, the highest annual rate since 1954.[11]

There are now more competitors to choose from in telephone service, and the quantity of service is also up since deregulation. The number of long-distance competitors rose from 42 in 1982 to 611 in 1991, and interstate switched access minutes rose 111 percent between 1984 and 1991.[12]

Finally, no one can overlook the explosion in new telephone services which have arrived since 1984, such as speed dialing, call waiting, and call stop. This is evidence that competition is the mother of innovation. Also, service quality, as measured by dial-tone delays, appears to have improved since deregulation, and consumer satisfaction surveys showed improvement in the late 1980s.[13]

Trucking

Our next stop in the deregulation caravan is trucking. Prior to 1980, the trucking industry was regulated in a way similar to the airline industry. A federal agency, the Interstate Commerce Commission, controlled the industry by re-

Figure 9-2   Real Telephone Service Price Indices (1984 = 100)

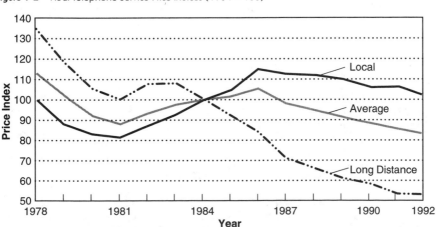

Source: U.S. Bureau of Labor Statistics, *Consumer Price Index Detailed Report*, June issues for 1978–1992.

stricting entry, restricting routes traveled by trucking firms, and regulating rates. Like the airline industry, the trucking industry operated almost as a branch of government.

The Motor Carrier Act of 1980 changed that. The act ended the tight rein that the Interstate Commerce Commission had over the interstate trucking industry. Trucking firms are now free to enter the industry, establish routes, and set their own prices. However, deregulation has not been complete. Individual states are able to regulate intrastate trucking, and to date, most of them still choose to do so.[14] Consequently, the deregulation of the trucking industry has occurred only in interstate trucking.

What's been the impact? Well, at the risk of sounding like a broken record, the results are essentially the same as with airlines and telephone service: lower prices, more activity, improved productivity, and, importantly, improved safety records. Real trucking prices are estimated to be 12 to 25 percent lower with deregulation.[15] With no restrictions on entry, the number of interstate truckers doubled between 1980 and 1986.[16] With no restrictions on routes, deregulation has led to more efficient routes, which in turn has led to a more efficient use of the trucking fleet. Service has also improved. Under regulation, trucking firms were forbidden to give performance guarantees to clients. Under deregulation, performance guarantees have become commonplace. (For example, trucking firms promise rebates on rates if schedules aren't met.) This has led to better inventory management and lower inventory costs by client firms.[17] The net result is that the economy is saving an estimated $23 billion (1992 dollars) annually due to deregulation of surface freight movement.[18]

There are, however, two alleged problems that are associated with trucking deregulation. One is that trucking deregulation has led to lost trucking service in rural areas. Fortunately, there is no evidence that this has occurred, and one study even finds improved service to rural areas after deregulation.[19]

The second potential problem is safety. The concern is that with trucking firms competing for customers and trying to keep costs low, safety will be the first caution thrown to the wind. Again, fortunately, the evidence doesn't support this concern. Several studies have found that every major measure of trucking highway safety, including accident, injury, and fatality rates per truck mile traveled, have fallen since deregulation![20] Trucking firms obviously know that, although safety costs money, it also pays off because a client won't be happy if the goods aren't delivered due to an accident.

One clear loser from trucking deregulation is the number of unionized workers. Since deregulation, the number of unionized truckers has fallen. Real wages in trucking have also fallen, although they still remain above the average for all manufacturing.[21]

Cable Television

Finally, let's look at deregulation's impact on the cable television industry. On the surface, deregulation of cable television appears to have been a failure. The Cable Act of 1984 removed price controls on cable television. However, after watching cable television rates rise 61 percent in the first 4 1/2 years of deregulation, Congress reregulated cable television rates with the Cable Television Consumer Protection and Competition Act of 1992.[22]

Is cable television the first example of a major industry in which deregulation failed? Is cable television an example of an industry in which unchecked competition doesn't work and government controls are needed?

The answers are "no" to both questions for two reasons. First, when the increased quality of cable television is taken into account, it's not clear that cable television prices rose out of control during their deregulation. The average number of channels available on cable increased 30 percent during deregulation. Hazlett estimates that the increased number of channels kept the real (inflation-adjusted) price per channel almost constant during deregulation.[23]

More importantly, the cable television deregulation act in 1984 only went halfway in deregulation. It gave cable television companies more power to set their prices, but the act didn't open up the industry to competition from new entrants. Specifically, under deregulation, cities were still able to give exclusive right to a particular cable television company to provide service within the city's boundary. That is, cities were able to set up cable television monopolies, and most of them did just that. Thus, under the halfway deregulation, local cable television companies had the best of all worlds—no effective competition and the ability to set their rates. In cities which have allowed competition in the provision of cable television service, cable television rates are significantly lower than in cities which have established cable television monopolies.[24]

What needs to be done in the cable television industry is complete deregulation, that is, price and entry deregulation, combined with abolition of cities' rights to establish exclusive cable television providers. Unfortunately, the 1992 cable television act didn't do this.

So the verdict on deregulation is in, and the consumer wins. Deregulation has resulted in more competition, more service, and lower prices. In a comprehensive study of deregulation, Clifford Winston calculates between $36 billion and $46 billion annually in savings to consumers and producers due to deregulation. And the good news is that this may not be all. Winston estimates further annual savings of $22 billion as deregulation spurs more efficiencies and competition in the economy.[25]

HAVE MERGERS HURT THE ECONOMY?

There is no question that merger and acquisition activity increased in the 1980s. Figure 9-3 shows the annual number of mergers and acquisitions since 1900. These data are pieced together from a number of individual data series. As can be seen, there have been four major waves of mergers: the turn of the century, the 1920s, and 1960s, and the 1980s. Clearly the annual number of mergers and acquisitions in the 1980s exceeded those of the previous waves.

It stands to reason that merger and acquisition activity, measured by the number of mergers and acquisitions, would be greater today than in earlier waves because the economy is larger today than in earlier years.

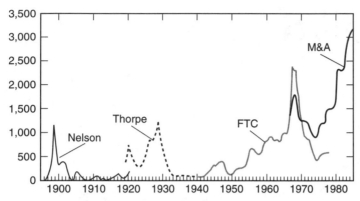

Figure 9-3   Annual Numbers of Mergers and Acquisitions

Ravenscraft has measured the size of mergers and acquisitions by calculating the annual average value of manufacturing and mining assets (where the bulk of mergers occurs) acquired via mergers and acquisitions as a percentage of gross national product. Ravenscraft's results are shown in Table 9-1. As can be seen by this measure, which I argue is the correct measure, the wave of the 1980s was actually the smallest of the four twentieth-century merger waves.

So-called hostile takeovers, that is, acquisitions that are opposed by management of the target firm, have received much attention by the media and public. But this attention has been out of proportion to the relative importance of hostile takeovers. For example, Browne and Rosengren report that hostile takeovers accounted for only 1 percent of total acquisition announcements in 1986.[26]

Why do mergers and acquisitions occur and why do they come in waves? Mergers and acquisitions occur when new buyers think they can better manage a company and earn higher profits. These expectations are most likely to occur when there are major changes occurring in the econ-

Table 9-1   Annual Average Real Value of Manufacturing and Mining Assets Acquired as a Percentage of Real GNP

YEARS	RATIO
All Nonwave Years	0.33
1898–1901	6.10
1926–1930	1.28
1965–1970	0.86
1981–1986	0.77

Source: David Ravenscraft, "The 1980s Merger Wave: An Industrial Organization Perspective," in Lynn Browne and Eric Rosengren, eds., *The Merger Boom* (Boston: Federal Reserve Bank of Boston, 1987), p. 19.

omy, which will cause differing outlooks among owners and managers. Interestingly, tax savings have *not* been found to be a primary motivation in most mergers.[27]

What, then, was going on in the 1980s to stimulate a new wave of mergers? The answer, in a word, is plenty. In the early 1980s the inflation rate peaked at double digits, then plunged to 1 percent by 1986. Interest rates fluctuated as much as inflation. A very severe recession occurred in the early 1980s, but it was followed by the second longest peacetime economic expansion in the nation's history. U.S. manufacturers faced increased competition in the early 1980s due to a stronger dollar lowering the prices of imports. Finally, the deregulation of some key industries certainly created opportunities for mergers and restructuring. So there was no shortage of economic change during the 1980s.

Probably the biggest issue about mergers is whether they help or hurt the economy. Although they can be wrong, economists suspect that mergers help the economy. Presumably, new buyers take over a company because they think they can run it more efficiently and create bigger profits for shareholders. Also, the mere *threat* of a merger or takeover may motivate managers of potential target companies to work harder for more efficiency and higher returns.

As you might expect, economists have conducted many studies attempting to measure the impact of mergers. These studies are of two types. The first type of study has looked at the impact of mergers and acquisitions on stock prices of both the target firms (the firm being acquired or merged) and the acquiring firms. These studies are surprisingly consistent in their findings. Stock prices of target firms rise and shareholders of target firms gain as a result of the merger. Stock prices of acquiring firms change little as a result of the merger.[28] These results seem to be saying that the stock market expects better performance from the target firm as a result of the merger.

The second type of study has tried to directly measure changes in company performance as a result of a merger or acquisition. The most comprehensive of these studies is by Healy, Palepu, and Ruback.[29] They examined postmerger performance for the 50 largest U.S. mergers between 1979 and mid-1984. They reached two major conclusions. First, merged firms showed significant improvement in their productivity and cash flow returns compared to other firms in the same industry. Second, mergers did not lead to reductions in long-term capital and research and development investments.

Studies of particular industries have reached similar conclusions. Schranz found that mergers improve the economic performance of banks.[30] Also, a study of RJR Nabisco, which went through a buyout in 1989, found that contrary to the dire predictions of havoc and decline, RJR Nabisco actually experienced greater productivity and profitability following the reorganization.[31]

Other concerns expressed about mergers and acquisitions have received attention in research studies. Jensen concludes that merger and acquisition activity has *not* resulted in increased industrial concentration and the creation of monopoly power.[32] Also, Becketti reports that junk bonds (i.e., high-risk bonds which financed many takeovers in the 1980s), didn't significantly increase corporate debt.[33]

So although the alleged evils of mergers and takeovers make for good movie material, the facts suggest that these activities are a natural consequence of change and, in fact, are good for the economy.

ARE CEO SALARIES OUT OF TOUCH WITH REALITY?

Perhaps nothing can raise the ire of the average American more than to hear about the large salaries and perks of America's chief executive officers (CEOs). For example, the average CEO salary and bonus in the 1980s (1982–88) at leading companies listed on the New York Stock Exchange was $843,000 (1988 dollars).[34] Total compensation at the largest publicly owned U.S. corporations rose 212 percent in the 1980s, and this was four times greater than the growth in the pay of the average factory worker.[35] Finally, foreign CEOs apparently earn much smaller salaries relative to the pay of the average worker than do American CEOs.[36]

These data seem to confirm the suspicions of the average American: that American CEOs are overpaid, and their exploitation of the economic system increased in the 1980s. But as you've learned in other chapters in this book, it's dangerous to stop at the surface; you must probe below the surface statistics to reach the real relationship.

In the case of CEO pay, the surface statistics are misleading. Jensen and Murphy show that the average CEO compensation in the 1980s ($843,000) was actually slightly lower than the average CEO compensation in the 1930s when adjustments are made for inflation.[37] Most importantly, numerous studies across countries (including Japan) and across time have demonstrated that the level of CEO compensation is directly related to the size of the company which the CEO directs. In general, CEO compensation (salary + bonus) increases 2.5 percent to 3.5 percent for every 10 percent increase in company assets.[38] This makes a lot of sense. The bigger the company, as measured by assets, the more important are the CEO's decisions because they affect more money. To attract better qualified CEOs, larger companies pay CEOs more.

Of course, factors other than company size should affect CEO compensation. In a massive study involving 20,000 executives at over 400 firms between 1981 and 1985, Leonard was able to statistically "explain" 87 percent of the differences in executive compensation by a variety of factors, including size of firm, degree of responsibility in the firm, and educational and experience characteristics of the executive.[39]

An important factor explaining differences in CEO compensation for the *same-sized* company between Japanese executives and American executives is the degree of control and responsibility of the CEO in the two countries. In general, American CEOs have more power and control than Japanese CEOs. In Japan, decision-making authority is lower in the organization than in American firms. Japanese CEOs must acquire consensus throughout the firm for their decisions, whereas American CEOs do not. In short, Japanese CEOs don't "run" their companies in the same way that American CEOs do. The diminished responsibility of Japanese CEOs compared to American CEOs goes a long way in explaining the lower compensation of Japanese CEOs.[40]

Perhaps the biggest controversy about CEO pay is whether CEOs are rewarded when their companies perform well, but also punished when the companies do poorly. There have been many studies which have addressed this issue, and they are summarized in Table 9-2. As the table shows, there is a link between CEO compensation and firm performance. In general, CEO compensation rises between 1.5 percent and 2 percent for every 10 percent increase in company performance.

A couple of the studies deserve special comment. Note that the Kaplan study of Japanese CEOs finds a pay-performance relationship similar to that of American CEOs. The Gibbons and Murphy study found that, in addition to company performance, performance of all companies in the industry influenced CEO compensation. This finding can explain why a CEO could get a pay raise even if the CEO's company lost money. The pay raise could occur if the CEO's company lost relatively less money than the average company in the industry lost. Making a CEO's compensation dependent on how his or her company performed relative to other companies in the industry protects the CEO from economywide or industrywide changes beyond the CEO's control.

The Leonard study finds evidence of a U-shaped relationship between CEO compensation and firm performance. This means that the biggest pay raises are earned by CEOs in companies with both the highest performance and the lowest performance. Although this relationship may seem odd, there are two reasons why companies with the poorest performance may give large raises to their CEOs. First, failing firms may have to pay more to keep the best executives, who in turn can work to minimize the firm's losses. Second, exec-

Table 9-2   CEO Pay and Performance Studies

STUDY	SAMPLE SIZE AND YEAR	COMPENSATION MEASURE	PERFORMANCE MEASURE	COMPENSATION CHANGE RESULTING FROM 10% IMPROVEMENT IN COMPANY PERFORMANCE°
Murphy	73 firms, 1969–81	salary + bonus	shareholder rate of return	+1.2% to 1.6%
Coughlin and Schmidt	40 firms, 1978–80	salary + bonus	stock return	+1% to 1.5%
Kaplan	119 Japanese firms, 1980	salary + bonus	stock price	+1.8% to 2.3%
Gibbons and Murphy	1,668 CEOs, 1974–86	salary + bonus	•shareholder rate of return, own firm	+1.8%
			•average shareholder rate of return in industry	-0.8%

Table 9-2   continued

STUDY	SAMPLE SIZE AND YEAR	COMPENSATION MEASURE	PERFORMANCE MEASURE	COMPENSATION CHANGE RESULTING FROM 10% IMPROVEMENT IN COMPANY PERFORMANCE[a]
Gibbons and Murphy	73 firms, 1969–81	salary + bonus + stock benefits	•shareholder rate of return, own firm	+2.0%
			•average shareholder rate of return in industry	-3.3%
Leonard	CEOs in 439 firms, 1981–85	salary + bonus	profits	Compensation rises 22¢ for a $1 rise in profits; but U-shaped relationship.
Abowd	16,000 top managers, 1981–86	salary + bonus	after-tax gross return	10% bonus is associated with a 0.3% to 0.9% increase in performance next year.
			shareholder return	10% raise is associated with a 0.4% to 1.2% increase in performance next year.
Jensen and Murphy	2,213 CEOs, 1974–86	salary + bonus	shareholder wealth	+0.03%

[a]Unless otherwise indicated.

Sources:

Kevin J. Murphy, "Corporate Performance and Managerial Renumeration," *Journal of Accounting & Economics*, 7, no. 2, (1985), 11.

Anne T. Coughlin and Ronald Schmidt, "Executive Compensation; Management Turnover, and Firm Performance: An Empirical Investigation;" *Journal of Accounting and Economics*, 7, no. 2 (1985), 43–66.

Steven Kaplan, "Top Executive Rewards and Firm Performance: A Companion of Japan and the U.S.," NBER Working Paper No. 4065 (May 1992).

Robert Gibbons and Kevin Murphy, "Relative Performance Evaluation for Chief Executive Officers," *Industrial and Labor Relations Review*, 43, no. 3 (February 1990), pp. 30S–51S.

Jonathan Leonard, "Executive Pay and Firm Performance," *Industrial and Labor Relations Review*, 43, no. 3, (February 1990), 135–295.

John Abowd, "Does Performance-Based Managerial Compensation Affect Corporate Performance?" *Industrial and Labor Relations Review*, 43, no. 3 (February 1990), 525–735.

Michael Jensen and Kevin Murphy, "Performance Pay and Top-Management Incentives," *Journal of Political Economy*, 98, no. 2 (April 1990), 225–264.

utives in failing firms may require greater current compensation because they heavily discount any promises of future pay.

In conclusion, the fear that business activity in the 1980s, centered on deregulation, mergers and takeovers, and CEO pay, harmed the consumer is mistaken. The evidence indicates that deregulation and merger activity actually helped the consumer by increasing firm efficiency and performance and lowering prices. Furthermore, when examined carefully, American CEO pay is closely related to CEO responsibilities and to performance of the company. We'd be going against this evidence if legal limits were put on these activities.[41]

NOTES

1. This tells you how firms, once in an industry, can benefit from regulation. If regulations prevent other firms from entering the industry, then existing firms can possibly keep prices much above costs and can earn greater profits. See Roger Meiners and Bruce Yandle, eds., *Regulation and the Reagan Era* (New York: Holmes and Meier, 1989) for an excellent discussion of both the economic and political causes and consequences of regulation.

2. See Hobart Rowan, "Deregulation of Airlines Never Got Off Ground," *Washington Post Writers Group*, June 7, 1993.

3. Elizabeth Bailey, "Price and Productivity Change Following Deregulation: The U.S. Experience," *The Economic Journal*, 96, no. 381 (March 1986), 1–17; Julian Simon, *Airline Service Improves Under Deregulation*, Center for the Study of American Business, Washington University, St. Louis Occasional paper 114 (October 1992); William Evans and Ioannis Kessides, "Structure, Conduct, and Performance in the Deregulated Airline Industry," *Southern Economic Journal*, 59, no. 3 (January 1993), 450–467.

4. Evans and Kessides, "Structure, Conduct, and Performance in the Deregulated Airline Industry."

5. Ibid.

6. Simon, *Airline Service Improves Under Deregulation*.

7. Thomas Gale Moore, "The Myth of Deregulation's Negative Effect on Safety," in Leon Moses and Jan Savage, *Transportation Safety in an Age of Deregulation* (New York: Oxford University Press, 1989), pp. 8–20; Nancy Rose, "Fear of Flying? Economic Analyses of Airline Safety," *Journal of Economic Perspectives*, 6, no. 2 (Spring 1992), 75–94; Steven Morrison and Clifford Winston, "Air Safety, Deregulation, and Public Policy," 6, no. 1 (Winter 1988), 10–15; and David Sawers, *Competition in the Air: What Europe Can Learn from the USA* (London: London Institute of Economic Affairs, 1987).

8. Steven Morrison and Clifford Winston, *The Economic Effects of Airline Deregulation* (Washington, DC: The Brookings Institute, 1986). Morrison and Winston estimate annual savings of $8 billion in 1977 dollars. I have updated this number to 1992 dollars using the Consumer Price Index.

9. Evans and Kessides, "Structure, Conduct, and Performance in the Deregulated Airline Industry."

10. The monopolistic grip of the regional "baby Bells" may be crumbling as AT&T moves into the cellular network market; see *The Economist*, November 14, 1992, p. 75.

11. Robert W. Crandall, *After the Breakup: U.S. Telecommunications in a More Competitive Era* (Washington, DC: The Brookings Institution, 1991), p. 67.

12. Eli Noam, "Assessing the Impacts of Divestiture and Deregulation in Telecommunications," *Southern Economic Journal*, 59, no. 3 (January 1993), 438–449.

13. Ibid.

14. Kenneth Boyer, "Deregulation of the Trucking Sector: Specialization, Concentration, Entry, and Financial Distress," *Southern Economic Journal*, 59, no. 3 (January 1993), 481–495; Cassandra Chrones Moore, "Lift the Roadblocks to Intrastate Trucking," *The Wall Street Journal*, December 10, 1993, p. A14.

15. Thomas Gale Moore, "Rail and Trucking Deregulation," in Michael Klass and Leonard Weiss, eds., *Regulatory Reform: What Actually Happened* (Boston: Little, Brown, 1986).

16. Clifford Winston, Thomas Corsi, Curtis Crimm, and Carol Evans, *The Economic Effects of Surface Freight Deregulation* (Washington, DC: The Brookings Institution, 1990).

17. Boyer, "Deregulation of the Trucking Sector."

18. Winston, et al., *The Economic Effects of Surface Freight Deregulation*. Their 1988 dollars are updated to 1992 dollars using the Consumer Price Index.

19. Michael Pustay, "Deregulation and the U.S. Trucking Industry," in Kenneth Burton and Dennis Swann, eds. *The Age of Regulatory Reform* (Oxford: Oxford University Press, 1989), pp. 236–256; John Due, et al., *Transportation Service to Small Rural Communities: Effects of Deregulation* (Ames, Iowa: Iowa State University Press, 1989).

20. Donald Alexander, "Motor Carrier Deregulation and Highway Safety: An Empirical Analysis," *Southern Economic Journal*, 59, no. 1 (July 1992), 28–38; Organization for Economic Cooperation and Development, *Competition Policy and the Deregulation of Road Transport*, Paris, 1990, pp. 54–61; Thomas Gale Moore, "The Myth of Deregulation's Negative Effect on Safety," in Leon N. Moses and Ian Savage, *Transportation Safety in an Age of Deregulation* (New York: Oxford University Press, 1989), pp. 18–19.

21. Organization for Economic Cooperation and Development, *Competition Policy and the Deregulation of Road Transport*.

22. Thomas Hazlett, "In Cable War, Consumers Get Snagged," *The Wall Street Journal*, October 2, 1992, p. A14.

23. Ibid.

24. The Great Cable TV Battle," *The Wall Street Journal*, October 2, 1992, p. A14.

25. Clifford Winston, "Economic Deregulation: Days of Reckoning for Microeconomists," *Journal of Economic Literature*, 31, no. 3 (September 1993), 1263–1289.

26. Lynne Browne and Eric Rosengren, "Are Hostile Takeovers Different?" in Lynn Browne and Eric Rosengren, eds., *The Merger Boom* (Boston: Federal Reserve Bank of Boston, 1987), pp. 199–229.

27. David Ravenscraft, "The 1980s Merger Wave: An Industrial Organization Perspective," in Lynn Browne and Eric Rosengren, eds., *The Merger Boom* (Boston: Federal Reserve Bank of Boston, 1987), pp. 20–28.

28. Ravenscraft, "The 1980s Merger Wave"; Browne and Rosengren, "Are Hostile Takeovers Different"; Michael Jensen, "The Free Cash Flow Theory of Takeovers: A Financial Perspective on Mergers and Acquisitions and the Economy," in Lynn Browne and Eric Rosengren, eds., *The Merger Boom* (Boston: Federal Reserve Bank of Boston, 1987), pp. 102–143; and E. M. Scherer and David Ross, *Industrial*

Market Structure and Economic Performance (Boston: Houghlin-Mifflin, 1990), pp. 169–170.

29. Paul Healy, Krishna Palepu, and Richard Ruback, "Does Corporate Performance Improve After Mergers?" *Journal of Financial Economics*, 31, no. 2 (April 1992), 135–176.

30. Mary S. Schranz, "Takeovers Improve Firm Performance: Evidence from the Banking Industry," *Journal of Political Economy*, 101, no. 2 (April 1993), 299–326.

31. "Were Doomsayers Blowing Smoke?" *Business North Carolina* (March 1992), pp. 10–11.

32. Jensen, "The Free Cash Flow Theory of Takeovers," p. 104.

33. S. Becketti, "Corporate Mergers and the Business Cycle," *Economic Review*, Federal Reserve Bank of Kansas City, 71, (May 1986), 13–26.

34. Michael Jensen and Kevin Murphy, "CEO Incentives—It's Not How Much You Pay, But How," *Harvard Business Review*, 90, no. 3 (May–June 1990), 138–153.

35. John A. Byrne, "The Flap Over Executive Pay," *Business Week*, May 6, 1991, pp. 90–96.

36. Kevin Salwen, "Executive Pay May be Subject to New Scrutiny," *The Wall Street Journal*, May 16, 1991, p. A3.

37. Jensen and Murphy, "CEO Incentives," p. 139.

38. Based on the following studies: Sherwin Rosen, "Contracts and the Market for Executives," NBER Working Paper 3542 (1990); Jasen Barro and Robert Barro, "Pay, Performance, and Turnover of Bank CEOs," NBER Working Paper 3262 (February 1990); and Steven Kaplan, "Top Executive Rewards and Firm Performance: A Comparison of Japan and the U.S.," NBER Working Paper 4065 (May 1992).

39. Jonathan S. Leonard, "Executive Pay and Firm Performance," *Industrial and Labor Relations Review*, 43, no. 3 (February 1990), 135–295.

40. Paul Milgram and John Roberts, *Economics, Organization, and Management* (Englewood Cliffs, NJ: Prentice-Hall, 1992), p. 443.

41. In 1993 Congress did pass legislation limiting the federal income tax deductibility of CEO salaries over $1 million, unless that salary is related to company "performance."

10

The savings and loan bailout

The savings and loan bailout captured the headlines for many years in the 1980s and 1990s. Hundreds of saving and loan associations (S&L's) went bankrupt in the 1980s. Because deposits in those S&Ls were backed by federal insurance, the failures caused expenditures of hundreds of billions of dollars from a taxpayer-supported insurance fund. The majority of these failures came after the savings and loan industry was, to some extent, deregulated.

Many observers of the S&L bailout blame the problems on the partial deregulation of the industry. They cite the fact that only a handful of failures occurred before the strings were relaxed on the industry. An alternative viewpoint agrees but puts the emphasis on the *partial* in partial deregulation. These analysts say the industry's problems occurred from a misguided "have your cake and eat it too" public policy, which loosened the investment controls on S&L's but kept the federal insurance. The incentive structure created by the partial deregulation led to the bailout disaster.

Let's see what really happened in the S&L bailout.

ORIGINS

The savings and loan problem of the 1980s had its origins in the 1930s, when the federal government began to regulate the savings and loan industry. Of course, the 1930s was the decade of the Great Depression. Millions of Americans lost their life savings in failed banks and savings and loan institutions. Other Americans hurriedly removed their savings from still solvent banks and savings and loan institutions, creating "runs" on those institutions. (For a good example of bank runs, see the movie *It's a Wonderful Life*.) Consequently, business and consumer loans stopped, the economy ground to a halt, and the unemployment rate rose to 25 percent.

One of the "cures" that the federal government established in the 1930s to halt the bank and S&L runs was federal deposit insurance. Funded by premiums charged to banks and savings and loan institutions, the deposit insurance was meant to ease the fears of depositors by guaranteeing payment of savings (up to certain limits) in the event that the bank or S&L failed. To add strength to the insurance funds, the federal government pledged to supply money to the funds in the event they were depleted. Separate deposit funds were established for banks and for savings and loan institutions.

In addition to deposit insurance, other "cures" were imposed on the savings and loan industry by the 1930s reformers. The savings and loan industry had developed as an industry specializing in home loans to consumers. To continue this, the federal government established regulations, which essentially limited S&Ls to relatively safe home loans. Also, in order to provide a flow of low-interest-rate loans to homebuyers, federal regulations limited the interest rate which savings and loan associations could pay to depositors.

This regulatory system imposed on the savings and loan industry actually worked rather well through the 1960s; in fact, it created a rather boring industry. Market interest rates from the 1930s through the 1960s stayed fairly close to the limits which savings and loan associations could pay; therefore, S&Ls were able to attract funds. The savings and loan associations made fixed-rate loans to homebuyers, the vast majority of which were repaid on time with no complications. Thus, the savings and loan industry was on automatic pilot, and only a handful of institutions failed.

THE SYSTEM COMES CRASHING DOWN

Cracks appeared in the savings and loan regulatory system when inflation began to rear its ugly head in the 1970s. Skyrocketing inflation rates in the 1970s pushed market interest rates well above the ceilings allowed to be paid by S&Ls to depositors. For example, when the inflation rate hit its peak in the late 1970s and early 1980s, interest rates on ultrasafe three-month treasury bills were over twice as high as rates on 2 1/2-year CDs offered by savings and loan associations (see Figure 10-1). Investors stopped putting new funds in S&Ls, and many existing depositors withdrew funds from S&Ls and put them in higher-yielding, yet safe, treasury securities and money-market funds.

The withdrawal of deposits made many savings and loan associations strapped for cash with which to make new loans. At the same time, S&Ls were earning below-market interest rates on long-term mortgage loans, which they had made years earlier when interest rates were much lower. This double squeeze put many S&Ls in bankruptcy, at least on paper.

With hindsight, we can say what Congress and federal regulators should have done next. They should have closed the savings and loan institutions which had become bankrupt by the early 1980s, gotten rid of the in-

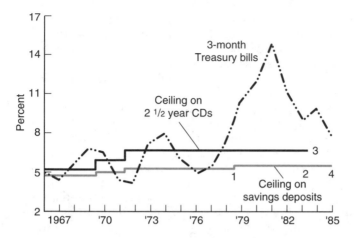

1: 6 month money market CD introduced November 1978.
2: Introduction of money market deposit account November 1982.
3: Ceiling on 2.5 year CDs eliminated October 1983.
4: Ceiling on savings deposits eliminated March 1986.

Source: *Federal Home Loan Bank Board Journal*, and the *Federal Reserve Bulletin*. Printed in Elijah Brewer III and Thomas H. Mondschean, "Ex Ante Risk and Ex Post Collapse of S&Ls in the 1980s," *Economic Perspectives*, Federal Reserve Bank of Chicago, 16, no. 4 (July/August 1992), 3.

Figure 10-1   Market Interest Rates versus Ceilings on Interest Rates
Offered by S&Ls

terest-rate ceilings which made it tough for S&Ls to attract funds in times of high market interest rates, and reformed the deposit insurance system to take account of the risk taken by S&Ls in their investments. There is more on all these reforms later.

Unfortunately, politicians including Congress and administrations of both major political parties chose to go in another direction, which ultimately made the situation worse. The premise of the new direction was to let the S&Ls grow out of their problems. To do this, new federal regulations allowed S&Ls to offer competitive interest rates to depositors. To finance these competitive (higher) interest rates, S&Ls were allowed to invest in riskier investments, such as commercial real estate. Accounting regulations were also relaxed for S&Ls. But the deposit insurance system was not correspondingly reformed. Deposit insurance fees charged to an S&L remained the same regardless of the risk taken by the S&L in its investments. In fact, federal deposit insurance was made more lucrative, as the insurance amount per account was increased from $40,000 to $100,000.[1]

So yes, the S&L industry was deregulated, but only halfway. The asset accounts of the industry, which govern the investments of the S&Ls, were deregulated to allow S&Ls to offer competitive interest rates to depositors. But the liabilities of the industry were not deregulated. S&Ls weren't required to take full responsibility for their investments because federal deposit insurance was still there as a backstop. Also, federal deposit insurance didn't distinguish between S&Ls which made cautious investments and S&Ls which made very risky investments. The same premiums were charged to each.

So, in essence, the new rules and regulations adopted by the federal government in the early 1980s said the following to S&L owners and managers: Take more risk in your investments and earn a higher rate of return in order to improve your balance sheet. But if your investments don't pan out, the federal government will bail you out.

As most of you can anticipate, this one-sided deregulation sowed the seeds for disaster. Actually, the booming economy of the mid-1980s delayed the disaster, and riskier real estate investments made by many S&Ls did improve their balance sheet. So all was well for a while. But commercial and speculative real estate is very much a boom-and-bust industry. The bust finally came in the late 1980s (helped along by the federal tax changes of 1986, which were very detrimental to real estate). Many of the riskier investments made by the S&Ls failed, or at least didn't provide the expected returns. S&Ls failed in bunches: 267 S&Ls failed between 1988 and 1991, compared to 51 failures between 1981 and 1987 (see Table 10-1), and deposit insurance losses mounted. Because the losses were so substantial, the federal deposit insurance fund became depleted, and supplementary funds ($127 billion by 1992) had to be provided by the U.S. Treasury. This was the S&L bailout.

So it wasn't greedy or shifty S&L owners and managers who caused the S&L bailout, despite the implication of many popular books and articles. Studies of the S&L bailout have consistently found that fraud accounted for

Table 10-1   S&L Failures and Federal Assistance

YEAR	NUMBER OF FAILURES	TOTAL COST OF FEDERAL ASSISTANCE[a] (CURRENT $MILLION)
1980	0	166
1981	1	760
1982	1	806
1983	5	275
1984	9	743
1985	8	1,026
1986	10	3,066
1987	17	3,704
1988	26	31,790
1989	30	5,914
1990	143	37,302
1991	67	34,506
1992	6	6,715

[a]Includes cost of government-assisted mergers of S&Ls.
Source: Congressional Budget Office, *Resolving the Thrift Crisis*, (Washington, DC: Government Printing Office, 1973), Table C-2.

only 5 to 15 percent of the total S&L losses.[2] Instead, S&L owners and managers were just following the *incentives* presented to them by federal laws and regulations. The incentive to take big investment risks with federally insured deposits was the underlying cause of the S&L losses and subsequent bailout. The problem was that politicians and federal regulators didn't want to bite the bullet in the late 1970s when it became evident that the regulatory system governing the savings and loan industry was beginning to unravel.

WHO BENEFITTED FROM THE S&L BAILOUT?

The savings and loan bailout is estimated to cost $180 billion if paid in one lump sum (1990 dollars).[3] It's popular to claim that this money is being used to pay off S&L owners and managers for the money they have lost in investments. To make matters worse, since much of the bailout money will come from taxpayers, critics also claim that the S&L bailout is a transfer from poor and middle-class taxpayers to rich S&L managers and owners.

Let me address these issues. Although I am not necessarily defending S&L managers and owners, the bailout did *not* directly benefit them. Instead, the bailout benefitted the *depositors* in failed S&Ls. Federal deposit insurance benefits *depositors*! The money lost in risky S&L investments was depositors' money. If the federal deposit insurance money had not been paid, then failed S&Ls would have been sold for only a fraction of their value, and depositors would have received only pennies on each deposited dollar.

It's also a misconception to think that the failed S&L investments only benefitted a few wealthy individuals. Consider a failed S&L which financed an office building. Most of the money was ultimately paid to hundreds of construction workers, architects, painters, designers, and so on. The money, in turn, was respent in the community. The entire local economy benefitted from the office building investment.

REFORMING THE S&L SYSTEM

Deregulation wasn't to blame for the savings and loan bailout. That's because complete deregulation wasn't tried. As I discussed, only halfway deregulation was implemented, in which S&Ls had greater freedom in their investments but still had the government underwriting of their losses.

In order to keep S&Ls financially viable and to prevent another bailout, incentives in the S&L industry must be changed. The biggest incentive to change is federal deposit insurance.[4] If S&Ls are to be free to pursue riskier investments in order to offer competitive interest rates, then S&L owners, managers, and depositors should be made to bear the risk of those investments. After all, this is the way the other sectors of the investment industry work.

This doesn't necessarily mean getting rid of federal deposit insurance for S&Ls. Federal deposit insurance can continue to be used if risk-based premiums are charged to S&Ls. This means that the premiums charged are directly related to the risk taken by the S&L in its investments, that is, the more risk taken in the investments, the greater the premiums. This is not a revolutionary concept. It is a standard technique used in the private insurance market.[5]

There are two benefits derived from using risk-based premiums. First, S&Ls taking more risk in their investments have a greater probability of failing and using money from the deposit insurance fund. It makes sense, therefore, that those S&Ls should pay more into the deposit insurance fund because they are more likely to use money from the fund. Second, the higher deposit insurance premiums associated with riskier S&L investments serve as an additional cost of those investments to S&L managers and depositors. S&L managers will have to evaluate the benefits of those riskier benefits against their added costs in the form of higher deposit insurance premiums.

Risk-based deposit insurance premiums were not used by federal regulators in the 1980s, and this is a big reason why the S&L bailout occurred. Fortunately, we have learned from that experience. As part of the Federal Deposit Insurance Corporation Improvement Act of 1991, a system of risk-based deposit insurance premiums was instituted in 1994. Although critics charge that the risk differential in the new system is too small, the new risk-based premium system is a step forward in changing the incentives which helped bring about the S&L bailout.[6]

Some economists have proposed doing away with federal deposit insurance altogether. Dowd argues that deposit insurance actually weakens S&Ls and banks and increases the chance they will fail by motivating them to make riskier investments.[7] Without the safety net of deposit insurance, he argues that banks and S&Ls would be motivated to maintain a strong financial position in order to keep the confidence of depositors. Also, banks and S&Ls would likely sort themselves into categories by the risk level taken in their investments. For example, S&Ls which wanted to offer no-risk investments would specialize in investing in short-term treasury securities and commercial paper. Depositors would realize, however, that such S&Ls would only pay lower interest rates. Other S&Ls would specialize in riskier investments paying higher interest rates.

LESSONS LEARNED

The conclusion of this chapter is simple, yet very important. The S&L bailout was not a raid of the federal Treasury by well-connected S&L owners and managers. The S&L bailout was not a result of deregulation because complete deregulation of S&Ls was not tried. Instead, the S&L bailout was ultimately the result of the failed S&L regulatory system established in the 1930s. The system did not come crashing down earlier only because interest-rate volatility remained modest until the 1970s.

The S&L bailout will not bankrupt our nation. In fact, the bailout is really a transfer of money from one group of citizens (taxpayers) to another group of citizens (S&L depositors). Nevertheless, we should learn from the mistakes which created the problem and reform the regulatory system accordingly. Fortunately, a step forward was made in this reform with the adoption of risk-based deposit insurance premiums in 1994.

NOTES

1. For evidence supporting the contribution of the increase in the deposit insurance to the S&L bailout, see Richard Cebula and Chao-Shun Hung, "Barth's Analysis of the Savings and Loan Debacle: An Empirical Test," *Southern Economic Journal*, 59, no. 2 (October 1992), 305–309.

2. Robert Litan, "Deposit Insurance, Gas on S&L Fire," *The Wall Street Journal*, July 29, 1993, p. A10; Paulette Thomas, "Fraud Was Only a Small Factor in S&L Losses, Consultant Asserts," *The Wall Street Journal*, July 20, 1990, p. A2; Statement of James R. Barth before the House Committee on Banking, Finance, and Urban Affairs, April 11, 1990; James R. Barth, Philip F. Bartholomew, and Carol J. Labich, "Moral Hazard and the Thrift Crisis: An Empirical Analysis," *Consumer Finance Law: Quarterly Report*, 44, no. 1 (Winter 1990).

3. Ibid., Table 1. The $180 billion is a present value (1990) cost. The actual nominal dollar costs will be greater because they will be spread out over many future years (e.g., 40 years) when dollar amounts are inflated.

4. This has been the most frequently cited recommendation for reforming the savings and loan system. See Lawrence White, "A Cautionary Tale of Deregulation Gone Awry: The S&L Debacle," *Southern Economic Journal*, 59, no. 3 (January 1993), 496–514; Edward J. Kane, *The S&L Insurance Mess: How Did It Happen?* (Washington, DC: The Urban Institute Press, 1989); Philip H. Dybvig, "Remark on Banking and Deposit Insurance," *Review*, Federal Reserve Bank of St. Louis, 75, no. 1 (January/February 1993), 21–24; Anjan Thakor, "Deposit Insurance Policy," *Review*, Federal Reserve Bank of St. Louis, 75, no. 1 (January/February 1993), 25–28; and Mark Flood, "Deposit Insurance: Problems and Solutions," *Review*, Federal Reserve Bank of St. Louis, 75, no. 1 (January/February 1993), 28–34.

5. For example, drivers with poor driving records, indicating they are greater risks, pay more for auto insurance than drivers with clean driving records. Similarly, individuals in poorer health pay more for life insurance than individuals in excellent health.

6. For an analysis of the new risk-based federal deposit insurance system, see Flood, "Deposit Insurance: Problems and Solutions."

7. Kevin Dowd, "Deposit Insurance: A Skeptical View," *Review*, Federal Reserve Bank of St. Louis, 75, no. 1 (January/February 1993), 14–17.

V.   STICKY PROBLEMS

In this section we'll explore several sticky problems facing American society: health care, poverty, and education. Each of these is a "hot-button" issue, which is frequently the topic of talk-show programs. Each of them also has an important and often overlooked economic dimension.

Health care has been elevated to one of the top issues of national discussion with President Clinton's far-reaching health care proposal and the proposals of several competing plans. Many politicians and others say that the nation faces a health care crisis. Is this the case? Is our health care system failing, or are the calls of crisis overstated? If there are problems in health care, are government solutions the answer, or are government programs and actions currently part of the problem in health care? We'll address these questions in Chapter 11.

Concerning the topic of poverty and welfare, the nation is almost divided within itself on this issue. On the one hand, most citizens are compassionate and want to help those "down on their luck." But on the other hand, those citizens are equally adamant about their unwillingness to provide "handsouts" for those unwilling to work.

So what's the story on poverty and welfare? Who's poor and how much poverty is there? How generous, or stingy, is our welfare system, and does it encourage or discourage continued dependence? Does the welfare system need to be overhauled, and if so, how? As you'll find, economic incentives have both much to do with current problems in the welfare system and with solutions.

Our final sticky problem is education. Perhaps no other institution in our country has gone from being held in such high esteem to being ridiculed and criticized as has public education. Has our public education system really failed, or are we reaping what we've sown in education? Are we not spending enough on public education, or are we simply spending the money in the wrong places? Will spending more money solve the perceived problems in public education, or is more radical surgery, like education vouchers and school competition, needed? Chapter 13 gives the answers.

There is a common thread running through these chapters. As I stressed in the introduction, in order to understand economic behavior, the best place to look is at incentives. Incentives are a key in all three of the systems—health care, poverty and welfare, and public education—studied in this section. Likewise, incentives will be a key to reforming all three systems in ensuring that the goals of each system are satisfied.

11

Are we getting what we pay for in health care?

The American health care system is primed for change. Blasted as being bloated, wasteful, run by high-cost doctors and hospitals, and not performing its functions of extending life and fighting disease for the majority of Americans, the system has come under attack from many sides. Fed up by escalating costs and hospital bills which don't make sense, Americans say they are ready for change.[1]

Yet there are contradictions in some of the proposed reforms. On the one hand, Americans say they want improved access to health care, high-quality health care, and the ability to choose their doctors. But on the other hand, Americans say they want all this with lower costs! As we will see, some health care reform proposals have catered to these contradictory desires and therefore have created unrealistic expectations about changes in the health care system.

It's also popular to argue that "health care is a right" which should be made available to everyone regardless of income. An extension of this view is that "health care is too important to be concerned with money"; after all, how can anyone put a price tag on a life? Therefore, the argument continues, although economics can apply to areas like international trade, regulation, and job creation, it must take a distant back seat to life and health when applied to the health care system.

Economics does apply to health care, and it's a big mistake to ignore economics in the health care system. The reason is simple. Economics exists only because resources are scarce and the potential uses for those limited resources are unlimited. The science of economics was developed to help us make decisions about resource use, that is, to help us use those resources in the best way to improve our lives. We can't ignore money in health care because there's always another use for that money. (For example, to really make you think, consider that $50,000 spent on heart bypass surgery for a 75-year-old person could have provided prenatal care for 20 low-income women!) In fact, because health care is so important, it's crucial that economics is applied in order to make sure that scarce resources are being spent in the wisest way.

There are two themes in this chapter. First, there's no "free lunch" in health care (just as there's no free lunch in any other part of our economy). If, for example, health care expenditures are limited, then health care services will also have to be limited. Second, putting incentives in the health care system which encourage consumers, doctors, and hospitals to "wisely" use health care resources by comparing the benefits of health care resources to their costs is the key to reforming the health care system in America.

PERFORMANCE OF THE HEALTH CARE SYSTEM

Before we talk about problems in the health care system and suggested reforms, it's useful to look at the recent performance of the health care system. Lost in all the debate about health care is a simple fact: The major measures of American health care continue to improve. There are many ways to measure health care, but three of the most widely used measures are life expectancy, infant mortality, and the incidences of major diseases. Figure 11-1 shows life expectancy for major groups in America. For each group, life expectancy has continued to trend upward over the past four decades. Similarly, Figure 11-2 shows infant mortality for African-Americans and for whites. Infant mortality has trended downward for the past 40 years.

Table 11-1 shows incidences of major diseases in America since 1950. As you can see, major improvements have been made in reducing the incidences of most of the diseases. For example, the incidence of tuberculosis was

Figure 11-1   U.S. Life Expectancy

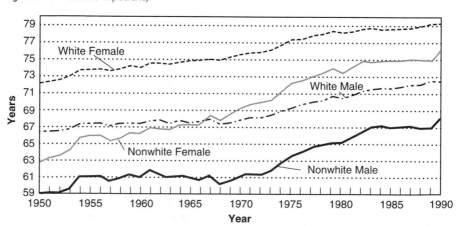

Source: U.S. Dept. of Health and Human Services, *Vital Statistics of the United States*, U.S. Government Printing Office, 1991.

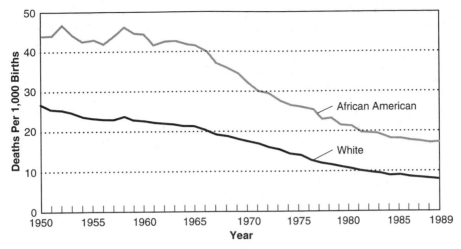

Source: U.S. Dept. of Health and Human Services, *Vital Statistics of the United States*, U.S. Government Printing Office, 1991.

Figure 11-2   U.S. Infant Mortality

reduced 88 percent from 1950 to 1989, the incidence of measles was reduced by 96 percent, and the incidence of whooping cough was reduced by 98 percent. Only for gonorrhea and hepatitis have dramatic improvements not been made.

Finally, although it's an input rather than an output of the health care system, the number of doctors per person also illustrates a country's commitment to, and progress in, health care. The number of doctors per capita (per 1,000 persons) has increased from 13.5 in 1950 to 21.1 in 1980 and to 23.3 in 1988.[2]

The American health care system cannot take credit for all of these improvements. A higher standard of living and better nutrition are at least

Table 11-1   Incidence of Major Diseases (cases per 1 million population)

	1950	1960	1970	1980	1989
Tuberculosis	802.4	308.6	183.2	122.3	94.8
Syphilis	1,538.9	681.2	438.5	304.6	447.6
Gonorrhea	2,035.9	1,398.5	2,855.0	4,432.7	2,955.6
Malaria	14.0	0.4	15.0	9.1	5.1
Typhoid	16.0	5.0	2.0	2.3	1.9
Streptococcal	427.1	1,761.2	2,394.5	1,510.8	Not Available
Hepatitis	24.9	234.4	320.3	212.4	238.7
Diphtheria	37.9	5.0	2.0	0.0	0.0
Measles	2,096.8	2,458.4	232.2	59.6	73.4
Meningococcal Infection	24.9	13.0	12.0	12.5	11.0
Acute Poliomyelitis	220.6	18.0	0.1	0.0	0.0
Whooping Cough	799.4	83.2	21.0	7.5	16.9

Source: U.S. Bureau of the Census, *Statistical Abstract of the United States*, various issues.

partially responsible for longer lives, lower birth deaths, and lower incidences of diseases. But there's no denying the vast improvement in the major measures of Americans' health over the last four decades.

HEALTH CARE COSTS

The dramatic rise in health care costs is the number-one health care concern of most Americans.[3] There's certainly no question that health care costs have risen dramatically since World War II. Figure 11-3 shows the rise in the real (inflation-adjusted) average cost per patient day since 1950. As the figure makes clear, the rise in patient costs is not a phenomenon confined to the 1970s and 1980s. In fact, in the 1950s, real average costs per patient day rose 60 percent; they were up 85 percent in the 1960s; real average costs rose 56 percent in the 1970s; and they jumped 71 percent in the 1980s. In 1990, health care expenditures took 12 cents of every dollar earned in the United States, double the rate in 1966 and more than in any other industrialized country in that year.[4] By 1993 the share had risen to 14.6 percent.[5]

Are the reasons for this dramatic rise in health care costs due to greed, inefficiency, incompetence, or a combination of the three? No, a closer examination shows that none of these factors is the answer. Instead, the major reasons for the rise in real health care costs are much less dramatic, but much more powerful. They are: (1) the natural inclination of a society to spend more on health care as real incomes rise; (2) the slow improvement in productivity in health care; (3) the increase in the quality of health care; and (4) the decoupling of the direct payment of health care services from the consumption of health care services.

It should make common sense to you that as a person becomes richer, he or she will choose to spend more on health care. Since countries are merely

Figure 11-3   Real Average Cost per Patient Day (1990$)

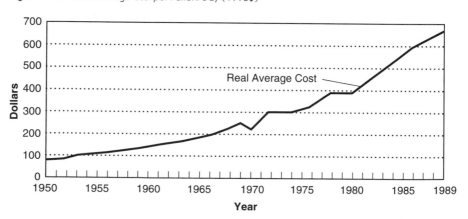

Source: U.S. Dept. of Health and Human Services, *Health Care Financing Review*, various issues.

aggregates of individuals, the same is true of countries. In fact, there is a very close relationship between a country's per capita income and that country's per capita spending on health care. Richer countries (those with higher per capita incomes) have higher per capita health care expenditures, and poorer countries (those with lower per capita incomes) have lower per capita health care expenditures. Because the United States is a rich country which has become richer over time, its per capita health care expenditures are high and growing.

But the per capita income of the United States cannot totally explain its per capita health care expenditures. When compared to other countries, the United States spends more per capita on health care than would be predicted by U.S. per capita income.[6] So other factors must be at work.

One other factor that may be at work is productivity, or specifically, the lack of productivity growth in health care. As I have emphasized in Chapter 6, improvement in productivity is one way to moderate price increases. Professor William Baumol argues that difficulties in improving productivity in health care is one reason for faster price increases in this sector.[7] Baumol isn't particularly worried about the slower productivity growth and consequent faster price increases in health care. As long as faster productivity growth occurs in other sectors of the economy, Baumol thinks the nation can afford a rising share of its real income going to health care.[8]

Another important factor is the quality of U.S. health care. Most objective analyses would suggest that the quality of U.S. health care has improved in recent decades. Health care today can do more than ever before. It can successfully treat more diseases and illnesses, it can perform operations never before thought of, and, as we have already seen, it has contributed to longer life expectancy and lower infant mortality rates. The quality of health care has improved, but better-quality health care costs more.

But how much has better-quality health care contributed to the increase in health care expenditures? As you might expect, this question has been the subject of considerable study by economists. The consensus answer seems to be 15 to 64 percent. Newhouse estimated that health care technology, which leads to better-quality health care, could be responsible for up to half of the increase in real (inflation-adjusted) health care expenditures between 1950 and 1980.[9] Wilensky studied data for 1965 to 1988 and concluded that new and improved health care technology accounted for 64 percent of the increase in medical expenditures unrelated to population and general price increases.[10] Finally, Rosko and Broyles's estimates are more modest, pegging improved health care quality as being responsible for between 15 and 33 percent of the increase in real health care expenditures between 1974 and 1984.[11]

So far our explanations for rising health care expenditures—higher real income, slow productivity growth in the health care sector, and better quality—have been rather boring and unsuspenseful! But the studies cited earlier still do not account for all of the rise in real health care expenditures. What else can be going on in the health care system to cause the jumps in real health care expenditures that we've seen in the past four decades? As the next section will show, the problem can be summarized as a lack of incentives.

THE PROBLEM OF LACK OF INCENTIVES

Incentives get to the heart of economics. For resources to be efficiently used in an economic system, incentives must be present. Producers must have the incentive to make profits in order to produce the products and services which consumers desire. Workers must face the incentive of earning more after-tax income in order to be motivated to work more or save more. Consumers must face the incentive of giving up income in the form of paying a price for products and services which they use in order to frugally use those products and services.

A major ongoing problem in the American health care system is the lack of incentives for both consumers and providers of health care to use resources in the system frugally. In fact, the current system does just the opposite in that it gives consumers and providers incentives to use resources with little concern for their costs. Let's see how.

For consumers, the culprit has been the *decoupling* of the *payment* of health care services from the *consumption* of health care services. Decoupling means consumers directly pay a very small part of the cost of health care, and it has a very important implication. If a consumer directly pays for health care (e.g., the consumer writes a check to the doctor or hospital for care received), then the consumer will frugally choose how much health care to use. In this case the consumer knows that more dollars spent on health care mean fewer dollars available to be spent on other goods or services that make the consumer happy. In contrast, if a consumer's health care is paid by a third party, such as the government or insurance, then the consumer won't be as frugal with those expenditures. In fact, the consumer won't care how much is spent because the tab is picked up by someone else.

Of course, consumers ultimately pay all the health care bills, since consumers ultimately pay all government taxes and all insurance premiums. But timing makes all the difference in affecting incentives. Taxes and insurance premiums have already been paid at the time that a consumer and his or her doctor are deciding on how many medical tests or procedures to use or how long to stay in the hospital. To the extent that these tests, procedures, and hospital stays will be paid by government or insurance, the immediate additional cost to the consumer is zero.

So the point is this. As third parties (government and insurance) pay a higher percentage of the health care bill, the percentage paid directly by the consumer falls, and consumers are motivated to use more health care and not worry about the expense because the additional cost to them is slight or zero. Stated another way, when consumers directly pay for health care, they will use additional health care as long as the benefits of care exceed the cost. When third parties pay for health care, consumers will use additional health care as long as the benefits of the care exceed zero! In the latter case, more health care will be used.[12]

An example may drive home this point. A doctor in Durham, North Carolina reported the treatment of a 70-year-old patient for a heart problem (a ruptured abdominal aortic aneurysm) and pneumonia. The patient was in the hospital for 3 1/2 months. The total bill was $275,000, but the patient wasn't concerned about this money because government paid it all. Then the patient needed new dentures so he could eat properly and continue his recovery. The dentures cost $75, but the cost would have to be paid by the patient. The patient refused to pay the $75 and get the new dentures, thereby putting in jeopardy the $275,000 operation. To the patient, $75 was a lot of money, but $275,000 wasn't because it was someone else's money![13]

The decoupling of the direct payment of health care services from the consumption of health care services is exactly what has happened during the past 40 years. Figure 11-4 shows the steady increase in the percentage of health care expenditures paid directly by government and insurance, from 39 percent in 1955 to 75 percent in 1991. The good news is that this has lessened the need for consumers to worry about paying doctor and hospital bills. The bad news is that it has simultaneously reduced consumers' need to carefully weigh the benefits and costs of health care and has thereby contributed to escalating health care costs.

The increase in third-party payments has given rise to three corollary effects. First are the charges of vast waste in the health care system. *Consumer Reports* estimated that 24 percent of health care expenditures were wasteful or unnecessary.[14] A study by the Rand Corporation claimed that 22 percent of medical procedures in their sample were inappropriate.[15]

There are reasons to question these high estimates of waste in the health care system.[16] The estimates are based on experts evaluating medical procedures and care after the fact, and as in anything, it's always easy to second-guess someone else's decision. Interestingly, in the Rand study, in only 12 percent of the time did seven of the nine experts agree that procedures were inappropriate.[17] But regardless of how much "waste" there is in health care, its understandable why the current system encourages more tests and procedures than many would deem appropriate. With third parties picking up most of the cost, doctors and patients have an incentive to use any test or procedure

Figure 11-4   Percent of Health Care Expenditures Paid by Government or by Insurance

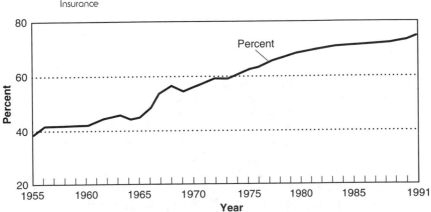

Source: U.S. Bureau of the Census, *Statistical Abstract of the U.S.*, various issues.

for which the benefits are greater than zero (rather than using a test or procedure only when its benefits are greater than its costs).

A second consequence of large and dominant third-party payments has been the motivation of doctors and hospitals to compete on service characteristics rather than on price. Doctors and hospitals are motivated to purchase the latest technology and equipment as a form of advertising to attract patients. Patients choose hospitals and doctors with the latest technology and equipment because they expect these characteristics to give them better care, and very importantly, patients don't care how much the equipment and technology cost because they don't directly pay for it. Some state governments have tried to stem the tide of technology and equipment purchases by requiring approval of certificates of need before a purchase is made, but because this bureaucratic procedure has not changed the incentives behind the motivations of doctors and hospitals, it is leaning against the wind.

A final outcome of the current incentives in the health care system is cost shifting. If any player in the health care system doesn't pay its bills, those costs will be shifted to other players.[18] For hospitals, cost shifting increased from $5 billion in 1980 to $11 billion in 1991 (both measured in 1991 purchasing power dollars).[19] Cost shifting has increased most recently in response to limitations in the reimbursements offered by the governmental-run Medicare and Medicaid programs. Costs not covered by Medicare and Medicaid are shifted to patients covered by private insurance. These shifted costs are sometimes factored into the bills of such patients in unusual ways, resulting in charges of $20 for boxes of tissues and $50 for bed linens!

Therefore, rather than placing the blame for escalating health care costs on high-cost doctors and wasteful hospitals, this section has pointed out the importance of a less ominous, yet no less powerful, factor: incentives. The incentives in the current health care system have encouraged the use of more tests and procedures, the purchase of the latest technology and equipment in order to compete by service and not by price, and the expansion of health care expenditures. So if we don't like the current health care system, how can it be changed? Read on!

ALTERNATIVE REFORMS

There's no shortage of suggestions for changes in the U.S. health care system. However, the proposals can generally be categorized into four groups: national health insurance, price controls, managed competition, and market-based solutions. Let's look at each in some detail.

National Health Insurance

National health insurance is lauded by many as the solution to our health care crisis. Under national health insurance, all consumers would have access to health care at no direct cost to them. National health insurance would be funded by taxes withheld from paychecks similar to the way social security is funded. National health insurance would completely decouple the payment of health care from the consumption of health care. That is, there would be no relationship between what a consumer pays from his or her income for national health insurance and how much health care the consumer uses. However, this is exactly what the proponents of national health insurance want: They don't want prices and costs to influence the decisions by consumers and doctors about how much health care to use.

But the decoupling of payment and consumption of health care caused by the rise of third-party payments is, as I've already stressed, one of the reasons behind the rising real cost of health care. National health insurance would effectively raise third-party payments (i.e., by the government) to 100 percent of all health expenditures. So national health insurance would exacerbate the current situation in health care. In fact, by raising the third-party share to 100 percent and reducing the direct consumer share to zero, national health insurance would motivate even greater consumption of health care services.[20]

The greater consumption of health care services under national health insurance would mean greater health care expenditures. If the politicians and managers of national health insurance didn't want more spent on health care, the only alternative is that health care would have to be rationed. That is, if the government establishes the total amount to be spent on health care, and if the direct price to the consumer is zero, then the only element that is left to limit total spending is the quantity of health care. Under national health insurance with a cap on total spending, consumers would find limits on the quantity and timing of tests, procedures, operations, and hospital stays.

The experiences of other nations which have instituted national health insurance give some forecasts of the consequences of a national health care system. Canada has a national health care system which is held up as a model by supporters of the same system in the United States. Yet Canada has even been less successful than the United States in controlling health care expenditures in recent years. Between 1982 and 1987, real Canadian health care spending per capita rose an average of 4.45 percent annually, compared to an annual rise of 4.15 percent in the United States.[21]

Rationing can also be seen in the Canadian system of national health insurance. Americans have much greater access to modern medical technology than do Canadians. For example, the United States has eight times more magnetic resonance imaging units, seven times more radiation therapy units, and three times more open-heart surgery units per capita than does Canada.[22] Although some claim this only means that the American system promotes too much technology use, doctors in Canada have publicly complained about the lack of modern medical technology in their country.[23]

Long waiting times (another form of rationing) for elective operations are also evident in the nationalized health care systems. In Canada, patients classified as needing elective (nonurgent) surgery can wait up to a year for the surgery to take place (see Table 11-2).[24] Of course, during the long wait, their condition can deteriorate. In the United Kingdom, which also has national health insurance, 25 percent of patients eligible for elective surgery will be kept waiting for a year, and men over the age of 55 cannot normally receive kidney dialysis.[25]

Table 11-2   Maximum Number of Waiting Days for Specified Elective Surgery, Ontario, Canada

	DAYS
CAT Scan	180
MRI (Magnetic Resonance Imager)	480
Cardiovascular Surgery	180
Eye Surgery	360
Orthopedic Surgery	360
Lithotripsy	720
Specified Physical Rehabilitation	60
Autologousbone Marrow Transplant	240

Source: Government Accounting Office, *Canadian Health Insurance: Lessons for the U.S.* (Washington, DC: U.S. Government Printing Office, June 1991), p. 55.

A system of national health insurance would have important implications for the control of decisions. If total expenditures are to be controlled under a nationalized system, then decision making must shift away from doctors and patients and to government bureaucrats. Government bureaucrats will ultimately decide on what medical technology to buy, what operations are to be performed and when, and how the national health care budget is to be divided.

I've not painted a very pretty picture of national health insurance. But a group of health care professionals in the United States claims it has developed a health care system which preserves the benefits of national health insurance (coverage to everyone without regard to income) without the "bad aftertaste," that is, without the rationing and bureaucratic control and with a maximum of patient control. The system is called *managed competition*. But before we see if managed competition is all it's cracked up to be, let's look at another potential solution which many think would be both simple and effective: price controls.

Price Controls

An immediate reaction of many of you to rising health care costs may be to propose a simple solution, that is, slap price controls on health care costs. You might be thinking, since health care is so important, we ought to limit price increases so as to keep health care affordable.

Price controls are frequently offered as a solution when the price of some product or service is thought to be rising too rapidly. Price controls were imposed on all products and services in the early 1970s when inflation reached the unheard level of 5 percent (!), and until the mid-1980s, price controls were kept on energy. Many communities still impose price controls on rents.

But whenever they have been tried, price controls haven't worked, and there's no reason to think they will work in health care. If price controls keep a product's price under what is necessary to recover costs and make an acceptable profit, companies will simply reduce production of that product. Therefore, price controls usually result in shortages of the products and services being controlled. Also, another way for companies to reduce production of a product or service is to reduce its quality. That is, a lower-quality product is really less of the product. So price controls on health care would likely result in doctors and hospitals providing lower-quality care.

If price controls are to be taken seriously, they require a bureaucracy to monitor prices and enforce controls. Already 24 percent of health care expenditures are estimated to be spent on administrative costs, overhead, and billing.[26] A new layer of costs would be added to both enforce and comply with price controls.

Advocates of applying price controls to health care have most frequently discussed them in reference to prescription drugs. Patients frequently complain about high and rising prescription drug prices. Are price controls the answer?

Actually, a closer look at the evidence suggests something far short of a crisis in prescription drug prices. Prescription drug costs as a percentage of total health care expenditures have actually declined in the past 30 years, from 10 percent in 1960 to 5 percent in 1991.[27] A detailed examination reveals that prescription drug prices did not skyrocket in the 1980s when the prices of generic pharmaceutical drug prices are included.[28] Also, drug industry profit margins have remained stable since 1982.[29] Finally, when compared to the cost of surgery, prescription drug costs often appear quite reasonable.[30]

Critics of the prescription drug industry overlook the costs and risks of developing prescription drugs. It's estimated that it costs $230 million (1990 dollars) and 12 years to develop a new drug.[31] Furthermore, only two of every ten drugs are approved by the Federal Drug Administration, and of these, only 30 percent recover their research and development costs.[32] So the prescription drug business is a very risky business indeed.

If the prices of prescription drugs are a concern, then there are policies much better than price controls to address the issue. First, public policymakers could work on reducing delays in the Federal Drug Administration, which contribute to the 12-year lag between start and finish of drug development. Second, laws could be changed to permit advertising of prescription drug prices. In other consumer markets it's been found that the introduction of advertising resulted in lower prices.[33]

Managed Competition

Supporters of managed competition claim it combines the best elements of government regulation of the health care system with market incentives for efficiency and low costs. Proponents of managed competition claim it's the answer to insuring all citizens at reasonable cost, controlling the growth of overall costs, and yet doing all this without a total government takeover of the health care system. Critics of managed competition say it's a contradiction in terms that won't work; as one economist said, managed competition is like mixing oil and water! Who's right?

First, what specifically is managed competition?[34] On the "competition" side, managed competition would allow businesses to band together into large purchasing groups and purchase health insurance for their employees as a group.[35] It's believed this would lower costs because the purchasing groups would have greater bargaining power with insurers than if each acted alone. In particular, it would especially help small businesses that often must pay very high premiums for coverage.

But this pro-competitive feature of managed competition would come at the expense of many mandates and controls. On the "managed" side, managed competition would require that employers provide insurance to all employees; no one could be excluded. Furthermore, insurers could not charge differential rates to individuals based on their health status. Instead, insurers would charge premiums based on *community health ratings*, that is, the average health status of people in a given geographical area. Everyone in a given geographical area would pay the same premium based on the community health rating. This means healthier people would subsidize sicker people, and the young would subsidize the old. Also, all insurers would be required to offer the same standardized policy that includes the same features and coverage. The rationale is that such a requirement would force insurers to compete on price and not features.

Who would pay the bills in managed competition? Employers would be required to pay for the cost of health insurance for their employees, and the government would subsidize the cost for low-income persons and unemployed persons. The money would go to the purchasing groups (the alliances of businesses in a local area) that have contracted with insurers.

Some versions of managed competition include a final mandate, which is a global budget for health care spending in the country. The global budget, in turn, would be split into separate budgets for each region in the country. Total health care spending in each region could not exceed the budget for that region.

What's the verdict on managed competition? Is it the savior for the health care system which avoids the centralized control of national health insurance? On the one hand, the competitive feature of managed competition is laudatory. Allowing firms, especially small firms, to band together and collectively purchase health insurance is a step in the right direction. This will allow firms to take advantage of price discounts associated with quantity purchases, and it will allow small firms to pool their risks over a larger number of people. Some states already have laws which permit such pooling arrangements by firms in the purchase of health insurance.

But the managed components of managed competition are misguided and miss addressing the essential reasons behind cost escalation in health care. The standardized health insurance policy, which all insurers would be required to offer, forces all consumers into one pool based on the premise that one size (policy) fits all. Yet why should this be the case in health insurance, since it's not the case in any other consumer market? American consumers are marked by a great diversity of desires and demands. Some consumers probably want a bare-bones, low-cost health insurance policy, while others want a deluxe high-cost policy. Insurance markets should be able to respond to these different desires and demands.

The community-rating mechanism of insurance policy pricing in managed competition is contrary to the most elementary principles of efficiently operating insurance markets. Insurance markets work best when policy premiums are based on the health risk of the policyholder. Policyholders with greater health risk have a greater probability of using the health insurance policy; therefore, in an efficient insurance market, their premiums will be higher. Similarly, policyholders with a lower health risk have a lesser probability of using the health insurance policy; therefore, their premiums will be lower.

If policyholders are charged some average premium, based on the average health risk in the community, then three results follow. First, high-risk policyholders will pay less than their expected costs to the insurance company, and low-risk policyholders will pay more. This means low-risk policyholders will subsidize the costs of high-risk policyholders. Second, in an efficient insurance market, high premiums charged to high-risk policyholders act as an incentive for them to reduce their health risk (maybe by losing weight, eating right, and not smoking) and to be rewarded with lower premiums. Under community-based ratings, this incentive will no longer be present. Third, with low-risk policyholders paying more than their cost to insurers, such low-risk policyholders will have an incentive to avoid being insured.

Versions of managed competition which include a global budget suffer from the same problem of global budgets in national health insurance plans. That is, with no motivation for frugality on the part of patients, rationing will have to result. Some level of bureaucracy, either at the national level or at the regional levels, will have to consciously ration the budgets for health care among the unlimited demands. For example, under President Clinton's health care proposal, a National Health Board would be established to set global budgets and control insurance premiums, and regional alliances would have the power to control payments to all health care providers.[36]

Yet the most important shortcoming of managed competition is its failure to address the essential problem in health care—the lack of direct incentives for patients and doctors to take account of the resources used in health care and to carefully use those resources. Fortunately, addressing these individual incentives is the hallmark of the next approach to the health care issue, the market-based approach.

Market-Based Approaches

The health care tiger won't be tamed with new bureaucratic structures and calls for providing all the care needed without regard to cost. Instead, no serious reform of the health care system can succeed without addressing incentives. Consumers of health care must be given the incentive to frugally use health care resources and realize trade-offs between more spending on health care and more spending on other goods and services which they like. Doctors and hospitals must have an incentive to efficiently use medical resources and to compete for patients' business.

For consumers, the best way to introduce incentives for careful resource use in health care is to recouple the payment of health care with the consumption of health care. As I've stressed, one of the big problems in health care today is the use of "other people's money" at the point of consumption of health care. Although consumers ultimately pay all the health care bills, when consumers are using health care, there is often very little relationship between what a consumer has paid in the past and the cost of health care in the present. When someone else is paying, the incentive is to use more resources.

Am I suggesting that we do away with insurance and government health care programs and have everyone pay for health care directly out of their own pocket? No! But what I am suggesting is that we return private and government insurance programs to their original purpose, which is to pay for catastrophic health care expenses, and not to pay for relatively small or initial expenses. By making consumers responsible for small or initial expenses, they will be using their own money for this care, and presumably they'll be more careful about the demands they place on the health care system. They'll be motivated to use the health care system only if the benefits they perceive from health care are greater than the benefits they perceive from other uses of their money. Consumers will only be able to use other people's money once they've put some of their own money on the line.

Some of you may think my prescription is very cold-hearted for three reasons. First, you may still cling to the notion that money shouldn't be a concern when health is the issue. But, again, unfortunately we live in a world where money and resources are limited, so we *always* must worry about trade-offs and alternative uses of money.

Second, you may worry about leaving health care decisions in the hands of consumers when consumers must use some of their own money to pay for the care. Won't many consumers always opt for spending money on other things they like, or need, even though spending money on health care might be best for them in the long run?

This is a philosophical issue which really gets to the heart of what kind of economic system we want. There are many areas of life where a consumer's behavior may not be what's best for him or her in the long run. Many consumers smoke, have poor diets, don't exercise, or engage in dangerous activities. Should such consumers be prohibited from making their own decisions and be put under the care of a "big brother or sister"? If not, then the alternative is to entrust personal decision making to individuals, relying on education, advice, and information to guide them to their own best long-run decisions.

The third concern some of you may have about my recommendation is money. Where will many families, who are already stretching their budget, find maybe two or three thousand dollars in a given year to meet a medical expense? There are three ways. First, families will save money on health insurance because health insurance policies which require a large initial payment by the policyholder for medical expenses (called large-deductible policies) are considerably cheaper than policies without such deductibles. For example, data from insurance companies show that families increasing their deductible from $250 to $2,500 annually can reduce annual premiums by over $1,700.[37] Second, as I will detail, the large deductibles can, in many cases, be provided by employers as part of their benefits package with little additional cost to them. Third, for families below the poverty line, the large deductibles can be provided by government subsidy.

Let's look at specific market-based proposals. The most interesting market-based approach which gives incentives for consumer oversight of health care expenditures is the *medical savings account*.[38] Under this plan, employers would be required to annually place a certain amount of money (say $3,000) for each employee into a medical savings account. Interest earnings on money in the medical savings account would accumulate tax free.[39] Any expenditures which the employee had for health care would initially come from the medical savings account, so it would act like a large deductible. Only when the medical savings account was exhausted would a backup health insurance policy pay the bills.[40] The employee could tap money in the medical savings account for other expenditures as long as taxes and a penalty were paid on the withdrawn funds. However, funds remaining in the medical savings account when the employee reached a certain age (say 59 1/2) could be withdrawn with no penalty but with taxes due on the accrued interest and used for any kind of expenditure.

Notice what this system would do to consumer incentives compared to a system of national health insurance or compared to the current system. Since consumers are using money which they could use later for something else they want, they would have an incentive to be frugal with their consumption of health care. They would recognize the trade-off between spending more money on health care and more money on other things.[41] However, for catastrophic health care costs, insurance would still pick up the bill.

Notice also what a system of medical savings accounts does to the locus of decision making. Since consumers control the money, and since their money is on the line, consumers of health care will control the shots (no pun intended). Since there won't be an automatic line of money from insurance companies and the government (at least for small or noncatastrophic health care expenditures), doctors and hospitals will have an incentive to compete for consumers' health care business, to advertise prices, and maybe even to prepare preapproved bills.

There are other changes which would introduce more incentives for cost-consciousness in the use of health care. A review and revision of state regulations of health insurance policies would help in the fight against rising health care costs. Most states tell insurance companies operating within their boundaries which provisions to include in their policies. In 1970 there were 48 such regulations; today there are 1,000.[42] The problem with such state regulations is that by requiring specific provisions and coverages, they raise the cost of insurance policies.[43] Reducing these insurance mandates would enable more access to no-frills and low-cost health insurance.

Although there is significant disagreement about the role of malpractice claims in raising the cost of health care, there's no question that malpractice insurance for doctors and hospitals is substantial. For example, average annual malpractice premiums for obstetricians rose 215 percent in real (inflation-adjusted) dollars from 1982 to 1989.[44] One association estimates that physicians spent $17 billion in 1989 on malpractice insurance premiums and defensive medicine designed to deter malpractice suits.[45]

Economists John Goodman and Gerald Musgrave make the excellent observation that medical malpractice is an issue which cries for voluntary solutions between patients and hospitals (and doctors). One solution, which they expect would lower total malpractice costs, would be for a hospital to purchase a life insurance policy on a patient prior to surgery. The patient and the patient's family would then voluntarily agree that if the patient dies for any reason during surgery, the family would take the proceeds from the life insurance policy as compensation for the death even if malpractice was the cause. That is, the family would give up any right to sue (with risk of not winning) in exchange for the certainty of receiving the life insurance money in the case of death. Unfortunately, according to Goodman and Musgrave, such voluntary malpractice agreements are now not legal.[46]

How would these reforms help the estimated 37 million uninsured Americans? First, it's important to recognize that the 37 million uninsured include individuals who don't have health insurance for only part of a year. Two-thirds of the uninsured are without insurance for less than a year, and only 15 to 18 percent are without insurance for over two years.[47] A major reason people are uninsured is they are between jobs, and their employer-provided health insurance has ended.

Medical savings accounts and reducing state mandates would help the uninsured in two ways. First, the accounts would be owned by individuals, not companies, so they would be completely portable. The funds in the accounts would be available to individuals for health care expenditures incurred between jobs. Second, reducing state mandates on health care policies would reduce health insurance premiums and make health insurance policies more affordable. Goodman and Musgrave estimate that 25 percent of the uninsured lack health insurance because of state mandates.[48]

Finally, we shouldn't forget the role of supply in health care economics. In any market, one way to reduce prices or to cause prices to rise at a slower rate is to increase supply at a faster rate. In the health care market, there are two ways to increase the number of practitioners at a faster rate. One way is to pressure medical schools to increase enrollments. Another way is to pressure state legislators to expand the authority of nurses and physician assistants, who aren't medical doctors, to perform more independent care without the direct supervision of a doctor.

FINAL THOUGHTS

Because health care deals with our number-one goal, survival, we're tempted to put economics aside and say "money shouldn't be involved when life is at stake." But this is wishful and faulty thinking. With resources limited, we make trade-offs between life and resources all the time. For example, lives could be saved on the highway by dramatically reducing speed limits but because time (as a resource) is limited, we take life-threatening risks by driving at high speeds in order to save time. Likewise, homeowners could reduce the risk of death or injury from fire by only building or buying homes with special fireproofing materials. But most homeowners choose not to do this because of the added expense.

Health care uses scarce resources, and the only way to ensure that these resources are used efficiently is to have economic incentives in the system which encourage cost-consciousness and wise spending. Importantly, those incentives must also apply to the consumer of health care.

NOTES

1. Polls have shown that over 80 percent of Americans want the health care system significantly changed; see Robert Blendon and Karen Donelan, "The Public and the Emerging Debate Over National Health Insurance," *The New England Journal of Medicine*, 323, July 19, 1990, 208–212.
2. U.S. Bureau of the Census, *Statistical Abstract of the U.S.*
3. The 1992 Kaiser/Commonwealth Health Insurance Survey.
4. In 1990, industrialized countries spent an average of 7 1/2 cents out of every dollar earned on health care. Organization for Economic Cooperation and Development, *U.S. Health Care at the Crossroads* (Paris, 1992), p. 22.
5. Congressional Budget Office, *Trends in Health Spending: An Update* (Washington, DC: Government Printing Office, June 1993), p. 51.
6. Organization for Economic Cooperation and Development, *U.S. Health Care at the Crossroads*, p. 17.
7. William Baumol, "A Growing Economy Can Pay Its Bills," *The Wall Street Journal*, May 19, 1992, p. A-14. Of course, this factor is probably also at work in other countries.
8. In other words, if real income is rising sufficiently fast, then a rising share going to health care can still leave more real income for other goods and services. For example, if real income in 1993 is $6 trillion and the share going to health care is 15 percent, then this results in $900 billion being spent on health care and $5.1 trillion being spent on other things. If, by 2000, real income rises to $9 trillion and the share being spent on health care rises to 20 percent, then this results in $1.8 trillion being spent on health care and $7.2 trillion being spent on other goods and services. So although health care's share rose, more was still left over for nonhealth care spending.
9. Joseph P. Newhouse, "Medical Care Costs: How Much Welfare Loss?" *Journal of Economic Perspectives*, 6, no. 3 (Summer 1992), 3–21.
10. Gail R. Wilensky, "Technology as Culprit and Benefactor," *Quarterly Review of Economics and Business*, 30, no. 4 (Winter 1990), 46–53.
11. Michael D. Rosko and Robert W. Broyles, *The Economics of Health Care* (New York: Greenwood Press, 1988).
12. For empirical evidence on the impact of health insurance on consumer demand for health care, see Willard Manning, Joseph Newhouse, Naihua Duan, Emmett Keeler, Arleen Leibowitz, and M. Susan Marquis, "Health Insurance and the Demand for Medical Care: Evidence from a Randomized Experiment," *American Economic Review*, 77, no. 3 (June 1987), 251–277.
13. James Weaver, "The Best Care Other People's Money Can Buy," *The Wall Street Journal*, November 19, 1992, p. A14.

14. Consumer Union, "Wasted Health Care Dollars," *Consumer Reports* (July 1992), pp. 435–448.

15. Cited in John Goodman and Gerald Musgrave, *Patient Power* (Washington, DC: Cato Institute, 1992), p. 115.

16. See Brant S. Mittler, "The Myth of Unnecessary Care," *The Wall Street Journal*, March 1, 1993, p. A14.

17. Goodman and Musgrave, *Patient Power* p. 116.

18. For an example of cost shifting, see Sidney Marchasin, "Cost Shifting: How One Hospital Does It," *The Wall Street Journal*, December 9, 1991.

19. This measure of cost shifting is based on the dollar amount of unsponsored care. Unsponsored care is the cost of bad debt and charity care, less subsidies from state and local governments. From Congressional Budget Office, *Trends in Health Spending: An Update* p. 58.

20. Under some national health insurance plans, there may be a modest direct payment by consumers in the form of small deductibles (initial money which the consumer must pay for health care before the national insurance "kicks in") and/or small coinsurance payments (percentage of the health care bill, up to some limit, which the consumer pays).

21. Edward Neuschler, *Canadian Health Care: The Implications of Public Health Insurance* (Washington, DC: Health Insurance Association of America, 1989), p. 41.

22. Data are for 1987 for the United States and 1989 for Canada; from Dale Rublee, "Medical Technology in Canada, Germany, and the U.S.," *Health Affairs* (Fall 1989), p. 180.

23. Goodman and Musgrave, *Patient Power*, p. 492. Also, one study has found the quality of life for Canadian heart attack patients to be inferior to the quality of life for American heart attack patients, see Ron Winslow, "Study Raises a Warning Flag About Canadian Health Care," *The Wall Street Journal*, November 11, 1993, p. B1.

24. In the Canadian system, patients are classified as needing emergent (life-saving), urgent, or elective surgery. However, the definitions for emergent, urgent, and elective can be changed over time.

25. Terree P. Wasley, *What Has the Government Done to Our Health Care?* (Washington, DC: Cato Institute, 1992), p. 90.

26. C. Jackson Grayson, Jr., "Experience Talks: Shun Price Controls," *The Wall Street Journal*, March 29, 1993, p. A12.

27. Congressional Budget Office, *Trends in Health Care Spending: An Update*, p. 38.

28. Robert Goldberg, "The Myth of High Drug Costs," *The Wall Street Journal*, September 29, 1992, p. A16. Goldberg's analysis shows prescription drug prices rising 5.7 percent annually from 1984 to 1989 compared to 3.7 percent for all consumer goods and services, after including prices of generic pharmaceutical drugs. See also Lindley Clark Jr., "Drug Price Rise May Be Exaggerated," *The Wall Street Journal*, October 8, 1993, p. A14.

29. Ibid., based on U.S. Commerce Department statistics.

30. For example, the annual cost of treating ulcers with prescription drugs (H-2 antagonist drug therapy) is $900, compared to $28,000 for ulcer surgery; from Murray Weidenbaum, *Restraining Medicine Prices: Controls vs. Competition*, Center for the Study of American Business, Policy Study Number 116 (April 1993), St. Louis, Washington University, p. 15.

31. Ibid., pp. 10–11.

32. Goldberg, "The Myth of High Drug Costs."

33. See Lee Benham, "The Effect of Advertising on the Price of Eyeglasses," *Journal of Law and Economics*, 15 (1972), 337; and Paul Farris and Mark Albian, "The Impact of Advertising on the Price of Consumer Products," *Journal of Marketing* (Summer 1980), p. 17.

34. References to the concept of managed competition include Stuart Butler, "The Contradictions in the Clinton Health Plan," *The Heritage Foundation Backgrounder* (Washington, DC: The Heritage Foundation, January 12, 1993); John Goodman, "Managed Competition—Too Little Competition," *The Wall Street Journal*, January 7, 1993, p. A14; and Congressional Budget office, *Managed Competition and Its Potential to Reduce Health Spending* (Washington, DC: Government Printing Office, May 1993).

35. The large purchasing groups are called Health Insurance Purchasing Cooperatives (HIPCs).

36. *Health Security Act* (Washington, DC: U.S. Government Printing Office, 1993). See also Elizabeth McCaughey, "Price Controls on Health Care," *The Wall Street Journal*, November 22, 1993, p. A14.

37. Goodman and Musgrave, *Patient Power*, p. 240.

38. References to the medical savings account idea can be found in Goodman and Musgrave, *Patient Power*, pp. 94–97, pp. 249–261; J. Patrick Rooney, "Give Employees Medical IRAs and Watch Costs Fall," *The Wall Street Journal*, January 28, 1992, p. A14; and Milton Friedman, "Gammon's Law Points to Health-Care Solution," *The Wall Street Journal*, November 12, 1991, p. A20. For an example of an actively working medical savings account, see Ken Davis, "Now the Good News on Health Care," *The Wall Street Journal*, September 20, 1993, p. A14.

39. Some promoters of medical savings accounts also recommend the annual deductible provided by the employer (the $3,000 in our example) be tax free to the employee. However, other health policy analysts want health care benefits provided by employers to be fully taxable to remove the current bias in the laws toward providing health care fringe benefits instead of extra salary. These analysts want employees to weigh the pros and cons of health care spending and insurance versus other kinds of spending without influence of the tax system, see Friedman, "Gammon's Law Points to Health-Care Solution."

40. Rooney argues that the medical savings account plus backup insurance policy would in most cases cost the average employer no more than current employer-provided health insurance. For example, in average cost of living cities, employer-provided health insurance with a $100 to $250 deductible costs $4,500 annually. A policy with a $3,000 deductible costs $1,500 annually. This leaves $3,000 for the medical savings account, see Rooney, "Give Employees Medical IRAs and Watch Costs Fall."

41. Some employers currently offer something like a medical savings account, but since unspent funds in the account revert to the employer at year's end, employees don't face the opportunity cost of using those funds for nonhealth spending in a later year, see Rooney, "Give Employees Medical IRAs and Watch Costs Fall."

42. John Goodman, "Health Insurance: States Can Help," *The Wall Street Journal*, December 17, 1991, p. A20.

43. For evidence, see Michael Walden and M. B. Hossain, "The Implicit Prices of Long-Term Health Care Policy Characteristics," Proceedings of the 38th Annual Conference of the American Council on Consumer Interests, Toronto, Canada, March 25–28, 1992, pp. 61–66.

44. Martin, L. Gonzales, ed., *Socioeconomic Characteristics of Medical Practice* (Chicago: American Medical Association, 1991), p. 147.

45. Ibid.
46. Goodman and Musgrave, *Patient Power*, p. 64.
47. Data from Katherine Swartz of the Harvard School of Public Health, cited in Greg Steinmetz, "Number of Uninsured Stirs Much Confusion in Health-Care Debate," *The Wall Street Journal*, June 9, 1993, pp. A1, A7.
48. Goodman and Musgrave, *Patient Power*, p. 348.

12

Why can't we eliminate poverty?

One of the most controversial and intractable problems we face is poverty. Despite being one of the richest nations in the world, the United States still has a substantial population which is considered poor. Although we have come a long way since the 1930s when President Franklin Roosevelt observed that one-third of the population was "ill-housed, ill-fed, and ill-clothed," most of us have seen families and individuals living in poverty. Furthermore, the reduction in poverty as measured by the poverty rate seems to have ground to a halt in the 1980s.

However, as we saw in Chapter 4, the fight against poverty has not ended, and indeed by many measures it expanded in the 1980s. The percent of our total economic resources devoted to assisting the poor actually increased in the 1980s. Yet poverty for many remains entrenched. This has led some observers to argue that poverty spending may be the problem rather than the solution because it has created a dependency class.[1]

Indeed, the issue of incentives is central to the debate about poverty and poverty policy. Have our poverty programs destroyed the incentive for many on poverty to work and lift themselves out of poverty? Should those receiving assistance be required to participate in skill training and eventually work in order to continue receiving benefits? Should those poor not working (assuming they are physically able to work) be cut off from receiving further assistance? If so, what happens to their dependents, that is, to their children? These are tough questions which many states are now wrestling with. We'll wrestle with them also.

Finally, a new kind of poverty has emerged in the past decade called homelessness. Who are the homeless and why did they apparently emerge in significant numbers in the 1980s? Is homelessness a problem significantly different from the general problem of poverty as to require a different set of solutions? We'll conclude this chapter by tackling the difficult problem of homelessness.

MEASURING POVERTY

Before we can talk about poverty we must know how many poor there are. To accomplish this, we have to measure poverty. This is no small order because there are many ways to measure poverty, and there are conflicting views about which is the best measure.

The official government measure of poverty was developed in the early 1960s and is based on the cost of an adequate diet.[2] The dollar cost of an adequate diet is divided by the typical proportion of a family budget spent on food to obtain the minimal level of total income necessary to afford the adequate diet. Calculations are done for each family size, and the income levels are adjusted upward each year by the annual rate of inflation. In 1991, this official measure of the poverty level resulted in a poverty line of $13,924 for a family of four. That is, families of four with incomes below $13,924 in 1991 were considered poor by this official definition.

Needless to say, not everyone agrees with this way of measuring poverty. Many critics want the poverty level determined by all spending and not only by spending on food.[3] The official poverty level is an absolute level. Some would prefer the poverty level to be based on a relative scale; for example, poverty would include all those making, say, 50 percent of the average income.[4] This would mean that poverty would never disappear because there will always be some households earning less than x percent of the national average income.

Other critics have focused on the fact that the official poverty measure looks at family income summed over a year. But households may slip in and out of poverty during the year. Ruggles estimates that over twice as many people may be poor sometime during a year than is indicated by the official poverty rate.[5] Finally, the official poverty measure only looks at income and not at assets. Theoretically, a household could be considered poor if it had low annual income even if it had hundreds of thousands of dollars of assets.[6]

Nevertheless, despite its critics, the official poverty measure is the standard poverty calculation. But once the official poverty level is accepted for a family of a given size in a given year (e.g., $13,924 for a family of four in 1991), a further issue remains of what to count as income for a family in determining if the family is poor. Three alternatives are presented here.[7] Definition 1 considers income as money income from all sources, including money income from privately earned wages and salaries and money income from government transfers, such as social security, unemployment compensation, and welfare cash payments. This is the alternative used by the government in determining the official poverty rate in any year.

A second definition uses only the money income from private sources in determining if a family is poor. Money income from government transfers are not included. The poverty rate calculated using this alternative will give a higher rate than obtained using definition 1.

A final alternative (definition 3) uses the most comprehensive measure of a family's income. This measure includes money income from both private and government sources (like definition 1) plus the cash equivalent of so-called in-kind government programs, such as Food Stamps, Medicare, Medicaid, rent subsidies, and school breakfasts and lunches.[8] Obviously, this is the most comprehensive of the three alternative definitions of a family's income, and so it will result in the lowest poverty rate.

Figure 12-1 shows the percentage of persons considered poor using the three alternative definitions of income. Unfortunately, the poverty rates using definitions 2 and 3 are only available since 1979. The poverty rate using definition 1 shows a sharp decline in the 1960s. However, since 1970 there's been virtually no improvement on trend in definition 1's poverty rate. The poverty rate rose during recessions (1969–70, 1973–75, 1980–83, and 1990–91) and during the rapid rise in inflation in the late 1970s, and fell during economic expansions (1971–72, 1984–89). Yet over the entire period, little change occurred.

As expected, definition 2's poverty rate is consistently higher than definition 1's rate, and definition 3's poverty rate is consistently lower than definition 1's rate. For example, in 1991, the poverty rate by definition 1 was 14.2 percent, the poverty rate by definition 2 was 21.8 percent, and the poverty rate by definition 3 was 11.4 percent. However, interestingly, the trends in all three rates have been very similar since 1979.

So how much poverty exists depends on how poverty is defined. If the concern is how much poverty exists after taking account of all government assistance programs, then clearly definition 3 is the appropriate measure and the answer is that slightly over 11 percent (in 1991) of persons are poor. If the concern is how much poverty exists without any government assistance pro-

Figure 12-1   Alternative Poverty Rates

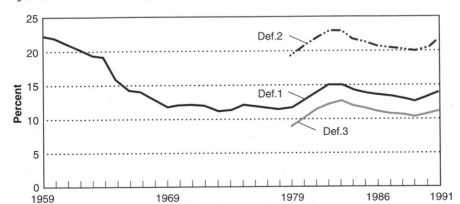

Source: U.S. Bureau of the Census, *Measuring the Effect of Benefits and Taxes on Income and Poverty: 1979–1991.*

grams, then the answer is that slightly over 20 percent (in 1991) of persons are poor. But whatever definition is used, clearly one concern is the lack of re-duction in the poverty rate over the past two decades.

One other issue remains in our discussion of measuring poverty. This is the issue of long-run or persistent poverty. The preceding poverty measures take a "snapshot" of poverty at a single point in time. But many people (hope-fully) are only temporarily poor. How many people are poor for long periods of time? This is a harder question to answer because it requires following in-dividuals and families over a long period of time. Fortunately, some re-searchers have been able to do this, and their research shows there is a significant population who is persistently poor. The consensus seems to be that somewhere between 20 and 50 percent of the poor population at any point in time are persistently poor (poor for eight or more years) rather than tem-porarily poor.[9]

Furthermore, there also appears to be some significant degree of in-tergenerational transmission of poverty. For example, research shows that women growing up in welfare families are from two to seven times more likely to be on welfare themselves as adults compared to women growing up in non-welfare families.[10]

These statistics on persistent poverty and intergenerational transmis-sion of poverty indicate failure in incentives and/or opportunities for a sig-nificant number of the poor to escape poverty. This has important implications for the design of programs to assist the poor. We'll return to this issue in later sections.

WHO ARE THE POOR?

Are the poor a cross section of the general population, or are the poor from specific parts of the population? Again, this question is important because the answers can be useful in thinking about programs and policies to assist the poor.

Table 12-1 summarizes the key characteristics of the poor. Although two-thirds of the poor are white, the poverty rate among African-Americans is almost three times higher than the poverty rate among whites. In 1991, 11.3 percent of whites were classified as poor compared to 32.7 percent of African-Americans.

Children are overrepresented among the poor. Over 40 percent of poor persons in 1991 were children under the age of 18. In contrast, only 24 percent of the nonpoor in 1991 were children under the age of 18. The elderly are slightly underrepresented among the poor. In 1991, 10.6 percent of the poor were persons over age 65, whereas 12.4 percent of the nonpoor were persons over age 65.

The household relationship of the poor points out a key problem. Thirty-four percent of poor persons in 1991 were in husband/wife households, and almost 22 percent of poor persons were unrelated individuals. But almost 39 percent of poor persons in 1991 were in female-headed households where no male spouse was present. This is sharply different than the 9.7 percent of

Table 12-1   Profiles of the Poor, 1991

	PERCENT OF POOR PERSONS
Race	
African-American	28.7
White	66.5
Other	4.8
Age	
Under 18	40.2
18–65	49.2
Over 65	10.6
Household Type	
In husband/wife household	34.8
Unrelated individuals	21.8
In female-headed households	38.7
In other households	5.5
Work Status (15 years and older)	
Worked sometime	40
Worked full-time all year	9

Source: U.S. Bureau of the Census, Current population Reports, Series p. 60, no. 181, *Poverty in the United States: 1991* (Washington, DC: U.S. Government Printing Office, 1992).

nonpoor persons in 1991 who were in female-headed households. Furthermore, 54 percent of all poor families in 1991 were female-headed families compared to 12.7 percent of all nonpoor families being female-headed families. This is up from 23 percent of all poor families being female-headed families in 1959. Clearly, among all the demographic relationships, being in a female-headed family is the characteristic most associated with being poor.

Finally, the working status of the poor clearly highlights a problem. Among poor persons 15 years and older in 1991, only 40 percent worked sometime and a mere 9 percent worked full-time all year. This is in sharp contrast to nonpoor persons, of whom 72 percent worked sometime and 45 percent worked full-time all year in 1991. The differences are just as striking among household heads. In 1991, only half of poor household heads worked sometime and just 16 percent worked full-time all year. These figures are much below the comparable percentages for nonpoor household heads, where 81 percent worked sometime and 61 percent worked full-time all year in 1991.

So the poor are not simply a cross section of the general population; instead, they have a definite profile. The typical poor person is a child or nonelderly adult in a female-headed household where the female head does not work full-time. To say the least, this profile presents a challenge for the designers of poverty programs.

HOW MUCH DO WE SPEND ON THE POOR?

In Chapter 4 we looked at trends in poverty spending and found that spending as a percent of the national economy was actually higher in the 1980s than in the 1960s and 1970s. In 1991, $149 billion was spent on various programs and payments to combat poverty, including food and nutrition programs, income support (but excluding social security), housing assistance, Medicaid (but not Medicare), training and employment programs, and social services. Divided among poor persons, this spending came to $4,174 per poor person.[11]

In this chapter we want to concentrate on poverty among the nonelderly and the nondisabled. Poverty among the elderly is addressed primarily by the social security and Medicare programs. Poverty among the blind and disabled is handled by the Supplemental Security Income program. Most of the controversy about poverty programs has focused on the nonelderly and the nondisabled who are physically able to work.

The main poverty programs for the nonelderly and nondisabled are Aid to Families with Dependent Children (AFDC), food stamps, Medicaid, and housing subsidies. AFDC is the basic welfare program, which provides cash to qualifying families. Originally only female-headed families with no husband present were eligible for AFDC, but recently husband/wife families have become eligible for AFDC (more on this later). Food stamps is a program which provides food coupons to eligible families and persons for the purchase of food. Similarly, Medicaid pays the medical bills of eligible poor families and individuals. Finally, housing subsidies assist eligible poor households to meet their rent payments. In 1992, $85.3 billion were spent on these four programs.[12]

A large percentage of poor households qualify for multiple program assistance. For example, in 1992, 86 percent of AFDC recipients received food stamps, 96 percent received Medicaid, and 30 percent received housing assistance.[13]

For households who qualify for assistance, how much assistance is typically received and how has it changed over time?[14] Figure 12-2 answers these questions by showing the real (1992 dollars) annual dollar amount of the major assistance programs received by an eligible three-person household. A number of interesting trends are revealed. The real annual amount of the main cash welfare program (AFDC) has fallen by 20 percent from 1977 to 1991.[15] In contrast, the real annual amount of food stamps rose by 20 percent from 1977 to 1991, and the real annual amount of Medicaid rose by 8 percent over the same time period.[16] Some economists speculate that states, which determine AFDC payments, may have lowered AFDC payments in response to the rise in federally controlled food stamp and Medicaid payments.[17] The real annual amount of housing assistance rose 53 percent between 1977 and 1991.

Figure 12-2 shows that for the three-person household receiving AFDC, food stamps, and Medicaid, the three-program sum changed very little from 1977 to 1991. In real terms, the three-program sum declined by 5 percent, meaning that increases in food stamps and Medicaid didn't quite counteract the decline in AFDC. However, for the three-person household receiving AFDC, food stamps, Medicaid, and housing assistance, the four-program sum rose slightly, by 5.7 percent in real terms, over the time period.[18]

Two corollaries must be made to the preceding findings. First, the numbers do not include costs of administering the programs. For the AFDC and food stamp programs, administrative costs take 11 to 12 percent of the

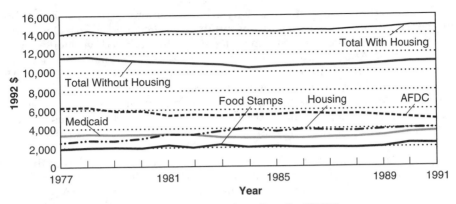

Medicaid adjusted by CPI medical care component; others adjusted by CPI-UX1.

Source: Committee on Ways and Means, U.S. House of Representatives, *1993 Green Book* (Washington, DC: U.S. Government Printing Office, 1993).

Figure 12-2   Real Annual Welfare Benefits for Three-Person Family

total budgets allocated for these programs, and the administrative bite is probably bigger in Medicaid.[19]

Second, the real Medicaid amounts in Figure 12-2 were derived by adjusting actual Medicaid spending by the Consumer Price Index for medical care. This was done because medical care prices have risen much faster than other prices in recent years. However, this means the real cash value to taxpayers of the Medicaid payments was much greater than the amounts shown in Figure 12-2. For example, if Medicaid payments had been adjusted by the average Consumer Price Index, then payments to a three-person household would have risen by almost 50 percent from 1977 to 1991.

Both of these points raise the issue of whether cash assistance to poor households by simply sending the poor cash rather than giving them food stamps and medical care would be a preferable way of helping the poor. We'll return to this issue later.

DO WELFARE PROGRAMS ENCOURAGE CONTINUED POVERTY AND DEPENDENCE?

This is *the* "hot-button" issue for many citizens when discussing poverty programs. On the one hand, most people are compassionate and want to assist households who are "down on their luck" and need help until they can "get back on their feet." But on the other hand, the same people worry that welfare programs may encourage some households to stay on welfare rather than work. This concern is particularly directed at those households who are permanently on welfare.

There is a considerable body of economic evidence which suggests that welfare programs do discourage work, although there is disagreement over the extent of the discouragement. The disincentives to work created by welfare programs come in three ways. First, numerous studies show that higher cash or quasi-cash welfare payments do reduce work effort. One study found that a 10 percent increase in welfare benefits reduced work effort by 1 to 2 percent.[20] Another study found that every $3 of additional welfare benefits only raised recipient income by $1 to $2 because recipients reduced work effort as a result of the increase in welfare benefits.[21] Also, the relative AFDC case load (AFDC case load per capita) rose steadily in the 1960s as the real (inflation-adjusted) AFDC benefit rose during that period. However, as the real AFDC benefit fell in the 1970s and 1980s, the relative AFDC case load stopped rising.[22]

The second way that welfare programs discourage work is in the *implicit tax rate* on welfare benefits that occurs when additional labor income is earned. The implicit tax rate (also called the *benefit reduction rate*) is the reduction in the dollar value of welfare program benefits per dollar of additional labor income earned. Each welfare program (AFDC, food stamps, Medicaid, and housing assistance) has its own rules regarding benefit reduction when more labor income is earned, and the rules interact. But economists agree that the implicit tax rate on benefits is high—at least 90 percent or more![23] That is, for every additional dollar of labor income that a welfare recipient earns, the recipient loses 90 cents or more of benefits. Needless to say, if the welfare recipient values leisure at all, and if there are expenses associated with working, then the implicit tax rate on benefits is a big disincentive to working for welfare recipients.

A specific example will dramatize this disincentive to work for welfare recipients. Figure 12-3 shows the disposable income available to a family of three in Pennsylvania at different levels of work earnings. Disposable income equals net work earnings plus AFDC benefits plus food stamp benefits. (Medicaid and housing assistance are not considered here.) Net work earn-

Figure 12-3   Annual Disposable Income at Various Earnings Levels for a Family of Three, Pennsylvania, January 1993

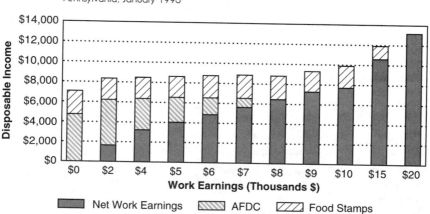

ings equal work earnings minus taxes on work earnings and minus work expenses. Work expenses are assumed to be 10 percent of earnings up to a maximum of $100 monthly, plus child care costs equal to 20 percent of earnings up to the maximum allowed by AFDC ($350 for two children).

The figure shows how net work earnings, AFDC benefits, and food stamp benefits change with higher work earnings. The figure clearly shows the disincentive to work up until $15,000 of work earnings. Disposable income rises from $7,497 to $8,662 as work earnings rise from $0 to $2,000 annually. However, disposable income rises from $8,662 to $9,907, an increase of $1,245, as work earnings rise from $2,000 to $10,000. That is, for increasing work earnings by $8,000, disposable income rises by only $1,245. This is some incentive for working more!

The third disincentive to work from welfare programs comes from a simple comparison of what a minimum-wage worker could earn by working full-time compared to what that person could receive in public assistance. In 1993 the minimum wage was $4.25. If an individual earning the minimum wage worked 40 hours per week for 52 weeks, total earnings would be $8,840. These are gross earnings, not subtracting any taxes or work expenses. However, as Figure 12-2 shows, a three-person family (say, one adult and two children) could receive $7,380 in just AFDC and food stamps in 1991. If Medicaid is added, the total is $10,941, and if Medicaid and housing are added, the total of public assistance is $14,886. So clearly, for minimum-wage family heads with few skills, public assistance can be financially preferable to working.[24]

There are two related incentive issues with welfare programs which are also "hot-button" items for many citizens. One issue is whether the welfare system encourages female headship. The second issue is whether the system encourages those female heads on welfare to have additional children.

Academic research on the first issue has given mixed results, but some studies have indeed found a link between welfare programs (particularly AFDC) and female headship.[25] The reason is simple—the AFDC program was traditionally targeted to families with female heads; husband/wife families were not eligible for AFDC benefits. Perhaps recognizing the incentive this restriction gave to the formation of female-headed families, the Family Support Act of 1988 mandated that states extend AFDC to eligible husband-wife families. However, the act only requires that benefits be paid for six months.

The incentive effects in welfare programs certainly aren't the only factor behind the rise of female family heads among poor households. Economists argue that marriage is not only an emotional union, but it is also an economic union. All other things equal, both women and men prefer mates with more income-earning potential. The increasing premium to education over the past two decades, which we have discussed frequently in earlier chapters, has reduced the income-earning potential of many men with no or few skills. This made such men less attractive as mates. Many economists have argued that this phenomenon has had an impact on the rise in female family heads among the poor population.[26]

Does the current welfare system encourage welfare mothers to have more children? There is no direct evidence that this is the case, but two incentives in the system appear not to discourage this activity. First, in 1993 a welfare mother received an average of $156 more per month ($1,872 annually) from AFDC and food stamps for each additional child.[27] In addition, Medicaid would cover medical expenses of the child, and with a larger family the mother may qualify for additional housing assistance. Although $1,872 annually for a child certainly isn't lavish, it isn't too far from the nonhousing and non-medical care expenses estimated to be required for raising a young child ($2,480 annually or $1,450 annually without transportation costs).[28]

The second possible incentive in the system for encouraging additional children by welfare mothers has to do with job training requirements for welfare recipients. As I will discuss in more detail in the next section, both the AFDC and food stamp programs have job training and work registration requirements. However, mothers with school-age children are generally exempt from these requirements. Therefore, welfare mothers who have an aversion to work may see an advantage in having additional children in order to avoid training and work requirements of welfare programs.

So there appears to be significant incentive problems in the welfare system which discourage work and may encourage female headship and additional births by female welfare recipients. So what's a better system? How should the welfare system be reformed to be compassionate and yet encourage economic independence? These questions are the topics of the next section.

REFORMING WELFARE

Everyone is in favor of welfare reform. In fact, there appears to be a consensus now that there are serious incentive problems in the welfare system which discourage work and encourage long-term dependence.[29] The task of welfare reform is to design a system which encourages skill acquisition and work without hurting innocent people (such as children). Some say this is an impossible task. We'll see!

Before we consider specific proposals for welfare reform, it's clear that structural changes in the economy may be making this task both more difficult and more important. As we discussed in Chapter 1, the premium to education has been increasing. Real wages have been rising the fastest for those with the most education. One major problem with the poor is that they have the least education. For example, in 1991, only 53 percent of poor family householders 25 years of age and older were high school graduates compared to 83 percent for nonpoor householders.[30] Also, the poverty rate is highest for those with the least amount of education. Twenty-four percent of householders without a high school degree were poor in 1991 compared to 11 percent for those with a high school degree and 7 percent for those with some college education.[31]

The relatively low level of education for poverty households is a double-edged sword. On the one hand, it shows that increasing education and skills has a direct relationship to reducing poverty. However, on the other hand, it shows that with the increased premium on education, those without education may fall even further behind. Economists who have studied the structural changes in the 1980s conclude that one reason why poverty rates didn't fall more during that decade of growth was that poor families who lacked education didn't benefit from the increasingly educationally focused growth.

A Five-Part Welfare Reform Program

Here I present a five-part welfare reform program. The program recognizes the desire to assist families who can't meet some minimum standard of living on their own, yet it provides strong incentives for self support.

1. Require Job Training.   When the Aid to Families with Dependent Children (AFDC) program was established in the 1930s, it was intended to help temporary widows and a small number of divorcees. The idea was that such women would receive assistance for a relatively short period of time so that the women could stay at home caring for the children rather than working. It was expected that the assistance would end when the women remarried. Designers of the program did not expect AFDC to become a permanent source of income for a significant number of families.

But times have changed in three important ways. First, women on AFDC today are not primarily widows. Ninety percent of women on AFDC today have never been married or are divorced or separated rather than widowed.[32] Second, as I have already documented, there is now a substantial long-term AFDC population, and some observers worry that a nonwork culture has developed among the long-term AFDC adults and dependents.[33] Third, unlike the 1930s, the majority of nonpoor mothers now work at least part-time. Society now doesn't expect mothers to remain at home engaged in child care.

Recent empirical evidence indicates job training efforts for welfare recipients can work in increasing the income of recipients, although the additional income earned is relatively small (no more than $1,500 annually).[34] Nevertheless, job training programs have been found to be cost-effective in that savings in welfare costs have exceeded training costs.[35]

Actually there already exists a job training requirement for welfare recipients (AFDC recipients) as part of the Family Support Act of 1988. This requirement is just being phased in, and in 1992 only 15 percent of eligible AFDC recipients participated.[36] Also, female heads with children under 3 years of age, with children attending school, or with children under 6 and no child care are *exempt* from the job training requirement. The problem is this exempts a large part of the AFDC population from required job training. For example, in 1991, 61 percent of the AFDC household heads were exempt from the job training requirements of the Family Support Act.[37] There's also a requirement for food stamp recipients to register for work and accept a suitable job if offered. However, recipients caring for children (under 12 years old) are exempt from the requirement.[38]

Therefore, to encourage independence and the work ethic among female heads on welfare and their children, the skill and job search training requirement of the Family Support Act should be extended to all able-bodied female heads. This would be a major departure from previous policy, but it would be made in the recognition of three facts: (1) most nonpoor mothers now work, (2) there is now a long-term, or permanent, welfare class, and (3) the nonwork of the permanent welfare class has created a culture of nonwork among a large number of the poor and their dependents. The extension of job training to female heads with children will, however, require additional child care resources for those families.[39]

Not too much should be expected from the jobs that welfare recipients are able to obtain. The jobs will likely be low paying, and recipients will likely continue to need assistance to supplement their labor income (more on this follows).[40] But the point is to get the poor and their dependents in a working environment and expect that future generations of today's poor will become self-supporting.

2. Institute Time Limits on Welfare Assistance. In order to provide further incentives for the development of work skills and work ethics among the poor, and particularly the permanent poor, time limits would be placed on the receipt of welfare assistance when the recipient is not working. This would guard against the case of a welfare recipient going through skill and job training and then not keeping a job. The time limit, say, two years, would tell the recipient that he or she had two years to obtain a job; if no job were found after this time, welfare assistance would end.[41] However, food and medical assistance to children would continue.

3. Fully Extend AFDC to Husband/Wife Families. To encourage husband/wife families, the general welfare cash assistance program, AFDC, would be fully extended to husband/wife families. Currently, eligible husband/wife families are only required to receive assistance for six months.

4. Reduce the Implicit Tax Rate on Welfare Benefits. This is probably the most important welfare reform. Hopefully, I've demonstrated convincingly to you that the current welfare system gives a big disincentive to work because welfare benefits are reduced virtually dollar for dollar with additional work earnings. As Figure 12-3 shows for one state, there's little incentive for welfare recipients to work if their earnings are $10,000 or less.

The solution to this disincentive is to reduce the implicit tax rate on welfare benefits when work income is earned. For example, rather than reducing welfare benefits 90 cents for every additional dollar of work earnings, reduce welfare benefits by, say, 33 cents for every additional dollar of work earnings. This would provide a powerful incentive for welfare recipients to earn more income.

There is a downside to this proposal. If current benefit levels are kept for those earning no income, then the proposal to reduce implicit tax rates would require higher benefit levels for those earning income and, furthermore, would likely require extending benefits to working families not currently receiving benefits. For example, in Figure 12-4, the top of each rectangular bar

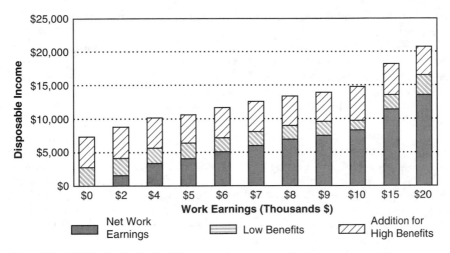

Source: Figure 12-3 and author's calculations.

Figure 12-4   Alternative Disposable Income at Various Earnings Levels for a Family of Three, Pennsylvania, January, 1993

shows the benefit levels and resulting disposable income at various levels of work earnings necessary to maintain the 33 percent implicit tax rate. As can be seen by a comparison to Figure 12-3, benefit payments to recipients would increase substantially. In other words, at least in the short run, welfare costs would increase.

Alternatively, total welfare costs could be maintained or reduced and the implicit tax rate lowered if benefit levels were reduced for those not working and for those having low levels of work earnings. This is illustrated by the "low benefits" rectangular in Figure 12-4. The downside of this alternative is that it hurts families whose benefit levels are reduced. Policymakers would have to choose between alternatives like the two discussed here. Part of the decision will hinge on how many resources policymakers are willing to devote to welfare assistance, and what subsistence standard of living policymakers are willing to support.

5. Convert All Assistance to Cash Assistance.   Of the $149 billion spent on assistance to poor households in 1991, only $21 billion (14 percent) was in the form of cash assistance. The other assistance was *in-kind* transfers, meaning the assistance was tied to certain kinds of spending. For example, food stamps can only be spent on food, rent subsidies can only be spent on rent, and Medicaid is only spent on reimbursing medical care expenses. There are two reasons why the majority of poverty assistance is in the form of in-kind transfers. First, interest groups lobby Congress for in-kind rather than cash transfers. Farm and food groups lobby for food stamps, building and real estate groups lobby for rent assistance, and doctor and hospital groups lobby for Medicaid. Second, taxpayers and Congress want recipients to use assistance in certain ways; they want "strings attached" to the assistance.

However, there are three advantages to moving to an all-cash form of assistance for the poor. First, if the purpose of poverty assistance is to improve the well-being of recipients, then allowing recipients to select what products and services make them happiest is the path to this goal.[42] For example, some studies show that Medicaid recipients value Medicaid transfers at only half of their dollar value.[43]

Second, all-cash assistance would remove the stigma faced by recipients with in-kind transfers. In-kind transfers are like a badge signaling to the outside world that the recipient is poor and requires help. Supermarket cashiers and other patrons know a family is poor when it pays for food with food stamps. So too do doctors and hospitals when a family's medical bills are paid by the Medicaid program. Such easy identification of welfare recipients may cause others to treat the recipients in a different (e.g., condescending) way. Such different treatment and any problems related to it could be avoided if the poor paid for their goods and services with cash just like the nonpoor.

Third, an all-cash assistance program could reduce the administrative costs in the current in-kind programs. As mentioned earlier, administrative costs are not insignificant, totaling 12 percent in the food stamp program. An all-cash assistance program could actually be implemented by the Internal Revenue Service. If a family's income tax return showed the family was earning income below eligibility levels, then the IRS would certify that assistance payments be made to the family.

So there you have it—a five-part welfare reform program, composed of required job training, time limits on receipt of welfare without a job, extension of full benefits to husband/wife families, reduction of the implicit tax rate to encourage work, and conversion to all-cash assistance. This is a reasonable program which will continue to provide compassionate help but at the same time will encourage work and self-sufficiency.

Before we leave the sticky problem of poverty, a new kind of poverty which deserves special attention is homelessness. Is homelessness a new problem? If so, how did it come about, and what can be done to solve this special problem?

HOMELESSNESS

Critics of the 1980s like to portray the decade with two contrasting images, one of investment bankers counting their money (or junk bonds), and the other of homeless persons sorting through garbage for food and sleeping in cardboard huts. The homeless nearly became a permanent fixture on nightly news programs and television talk shows in the 1980s. Who are the homeless, and why have they suddenly become an issue?

Before I address these questions, how many homeless are there? This is not an innocent question, as political tugs-of-war have been waged over the homeless numbers. Although no complete census of the homeless exists, the best estimates put the homeless population at between 500,000 and 1.2 million persons.[44]

Who are the homeless? Are they simply average people who are down on their luck, or are they a special population? The homeless population is definitely a special population. It is estimated from a number of sources that between 65 percent to 85 percent of the homeless population suffers from serious alcohol, drug, or mental problems.[45] Furthermore, only 10 percent of all homeless households are families.[46] So the homeless aren't a representative slice of American society; they are largely a population beset by serious problems which inhibit their ability to function in society.

Where did the homeless come from? Why did they suddenly appear in the 1980s? There are three right answers and one wrong answer to this question. The wrong answer is that the homeless population arose due to a reduction in spending on housing programs in the 1980s, particularly by the federal government. The reality is that federal housing assistance more than doubled in the 1980s, from $9.6 billion in 1980 to $17.5 billion in 1990 (both in 1993 dollars).[47]

Instead, there are three explanations for the rise in homelessness. First is the deinstitutionalization of mental patients. As a result of changes in professional and public attitudes about how the mentally ill should be treated, between 1955 and 1985 the nation's system of state mental hospitals was almost totally dismantled. In that 30-year period, an 80 percent decline in mental hospital patients occurred, from 550,000 to 110,000 patients.[48] The Community Mental Health Center Act of 1963 codified this dismantling and provided financial incentives to states for the patient releases. Furthermore, the least mentally ill patients were released in the early years; in the 1970s, the more severely mentally ill were discharged.[49]

The original intent of the 1963 legislation was not to release patients to the streets. Rather, the goal was to change the form of care for the mentally ill from large mental hospitals to a network of smaller and less restrictive community-based hospitals or care centers. But the new mental health care network was never fully built, and those centers which were built didn't take the released mental patients. Between 1968 and 1978, only 5 percent of the mental care center admissions were patients released from the state mental hospitals.[50] So the simple fact is that large numbers of today's homeless are people who traditionally would have been in mental institutions.

Another piece of federal legislation, the Uniform Alcoholism and Intoxication Treatment Act of 1971, is a second contributing factor behind homelessness. This act made public drunkenness a public health problem rather than a criminal problem. Again, the idea behind the legislation was laudable. Public drunks would be cared for in community detoxification centers rather than in jails. However, admission into the detoxification centers was voluntary and not required. Many persons afflicted with alcoholic problems have simply not used the detox centers. These persons too have taken to the street as a home.

The third explanation for the rise of homelessness in the 1980s is demographics. The baby-boom generation, born between 1946 and 1964, is a generation of 76 million individuals. Due to its sheer size, this generation has influenced everything from fashion to finance (see the discussion in Chapter 3 on borrowing and saving) during the past 20 years. Baum and Burnes argue that during the 1970s and 1980s, the baby-boom generation had reached the age when any generation sees some of its members experience alcohol and drug problems.[51] What made the experience different this time was the numbers due to the enormous size of the baby boomers.

So the explanations for the rise of homelessness are primarily institutional and demographic rather than economic. But economics does play a role in homelessness, albeit relatively minor. Two public policies affecting the supply of housing have had an impact on homelessness. First was the national policy of eliminating "slums" (also called urban renewal), especially in the large cities. Slum elimination was achieved with the bulldozer—slum areas were simply demolished. The problem is that along with the demolition of slums came the demolition of a significant part of the nation's low-cost housing supply. For example, single-room occupancy (SRO) hotels in slum areas were traditionally the home of persons with few financial resources. But between 1970 and 1982, half of the nation's supply of SRO hotels, over 1 million units, were destroyed.[52] These units were not replaced.

The second public policy which has adversely affected the homeless is rent control. To many, rent control sounds like a good idea. Limit the rent which landlords can charge and housing will be more affordable. But if the legal rents aren't high enough to allow landlords a sufficient profit (rate of return), then rent control will discourage residential construction and will cause the supply of housing to be lower than it would have been without the controls.[53] This means a lower supply of housing for everyone, including used housing which would be available for use by low-income households. Indeed, Tucker has found a statistically significant relationship between rent control and homelessness, that is, all other things equal, cities with rent control have higher rates of homelessness.[54]

So homelessness is largely a noneconomic problem which will have to be addressed with noneconomic solutions. But there are two economic public policies which communities can use to alleviate homelessness. First, communities who have strict zoning and housing code laws, which make it difficult for entrepreneurs to develop and market very low-cost housing (especially single-room occupancy housing), can relax those laws and restrictions. If there's a viable, profitable market for housing some of the homeless, entrepreneurs will find it. The problem is that many local laws and restrictions prevent this market from being met.

Second, communities who have rent controls should eliminate them. Rent controls distort the housing market and provide benefits to a lucky few. Ample evidence indicates that rent controls slow housing construction. Increasing the supply of housing is one part of the homeless solution.

NOTES

1. See, for example, Charles Murray, *Losing Ground, American Social Policy 1950–1980* (New York: Basic Books, 1984).

2. For discussion, see Mollie Orshansky, "Counting the Poor: Another Look at the Poverty Profile," *Social Security Bulletin*, 28 (January 1965), 3–29; and U.S. Department of Health, Education, and Welfare, *The Measure of Poverty: A Report to Congress as Mandated by the Education Amendments of 1974* (Washington, DC:, U.S. Government Printing Office, April 1976).

3. Patricia Ruggles, *Drawing the Line, Alternative Poverty Measures and their Implications for Public Policy* (Washington, DC: The Urban Institute Press, 1990), pp. 39–41.

4. Lee Rainwater, *What Money Buys: Inequality and the Social Meanings of Income* (New York: Basic Books, 1974).

5. Ruggles, *Drawing the Line*, p. 94.

6. Robert Rector, "How the Poor Really Live: Lessons for Welfare Reform," *Backgrounder No. 875*, The Heritage Foundation, Washington, DC: (January 1992).

7. The three alternative measures are from U.S. Bureau of the Census, Current Population Reports, Series p. 60, no. 182RD, *Measuring the Effect of Benefits and Taxes on Income and Poverty: 1979 to 1991* U.S. Government Printing Office, (Washington, DC: 1992).

8. The cash equivalent of in-kind government assistance programs is not necessarily the same as the dollar cost to taxpayers of the programs. Instead, the in-kind program benefits are counted as cash only to the extent that they free up resources that could have been spent on the product or service (like medical care) by the recipient; see Ibid., p. viii.

9. See Ruggles, *Drawing the Line*, pp. 107–108 for an excellent summary of these studies.

10. Greg Duncan, Martha Hill, and Saul Hoffman, "Welfare Dependence Within and Across Generations," *Science*, 239, (January 1988); and Martha Hill and Michael Ponza, "Does Welfare Dependency Beget Dependency?" Institute for Social Research, University of Michigan, mimeo. (Fall 1984).

11. Social security and Medicare are excluded from the total because their benefits are paid to eligible households regardless of the recipient's income.

12. There are other minor programs which assist the poor, including the school lunch program ($4.5 billion in 1992), the school breakfast program ($0.8 billion in 1992), the supplemental food program for women, infants, and children ($2.6 billion in 1992), and the low-income home energy assistance program ($1.5 billion in 1992). Also, the majority (69 percent in 1991) of Medicaid benefits is paid for the elderly and the disabled, see Committee on Ways and Means, U.S. House of Representatives, *Overview of Entitlement Programs—The 1993 Green Book* (Washington, DC: U.S. Government Printing Office, 1993), pp. 1633–1166; 1677–1698. The Medicaid benefits included in the $85.3 billion are only for AFDC adults and children.

13. Committee on Ways and Means, *Overview of Entitlement Programs*, p. 1603.

14. A related issue is how well the poor are able to live with public assistance. For an analysis, see Rector, "How the Poor Really Live."

15. A similar decline has been found in other studies; see Robert Moffitt, "Incentive Effects of the U.S. Welfare System: A Review," *Journal of Economic Literature*, 30, no. 1 (March 1992), 7; and Rebecca Blank, "Why Were Poverty Rates So High in the 1980s?" National Bureau of Economic Research, Working Paper No. 3878, Cambridge, MA (October 1991).

16. Medicaid benefits were deflated by the Consumer Price Index for medical care.

17. Gary Burtless, "The Economists' Lament: Public Assistance in America," *Journal of Economic Perspectives*, 4, no. 1 (Winter 1990), 57–78.

18. Similar results are found in Bureau of the Census data. The annual value of public assistance fell 7 percent in real terms for the poorest 20 percent of female-headed households with children under 18 (Bureau of the Census, *Measuring the Effect of Benefits and Taxes on Income and Poverty: 1979 to 1991*, pp. 46–50).

19. Committee on Ways and Means, *Overview of Entitlement Programs*, pp. 1588–1632.

20. Burtless, "The Economists' Lament", p. 64.

21. Gary Burtless, "The Work Response to a Guaranteed Income: A Survey of Experimental Evidence," in Alicia Munnell, *Lessons from the Income Maintenance Experiments* (Boston, MA: Federal Reserve Bank of Boston, 1987). Also see "Incentive Effects of the U.S. Welfare System: A Review" for an excellent review of other studies of work-incentive effects of welfare programs.

22. Blank also found a statistically positive link between the relative size of income transfers (measured by transfers/GNP) and the poverty rate, see Blank, "Why Were Poverty Rates So High in the 1980s?"

23. Burtless, "The Economists' Lament," p. 64.

24. A simple solution, you may say, would be to raise the minimum wage. However, as we discussed in Chapter 10, raising the minimum wage reduces the demand for labor and results in higher unemployment, particularly among low-skilled workers.

25. M. Honig, "AFDC Income, Recipient Rates, and Family Dissolution," *Journal of Human Resources*, 9 (1974), 303–322; H. L. Ross and J. Sawhill, *Time of Transition: The Growth of Families Headed by Women* (Washington, DC: The Urban Institute Press, 1975); and D. T. Ellwood and M. J. Bane, *The Impact of AFDC on Family Structure and Living Arrangements*, report prepared for the U.S. Dept. of Health and Human Services under grant No. 92A-82, John F. Kennedy School of Government, Harvard University, 1982.

26. Isabel Sawhill, "Poverty in the U.S.: Why Is It So Persistent?" *Journal of Economic Literature*, 26, no. 3 (September 1988), 1073–1119.

27. Committee on Ways and Means, *Overview of Entitlement Programs*, pp. 615–739, 1605–1632.

28. United States Dept. of Agriculture, Family Economics Research Group, *Expenditures on a Child by Families, 1992* (1993).

29. For a discussion of the evolution and politics of this consensus, see Lawrence Mead, *The New Politics of Poverty* (New York: Basic Books, 1992).

30. U.S. Bureau of the Census, Current Population Reports, Series P-60, no. 181, *Poverty in the U.S.: 1991* (Washington, DC: U.S. Government Printing Office, 1992), p. xv.

31. Ibid.

32. Judith Gveron, "Work and Welfare: Lessons on Employment Programs," *Journal of Economic Perspectives*, 4, no. 1 (Winter 1990), 81.

33. Myron Magnet, *The Dream and the Nightmare* (New York: William Morrow and Co., 1993).

34. Gveron, "Work and Welfare"; Judith Gveron and Edward Pauly, *From Welfare to Work* (New York: Russell Sage Foundation, 1991); Stephen Bell, John Enns, and Larry Orr, "The Effects of Job Training and Employment on the Earnings and Public Benefits of AFDC Recipients: The AFDC Homemaker-Home Health Aide Demonstrations," paper presented at the annual meeting of the American Economic Association (1987); and Center for Human Resources, "Food Stamp Work Registration and Job Search Demonstration," (Waltham, MA: Brandeis University, 1986).

35. Gveron, "Work and Welfare," p. 94.

36. Committee on Ways and Means, *Overview of Entitlement Programs*, pp. 642–644.

37. Ibid.

38. Ibid, p. 1609.

39. The additional resources for child care may not be substantial. Many welfare mothers will make informal arrangements for child care. See Dorothy Herbers, "Child Care," in Charles Garvin, Audrey Smith, and William Reid, eds., *The Work Incentive Experience* (Montclair, NJ: Allanheld Osmum, 1978), Ch. 10.

40. Some analysts have also worried about the accessibility of the poor to jobs, since many of the poor live in inner cities and jobs are increasingly located in suburbs, see John Kasarda, "The Regional and Urban Redistribution of People and Jobs in the U.S.," study prepared for the National Research Council, University of North Carolina, Dept. of Sociology (October 1986). However, many working low-income persons make use of car pools and public transit for transportation to and from jobs until they earn enough to buy a car. Also, studies of work programs for welfare recipients have found only minor problems with transportation, see Mead, *The New Politics of Poverty*, p. 169.

41. Time limits on receipt of welfare benefits have been proposed in at least two states, Wisconsin and California, see "Work Not Welfare," *The Wall Street Journal*, June 3, 1993, p. A14; and "Welfare Reform, California Style," *The Wall Street Journal*, February 25, 1993, p. A18.

42. Many people worry that cash assistance will result in recipients spending less on necessities, such as food, clothing, and housing. The majority of recent studies of replacing the food stamp program with cash assistance do show that recipients spend less on food when receiving cash. However, the nutrient value of the food bought by most of the cash-assisted recipients still exceeded the recommended daily allowances, see James Ohls and Harold Beebout, *The Food Stamp Program: Design Tradeoffs, Policy, and Impacts* (Washington, DC: The Urban Institute Press, June 1993).

43. The U.S. Census Bureau estimates the average household receiving Medicaid values those benefits at $2,249 annually in 1991. However, this compares to $3,762 actually spent annually on Medicaid benefits for a three-person (one adult and two children) AFDC household in 1991 and $7,579 actually spent for an elderly Medicaid recipient, see U.S. Bureau of the Census, *Measuring the Effect of Benefits and Taxes on Income and Poverty: 1979 to 1991*, p. xxi; and Committee on Ways and Means, *Overview of Entitlement Programs*, p. 1664.

44. U.S. General Accounting Office, *Homeless Mentally Ill: Problems and Options in Estimating Numbers and Trends* (Washington, DC: General Accounting Office, 1988), pp. 30–31; Peter Rossi, *Down and Out in America: The Origins of Homelessness* (Chicago: University of Chicago Press, 1989), p. 70; Martha Burt and Barbara Cohen, *America's Homeless: Numbers, Characteristics and Programs that Serve Them* (Washington, DC: The Urban Institute, 1989).

45. Committee on Health Care for Homeless People, Institute of Medicine, *Homelessness, Health, and Human Needs* (Washington, DC: National Academy Press, 1988), pp. 50–56; Interagency Council on the Homeless, *The 1989 Annual Report of the Interagency Council on the Homeless* (Washington, DC: U.S. Government Printing Office, 1989), pp. 5–11; National Institute on Alcohol Abuse and Alcoholism, "Homelessness, Alcohol, and Other Drugs," proceedings of a conference held by the U.S. Dept. of Health and Human Services in San Diego, CA, February 2–4, 1989, pp. 18–20.

46. Alice Baum and Donald Burnes, *A Nation in Denial: The Truth About Homelessness* (Boulder, CO: Westview Press, 1993), p. 141.

47. Committee on Ways and Means, *Overview of Entitlement Programs*, p. 1675.

48. Baum and Burnes, *A Nation in Denial*, p. 163.

49. Rael Jean Isaac and Virginia C. Armat, *Madness in the Streets: How Psychiatry and the Law Abandoned the Mentally Ill* (New York: The Free Press, 1990), p. 140.

50. Baum and Burnes, *A Nation in Denial*, p. 164.

51. Ibid., pp. 30–43.

52. Ibid, p. 139.

53. For one example of the impacts of rent controls on the housing market, see Lawrence Smith and Peter Tomlinson, "Rent Controls in Ontario: Roofs or Ceilings?" *Journal of the American Real Estate and Urban Economics Association*, 9, no. 2 (Summer 1981), 93–114.

54. William Tucker, *The Excluded Americans: Homelessness and Housing Policies* (Washington, DC: Regnery Gateway, 1990), pp. 34–67.

13

Solving the education puzzle

The American public education system, once held in high esteem, is in trouble. In a nutshell, the public elementary and secondary schools are thought to not be doing their job. Despite spending record amounts of money per student, the conventional wisdom holds that students aren't achieving what they should. National SAT scores are lower today than 30 years ago, and some students are graduating from high school without the skills necessary to function in today's complex society. Many citizens simply think they're not getting their money's worth in the public education system. This has created a demand for alternatives to the public education system, such as school choice and student vouchers.

Of course, an efficient and successful educational system is crucial to a nation's economy. I have documented many times the relationship between educational attainment and both a worker's compensation and a country's success in world trade. Everyone has a stake in the educational system. To the extent that the educational system is more successful, welfare spending should be lower, average incomes should be higher, and the average tax burden on everyone should be lower.

In this chapter we'll review and analyze the issues in public education. Is there an "education puzzle" created by the rise in real per pupil spending coupled with the decline in student performance, or have we reaped what we have sown in the educational system? What's really happened to student achievement? Although taxpayers have poured billions of new dollars into education in recent decades, where have these dollars gone? Have they gone into instruction or have they gone elsewhere? If we want to improve student achievement, what should be changed, and how much impact can schools really have? Finally, should the structure of public education provision in America be drastically changed? What role do school choice and education vouchers have in creating a "market" for education that will improve both efficiency and results?

WHAT'S REALLY HAPPENED TO STUDENT ACHIEVEMENT?

Most citizens base their perceptions of a decline in student achievement, and therefore by extension, a decline in the public education system, on the well-publicized decline in SAT (Scholastic Aptitude Test) scores. Indeed, between 1963 and 1980, SAT math scores fell 30 points, or 6 percent, and SAT verbal scores fell 50 points, or 11 percent. Both SAT math and verbal scores rebounded in the 1980s, but not back to 1963 levels.[1]

But the SAT is not necessarily representative of all student achievement since it is taken only by college-bound students. Charles Murray and R. J. Herrnstein, who have extensively analyzed student achievement, report on two alternative tests which are more representative of the entire student body.[2] One test called the preliminary SAT (PSAT) was administered to a nationally representative group of high school juniors between 1955 and 1983. The results show both math and verbal scores declining in the 1960s and 1970s but fully recovering by 1983. Also, when the scores of the PSAT are compared to the scores of the SAT, the scores converged in the 1970s and 1980s. That is, although college-bound students taking the SAT consistently scored higher than the "average" students taking the PSAT, the gap between the two has narrowed.

The second representative test reported by Murray and Herrnstein is the Iowa Test of Educational Development, which has been given to Iowa high school students for 50 years. Although the results are only for one state, they can show trends. The trends are clear. Student achievement improved in the 1950s and early 1960s, then declined until the late 1970s, but then fully rebounded in the 1980s. In other words, Iowa high school students were performing as well in the late 1980s as they were at their previous "best" in the mid-1960s.[3]

Another nationally representative test of student performance shows results similar to the PSAT and Iowa test. Since the early 1970s the National Assessment of Educational Progress (NAEP) test has been given to a nationally representative sample of 9-, 13-, and 17-year-old students.[4] The results tell the same story: Test scores fell in the 1970s but fully recovered in the 1980s. The NAEP test also shows that differences in test scores between white students and African-American students have considerably narrowed over the past 20 years.[5]

So the story on student achievement appears to be more complicated than the commonly accepted notion that "students aren't doing as well in school today as in the past." Results from several tests clearly show that the representative student is performing as well today as 30 years ago. (Figure 13-1 shows the performance of 17-year-olds on the NAEP test.) This is not to

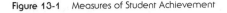
Figure 13-1   Measures of Student Achievement

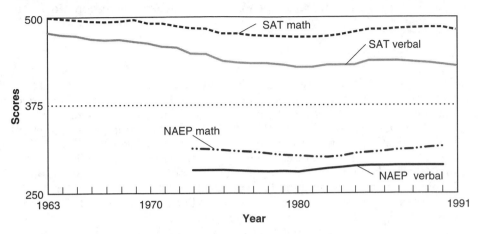

Sources: U.S. Department of Education, *Digest of Education Statistics*, Washington, DC, U.S. Government Printing Office, various issues; Congressional Budget Office, *The Federal Role in Improving Elementary and Secondary Education*, U.S. Government Printing Office, May 1993.

say that the average student is learning all he or she needs to know in today's competitive world; surely we would have liked performance to have increased. But as far as a decline in performance, it appears that it's the brightest students, that is, those college-bound students taking the SAT, where the slippage has occurred (Figure 13-1 also shows the trend in SAT scores), and the slippage has especially occurred in verbal skills. For example, the percentage of SAT takers scoring 700 or above on the verbal component fell 50 percent between 1967 and 1991.[6]

The reasons for the relative decline in academic performance by the top students are straightforward. Beginning in the late 1960s, an emphasis was placed on reaching the average and lower-performing student at the expense of the above-average student. Textbooks were reduced in difficulty and level. Some studies show that many textbooks have been reduced by two grade levels in the last 20 years.[7] This probably helped the average and below-average student at the expense of the above-average student. Teachers also stopped giving separate assignments for the academically above-average student. For example, one national survey found 84 percent of the teachers gave the same assignments to all students regardless of level.[8] As a result, academically gifted students report they are not challenged. One study found these students typically study only one hour daily.[9]

SPENDING AND RESOURCES: WE HAVE REAPED WHAT WE HAVE SOWN

The first rule in studying any issue or problem is to follow the money trail. If this is done in public education, then the student achievement results described in the previous section make a lot of sense. Let's examine where the public schools' two main resources, spending and teachers, have gone in recent decades.

Spending

There's no lack of spending on public elementary and secondary education. Expressed in real 1992 dollars, spending per pupil (exclusive of capital spending and interest on school debt) rose from $1,635 in 1960 to $2,740 in 1970 to $3,707 in 1980 and to $5,099 in 1991. Real spending per pupil rose 68 percent in the 1960s, 35 percent in the 1970s, and 37 percent in the 1980s.[10]

But not all educational spending is allocated to instruction (teacher salaries and benefits, textbooks and library books, and teaching supplies). Noninstructional spending, that is, spending on administration, plant maintenance, transportation, and student services like the cafeteria, is taking an increasing share of total per pupil spending. For example, in 1960, noninstructional spending per pupil was 32 percent of total spending per pupil. By 1991, noninstructional spending per pupil was 40 percent of total spending per pupil. Looked at another way, from 1970 to 1990, total real spending per pupil rose 85 percent, but real noninstructional spending per pupil rose 134 percent and instructional spending per pupil rose 62 percent.[11]

The spending story doesn't end here. In the past two decades there has been a concerted effort to provide more help to handicapped and educationally disadvantaged students. In 1988, $24 billion was spent nationwide on public elementary and secondary education for handicapped, special education, and low-income students out of a total education budget of $157 billion.[12] Prior to 1965, virtually no funds were spent on these special populations of students. In contrast, in 1990, $400 million was spent nationwide on academically advanced ("gifted and talented") students.[13]

The reason this distinction in spending is important is because it costs much more per pupil to educate a handicapped or special education student. For example, in 1988, instructional costs per handicapped or special education student were $5,203 compared to $2,895 per other student (expenditures in 1992 dollars).[14] Since the passage of the Education of the Handicapped Act in 1975, which mandated that disabled children be given "free, appropriate education designed to meet their individually determined needs", the number of students classified as handicapped or requiring special education has increased from 3.7 million in 1977 to 4.9 million in 1991.[15] This increase occurred at a time when the number of all public elementary and secondary students declined by over 3 million.

Therefore, to know how real instructional spending per nonhandicapped student has changed, we must subtract the resources spent on handicapped and special education students. Unfortunately, data for handicapped and special education spending are only available from school year 1982–83 to school year 1987–88. Using these data, real instructional spending per nonhandicapped and nonspecial education pupil (termed *adjusted instructional spending per pupil*) is calculated to have increased from $1,981 in 1982–83 to $2,355 in 1987–88 (all in 1992 dollars).[16] The per pupil instructional spending

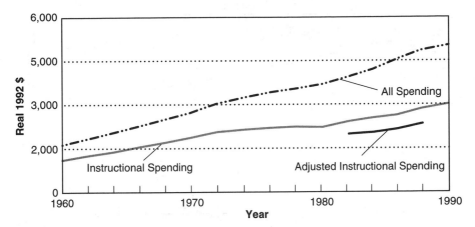

Source: U.S. Dept. of Education; author's calculations.

Figure 13-2   Measures of Real Instructional Spending per Pupil

of $2,355 in 1987–88 is $540 less the per pupil instructional spending if adjustments aren't made for handicapped and other special spending.

Figure 13-2 summarizes these alternative measures of educational spending. All measures show real per pupil spending increasing. But the rate of increase is much less if only instructional spending is considered, and the rate of increase is even less if per pupil instructional spending is considered for only nonhandicapped and nonspecial education students. Indeed, compared to 1964, before targeted spending for special student populations began, adjusted per pupil spending was 67 percent higher in 1988, compared to 106 percent higher if all instructional spending per pupil is compared.

Teachers

Teachers are the major resource of the educational system. In addition to real instructional spending per pupil, the other major measure of resource commitment to education is the pupil/teacher ratio. Lower teacher/pupil ratios indicate more teacher time being devoted to each student.

There has been a dramatic decline in the overall pupil/teacher ratio (see Figure 13-3). The national pupil/teacher ratio has declined from 26 in 1960 to 23 in 1970 to 19 in 1980 to 17 in 1990.[17] From this trend we would have expected a noticeable improvement in student academic performance. But, as already discussed, at best average student performance has stagnated over the past 30 years.

Yet there's the same problem in looking at overall pupil/teacher ratios as there is in looking at overall instructional spending per pupil. Both the Elementary and Secondary Education Act of 1965 (so-called "Chapter 1") and the Education of the Handicapped Act of 1975 have resulted in many teachers being hired to specifically teach handicapped and special education stu-

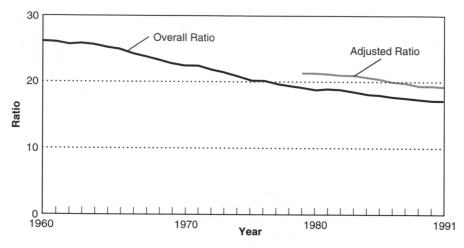

Source: U.S. Dept. of Education; author's calculations.

Figure 13-3   Pupil/Teacher Ratios

dents, and to teach students from low-income households. Usually these teachers instruct small groups of students (groups much smaller than the number of students in regular classrooms) for limited time periods in the day. That is, the targeted students are "pulled" from their regular classroom for perhaps 30 minutes daily for instruction in small groups by the resource teacher.

Therefore, the overall pupil/teacher ratio has, in part, declined since 1965 because it has included large numbers of resource teachers who instruct small groups of targeted students for part of the school day. What we'd like to know is how the pupil/teacher ratio has changed for the teachers and students who are not part of these targeted groups.

Figure 13-3 shows an adjusted pupil/teacher ratio, which takes out the handicapped and special education teachers and students from the overall pupil/teacher ratio. Unfortunately, data to construct the adjusted ratio are available only for the 1980s. The adjusted pupil/teacher ratio is designed to show the average number of students taught by a teacher who has not been hired to service the handicapped and special education student.[18]

As with the adjusted real instructional spending per pupil numbers discussed in the previous section, the adjusted pupil/teacher ratio shows a downward trend. However, the levels of the adjusted pupil/teacher ratios are approximately two students per teacher higher than the levels of the overall pupil/teacher ratios. Also, rather than being one-third lower than the pupil/teacher ratio in 1964 (before the targeted teacher programs were begun), the adjusted pupil/teacher ratio in 1991 is one-fourth lower than in 1964.

So the bottom line for this section is this. Resources devoted to public elementary and secondary education have increased over the past two decades, but a large amount of these resources have been devoted to noninstruction, and within instruction, a substantial amount has been devoted to targeted student populations, specifically handicapped students and students from poverty areas. In a sense then, we have reaped what we have sown in the public education system. The targeted spending has apparently helped improve the performance of poorer-performing students.

Nevertheless, after accounting for these allocations of resources, resources devoted to the instruction of nonhandicapped and nonpoor students have still increased. Why, therefore, hasn't achievement of the average student increased more, and why have the top students' performance slipped? To answer this question, we must look at the *education production function*.

THE EDUCATION PRODUCTION FUNCTION

Economists typically look at the relationship between output and the inputs used to produce that output in the form of a production function. For example, the production function for corn relates the output of corn on a farm measured in bushels of corn to the inputs of seed, fertilizer, rainfall, soil nutrients, and pest control. Economists are interested in how changes in the inputs affect the output. That is, in our corn example, agricultural economists try to measure the effect of changing seed varieties, of varying levels of fertilizers, and of differing levels of rainfall on the output of corn.

Student educational achievement measured by scores on standardized tests can also be considered in a production function format.[19] In this format, student educational achievement is not only related to the inputs of spending and the pupil/teacher ratio, but also to other inputs like the home environment of the student, the disciplinary condition of the classroom, the amount of student time spent on homework, the amount of student time spent on competing activities like television, and the relative number of academic courses taken by the student. Studies have found these other inputs determine 65 to 85 percent of student achievement, leaving only 15 to 35 percent determined by the traditional school inputs of instructional spending per student and the teacher/pupil ratio.[20] The point is that student achievement could stagnate or decline, even if spending and the teacher/pupil ratio are improving, if the other inputs affecting student achievement are deteriorating. So let's see what's happened to all the inputs of the education production function.

The Traditional Inputs

The traditional inputs of the education production function are real spending per student in instruction and the pupil/teacher ratio. The expectation is that student academic achievement should increase with increases in these two inputs.

But perhaps surprising to you, all studies which have examined the relationships between student achievement and spending per student and the pupil/teacher ratio have not found a positive impact on achievement of these two traditional inputs. In a comprehensive review of these studies, Hanushek found only 20 percent of the studies showing a positive relationship between student achievement and per pupil spending, and found only 8 percent of the studies showing a positive relationship between student achievement and the teacher/pupil ratio.[21]

However, not all of the studies are careful to separate the impacts of instructional spending and noninstructional spending. One study that did found a positive impact of instructional spending per student on student achievement and found a negative impact of noninstructional spending per student on achievement; that is, increasing instructional spending for each student improves performance, but increasing noninstructional spending for each student decreases performance![22] This finding obviously raises concerns about the tremendous increase in noninstructional spending in the public schools during the last three decades.

Likewise, a study which was careful to separately consider the impacts on student performance of teachers, teacher assistants, and nonteachers found some interesting results. More teachers per pupil (that is, a lower pupil/teacher ratio) was found to raise student performance. But the number of teacher assistants per pupil had no impact on student performance, and increases in the number of nonteachers per pupil was found to *decrease* student performance.[23]

How could an increase in nonteachers per pupil in the school system actually decrease student performance? Easy—ask any public school teacher. Nonteachers, such as central office bureaucrats and staff, can impose costs on teachers by requiring workshops, meetings, and seemingly endless completion of forms. These activities take time from teachers which could be used for teaching or lesson preparation.

So simply throwing more money and personnel into the education system won't necessarily pay off in higher student achievement. In fact, adding nonteaching personnel and noninstructional spending may actually be counterproductive and reduce what students learn!

Home Environment

There is substantial evidence that the socioeconomic status of families affects the academic performance of children. One study found that 58 percent of the student test scores was determined by the socioeconomic status of the students' families.[24] On average, students from poor families and students from one-parent families have more difficulty in school than students from non-poor families and students from two-parent families.[25]

On both of these measures, recent statistics indicate the student population has become more difficult to teach. The percentage of children living in poverty has trended upward since 1970, after declining in the 1960s (Figure 13-4).[26] But more revealing, the percentage of children living in single-parent families has more than doubled in 30 years, increasing from 10 percent in 1959 to 22 percent in 1990 (Figure 13-4).[27] This last trend is very important because surveys show that single parents spend significantly less time helping their children with homework than do families with two parents.[28]

Another major social trend has been the dramatic increase in mothers of school-age children who work outside the home. In 1970, 43 percent of school-age children had mothers in the labor force; by 1984 this rate had risen

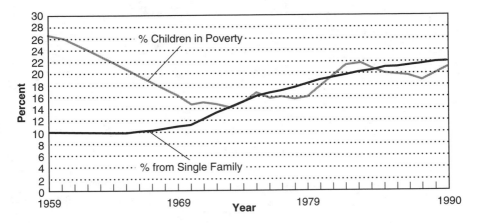

Sources: U.S. Bureau of the Census, *Statistical Abstract of the United States, 1992,* Washington,
DC, U.S. Government Printing Office, 1993; U.S. Department of Education, *Digest of Education
Statistics,* Washington, DC, U.S. Government Printing Office, various issues.

Figure 13-4   Changes in Socioeconomic Status of Children

to 60 percent.[29] However, a comprehensive review of the literature found no
consistent negative impact of this trend on student achievement.[30]

Finally, drug and alcohol use by students increased in the 1960s and
1970s and peaked in 1978.[31] This greater use could have contributed to some
of the decline in student achievement in the 1970s.[32] Fortunately, student drug
use declined in the 1980s.[33]

Disciplinary Environment

There is evidence that the more time spent by a teacher on disciplinary matters, the lower the achievement level of students. This makes sense because
the more time spent by a teacher on discipline, the less time available for teaching.[34]

What's happened to the disciplinary environment of the public
schools? The conventional wisdom (that is, the opinion of the average woman
and man on the street) is that the disciplinary environment has deteriorated.
The conventional wisdom seems to be confirmed from both teachers and students. In 1987, 44 percent of teachers surveyed reported that disruptive behavior was greater in that year compared to five years earlier, while only 27
percent reported disruptive behavior as lower in 1987 than in 1982.[35]

From students, one measure of the disciplinary environment is the
percentage of students reporting theft of their property in school. This measure tends to be cyclical, falling when the economy is improving and rising
when the economy is in recession. Nevertheless, Figure 13-5 shows this measure has trended upward in the 1980s compared to the 1970s.

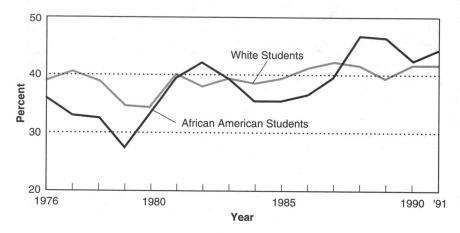

Source: U.S. Department of Education, *The Condition of Education, 1993,* Table 50.

Figure 13-5   Percentage of High School Seniors Reporting Thefts

What's the cause of this deterioration in the school disciplinary environment? Certainly some school disciplinary problems are related to the socioeconomic status of families, child abuse, and drug abuse. But school policies about student discipline also have an impact on the incentives of students to behave or misbehave. The facts are that both court rulings and administrative decisions by school boards have reduced the ability of the public schools to deal with disciplinary problems in a timely manner. This has reduced the cost to students of misbehaving. Since students respond to incentives like anyone else, if the cost of misbehaving is reduced, then misbehavior will increase.

What court rulings contributed to this? The most important was a U.S. Supreme Court ruling in 1975, which gave students the right to due process. The Supreme Court said students charged with misbehavior had to be given oral or written notice of the charges. If they denied the charges, they had to be given an explanation of the evidence against them and a chance to counter the evidence. Obviously, this ruling has increased the time and effort required of teachers and administrators to discipline students. In some cases, this has probably deterred teachers and administrators from taking disciplinary action against students, and in other cases the new policy has certainly taken time and effort away from academic duties.

With heightened attention to child abuse, school boards around the country have reduced the ability of schools to use corporal punishment (spanking) as a disciplinary device. Increasingly, teachers must use other disciplinary measures, such as "time-out" rooms, the removal of class privileges, or reasoning to deal with misbehavior. Although spanking can certainly be abused, it has the advantage of being swift and distasteful to most students. Alternatives, such as time spent in the "time-out" room, may not phase the student who is uninterested in learning and, therefore, would not be a major deterrent to this student.

Time Use by Students

The amount of time spent by students in schooling is a crucial input in the education production function. It doesn't take any fancy economic modeling to conclude that the more time spent by students on academic subjects, the better should be their academic performance.

Two types of time use by students are important in impacting their academic performance. First is time use in the classroom, particularly in the types of courses taken. Second is time use outside the classroom in terms of time spent on homework and other competing activities. Let's see how each has changed.

There's bad news, but then good news, about time use by students in the classroom. Between 1969 and 1982, there was a 7 percent decline in the number of academic courses taken by white students.[36] There was no change over this time period in the number of academic courses taken by African-American students. However, between 1982 and 1987, there was a full recovery to 1969 levels in the number of academic courses taken by white students, and the number of academic courses taken by African-American students also increased. So a very straightforward explanation for the decline in academic achievement in the 1970s, at least among white students, is their reduction in classroom time taking academic courses.

The published trends on homework have actually been encouraging. For example, the percentage of 17-year-olds reporting they had no homework or they didn't do their homework declined from 45 percent in 1978 to 14.8 percent in 1990, and the percentage of 17-year-olds reporting they spent more than two hours nightly on homework rose from 0 percent in 1978 to 13 percent in 1990.[37]

Some studies have found that time spent by students watching television is a more important determinant of achievement than is time spent on homework.[38] Here, unfortunately, the statistics aren't as encouraging, although there are some positive trends. Television viewing among 17-year-olds has continued to trend upward. For example, the percentage of 17-year-olds who watch television six hours or more daily almost doubled from 1978 to 1990, rising from 4.8 percent to 8.5 percent. Likewise, the percentage of 17-year-olds watching television between three and five hours daily rose 15 percentage points over the same time period.[39]

However, among younger children, television viewing at least seems to have leveled off, although it is still substantial. In 1990, 69 percent of 13-year-olds and 63 percent of 9-year-olds watched three or more hours of television daily. These percentages are higher than the rates in 1982 but are lower than the rates in 1986.[40] So there's been some improvement (that is, decrease) in television viewing among younger children in the late 1980s, but the time spent is still high.

Even after adjusting for money and teachers targeted for special groups of students, real instructional spending per student and the pupil/teacher ratio have still improved in the past two decades. Why, then, hasn't student performance improved more? The answer is straightforward: Many of the other factors which influence student performance have changed in a way which would reduce student performance. The characteristics of students' families make them harder to teach today. The disciplinary environment of schools has deteriorated. Finally, many students have devoted less time to academic courses and more time to television viewing.

So in light of these other factors and changes, we could conclude that the public school system has actually been doing a good job just to keep average student performance constant over the past 30 years. But is what we're now doing enough? Are there no other structural changes which could be made in public education to improve the performance outcomes? Well, read on; these are the subjects of our next section.

ALTERNATIVES TO THE PUBLIC SCHOOL MONOPOLY

Public schools are virtual monopolies funded by taxpayers. A monopoly occurs when a single firm supplies a product or service in a market, and that firm faces no competition. Although there are private alternatives to public schools, the practical fact is that most families aren't willing to pay both taxes to support public schools and fees for a private school. This puts public schools into a virtual monopoly position in which they're the only provider of elementary and secondary education. Typically, a local public school system assigns students to a particular public school within the system or gives limited choice to school selection.

So what's wrong, you're thinking, with public schools being monopolies? There are three problems. First, economic theory predicts that monopolies will charge higher prices and produce less output than a firm which must compete with other firms for business.[41] Studies comparing public schools and private schools do find spending per student (a proxy for price) higher in public schools.[42]

The second problem with the public school monopoly is efficiency. Publicly supported monopolies don't have the same motivation to use resources efficiently as do firms who must compete for customers. Firms operating in a competitive market can only charge what the market will bear, that is, what customers are willing to pay. Such firms, therefore, are motivated to eliminate all unnecessary costs in an attempt to underprice competitors and attract more customers.

Publicly supported monopolies don't worry about keeping prices low because there are no competing firms. Instead, publicly supported monopolies begin by calculating what costs they deem necessary to provide the product or service, and then they try to convince public bodies (e.g., school boards) to fund these costs. However, because there's no competitor threatening to take away customers, there's no assurance the public monopoly will choose only necessary inputs and, therefore, there's no assurance the public monopoly won't include unnecessary costs.

Indeed, concern about the efficiency of public schools is indicated by the already noted substantial rise in noninstructional spending. If noninstructional spending per student had been kept at its 1960 level, then per pupil spending in 1992 would have been $1,500 lower. Economists Gary Anderson,

William Shughart, and Robert Tollison have speculated that the increase in noninstructional staff has been a result of income-maximizing behavior by public school administrators. Their argument goes like this. If school administrators' incomes are, in part, based on the size of the staff they control, then administrators may have an incentive to put additional resources into increasing their staff rather than putting those resources into the classroom.[43]

The third problem with the public school monopoly is limited choice. The public school bureaucracy has an inclination to impose the same structure and standards on all teachers and students—sort of a one-size-fits-all philosophy. In contrast, in a system where many firms are competing for customers, there's a natural drive for each firm to innovate and try new techniques. Each competing firm is constantly trying to find a new process, service, or product which customers will prefer and which the firm can use to attract new customers and make more money. With customers "up for grabs," competing firms are always trying to "build a better mousetrap." Although public monopolies may talk about improving service and output, with a captive clientele they just don't have the same drive to do so.

So how do we correct these problems with the public school monopoly structure? The answer is to develop a new structure which promotes competition in elementary and secondary education by giving choice to parents and students. Completely privatizing the public schools would be one way to accomplish this. Allow parents to keep the average $5,000 they pay annually in taxes to educate each child. Then let parents decide how much to spend on their children's education and to choose their children's schools. For poor parents who can't afford to spend $5,000 per child on education, income subsidies could be provided. This system would make education just like any other private market transaction. Parents could exercise their own tastes and preferences in education for their children. Parents would also have a strong incentive to monitor their children's education, since the parents' money (and not the government's money) is on the line.

One problem with the total privatization of elementary and secondary education is the positive externality aspect of education. A positive externality is a by-product of actions by an individual which have positive impacts on other individuals. With education, obviously the individual (call this person Joe) receiving the education benefits from that training. These benefits are usually in the form of a higher salary than without the education. But other people also benefit from Joe's education. They benefit from the greater work productivity that follows from Joe's greater education, from the higher taxes that Joe will pay with his greater salary, and from the reduced chance that Joe will need public assistance (welfare).

If education is totally privatized, the concern is that individuals won't acquire as much education as is socially desirable because they won't take into account the positive benefits that flow to others as a result of their education. This concern has been a major reason for the public funding and provision of elementary and secondary education (and, incidently, for the substantial public subsidies to higher education).

The most direct way to maintain the public funding of elementary and secondary education (therefore accounting for education's positive externalities) and at the same time to introduce competition and choice into the system is to establish a voucher system. Under a voucher system, the government would still tax citizens for funding of elementary and secondary education. However, these tax revenues would be returned on a per student basis to parents in the form of education vouchers. (For example, each parent would receive a voucher worth $5,000 for each child.) Parents could only use the vouchers to pay for education. However, parents could spend the vouchers on any school they chose for their children.

Therefore, under the voucher system, schools would act as individual firms competing for students. No school would be assured of a captive clientele. Schools would compete for customers (e.g., students), and schools which couldn't attract and keep customers would have to change or go out of business.

The voucher system would promote efficiency in schools. If the ABC School costs more than the XYZ School, and both schools deliver the same services, then the ABC School will have to use its resources (teachers, staff, classrooms) more efficiently in order to survive. If, as many suspect, the current public schools have a bloated bureaucracy which doesn't contribute to student achievement (and may even impede student achievement), then in a structure of school choice, schools will be motivated to eliminate this inefficient use of resources.

The voucher system would also promote innovation and experimentation in the schools. In order to attract customers, schools would be motivated to try new teaching techniques, to design courses which best meet parents' and students' needs, and to constantly monitor the satisfaction of their customers (parents and students) with the schools' performance. Under a voucher system, many schools would specialize in teaching certain kinds of children (the handicapped, the unruly child) and in teaching certain kinds of curriculum (international studies, vocational subjects, math and science).[44]

The voucher system of promoting choice and competition in schools is not without its critics. Let me deal with each of the major criticisms separately:

1. Vouchers favor the rich: Critics charge that vouchers favor the rich because the rich will be able to supplement the vouchers and send their children to elite schools. In response, voucher supporters counter that, without vouchers, only the rich can afford to send their children to private schools. With vouchers, all parents can choose schools, and the common interests of parents of all income levels can easily result in children of many income levels studying together.

2. Vouchers will promote fraud: With the government not directly running the schools, won't some "schools" run by unsavory characters simply take parents' money and then not teach children anything? In other words, won't there be some "rotten apples" in the marketplace of schools which some parents will be unfortunate to "bite into"?

This criticism can easily be handled by requiring schools in the education marketplace to be licensed by a governmental body, much like stock brokerage firms, insurance companies, and restaurants are licensed. The license would have to be periodically renewed.

3. The voucher system will hurt handicapped students: Voucher critics are concerned about handicapped students in a voucher system. As documented earlier, handicapped students cost almost twice as much annually to educate as do nonhandicapped students. If all parents receive the same voucher amount, won't handicapped students not be able to receive the services they need?

The answer to this concern is also simple. Vouchers can be higher for handicapped students, thereby allowing their parents to shop for and pay for the needed services.

4. Competition in the voucher system will only occur for elite schools and for students from high-income parents: In other words, this criticism says competition will only occur at the "high end" of the education spectrum, and there will be no competition for average and poor students and for students from low-income parents.

The response to this criticism is to cite experiences from other markets. For example, in the restaurant market, we don't observe competition only at the high end, that is, among the four- and five-star restaurants. We also observe stiff competition at the low-cost end; for example, we observe perhaps the greatest competition among McDonald's, Wendy's, and Hardees. The same is true in most other markets. Look at the retailing market. The greatest competition in recent years has occurred between the large discount retailers like Wal-Mart and K mart, and among the discount warehouses like Sam's and Pace. We would expect the same kind of competition among all ranges of the education market.

5. The voucher system will encourage segregation of students by race and ability: This is perhaps the most serious of the criticisms of the voucher system. With the ability of parents to choose schools for their children, the concern is that parents will be motivated to choose schools which cater to children of similar ability and similar race. This would reduce the role of the elementary and secondary schools as "melting pots," where children of all abilities and races interact and learn about the others' viewpoints.

The voucher system probably will encourage specialization by student academic ability. But this already occurs in the public schools. Students are frequently grouped by ability for reading and math classes. Teaching is often more effective if the class is homogeneous in ability than if the class is composed of students of widely differing abilities. If there are societal benefits to having students of differing abilities in the same classroom, these benefits must be weighed against the benefits of homogeneous grouping in teaching.

The issue of whether racial segregation will result from the voucher system is more difficult to address. Research on whether African-American students have benefitted from integrated classrooms with white students is inconsistent and controversial.[45] Nevertheless, if a sufficient number of African-American parents and white parents value and prefer integrated schools, then the education marketplace will respond. Indeed, racial relations would likely improve if parents are able to freely choose racially mixed schools for their children. Also, with parents motivated to find the best school for their children under the voucher system, this common drive for excellence will in many cases likely overcome racial concerns.

FINAL THOUGHTS

Our elementary and secondary school system is neither as bad as many think nor as good as it could be. Average student performance fell in the 1970s but fully rebounded in the 1980s. Minority students have improved their performance, but academic achievement of the top students has dropped.

In some sense, these results have directly followed the placement of resources. During the past 25 years, resources (both money and teachers) devoted to handicapped students and to students from poverty backgrounds have dramatically increased. Textbooks and other teaching materials have also been altered to be more accessible to average and lower-performing students. Consequently, top-achieving students have been less challenged.

The increasing amount of resources devoted to noninstructional inputs in the public schools (administrators, other bureaucrats, and so on) is also disturbing. This trend is consistent with the prediction by some economists of "empire building" in public bureaucracies, in which resources are devoted to activities unrelated to the stated mission (here, student achievement) of the public agency.[46] The conclusion is that the public schools are not using their resources in the most efficient manner.

Other factors and changes during the past 20 years, both inside and outside the classroom, have also affected student performance. Changes in family structure, in time use by students, and in discipline within the schools have probably had adverse effects on student achievement.

Obviously, we must worry about the external factors affecting student performance such as family structure, violence, and student time use (i.e., television viewing). But the resources now being devoted to education would be used more efficiently, and would be more responsive to parental desires, if the public school monopoly were ended. A way to do this is to make schools compete for students by introducing publicly funded education vouchers. Education vouchers would create a school marketplace which has all the advantages of any marketplace such as constant innovation and attempts to improve performance, elimination of wasteful expenditures, and attention to the needs and desires of the customer (parents and students). Some may say that education is too important to leave to a competitive market. The contrary response is that education is too important *not* to leave to the competitive market.

NOTES

1. The College Board.
2. Charles Murray and R. J. Herrnstein, "What's Really Behind the SAT-Score Decline?" *The Public Interest* no. 106 (Winter 1992), pp. 32–56.
3. Murray and Herrnstein also investigate whether the decline in the SAT can be accounted for by the "democratization" of the SAT, that is, more students from disadvantaged backgrounds are taking the SAT. However, the authors performed statistical analyses to adjust for changes in the socioeconomic status (parental education, gender, race) of SAT takers and found no difference in adjusted SAT scores and actual scores.
4. Congressional Budget Office, *The Federal Role in Improving Elementary and Secondary Education* (Washington, DC: U.S. Government Printing Office, May 1993).
5. For example, for 13-year-olds, the difference in math scores between white students and African-American students fell from 45 points in 1973 to 28 points in

1990, and the difference in reading scores fell from 40 points in 1973 to 21 points in 1990 (Ibid., pp. 14–15).

6. U.S. Department of Education, *Digest of Education Statistics* (Washington, DC: U.S. Government Printing Office, various editions). Also, the number of students with high scores (over 600) on the verbal SAT declined by 40 percent between 1972 and 1989, and the number of high scorers on the math SAT hasn't increased since 1972. See Office of Educational Research and Improvement, U.S. Department of Education, *National Excellence: A Case for Developing America's Talent* (Washington, DC: U.S. Government Printing Office, October 1993).

7. Office of Educational Research and Improvement, *National Excellence*, p. 19.

8. Ibid., p. 20.

9. Ibid., p. 21.

10. U.S. Department of Education, *Dept. of Education Statistics* (Washington, DC: U.S. Government Printing Office, 1993).

11. Ibid.

12. Office of Special Education Programs, U.S. Department of Education, *Fourteenth Annual Report to Congress on Implementation of the Individuals with Disabilities Act* (Washington, DC: U.S. Government Printing Office, 1992); U.S. Department of Education, *Digest of Education Statistics*, 1993.

13. Office of Educational Research and Improvement, U.S. Department of Education, *National Excellence*, p. 18.

14. Handicapped per pupil expenditures calculated from Office of Special Education Programs, U.S. Department of Education, *Fourteenth Annual Report to Congress*.

15. U.S. Department of Education, *Digest of Education Statistics*.

16. The adjusted per pupil spending formula is: (total instructional spending – handicapped spending – Chap. 1 spending)/[total pupils – (proportion of handicapped pupils self contained or in regular classroom ¥ number handicapped) – (proportion of handicapped in separate classroom ¥ number handicapped) – (proportion of school day that Chap. 1 pupils are in separate classroom ¥ number Chap. 1 pupils)]. The proportion of handicapped in separate or regular classrooms is 0.51 (Office of Special Education Programs); the proportion of handicapped in separate classroom for part of the day is 0.41 (Office of Special Education Programs); the proportion of school day in separate classroom for handicapped and Chapter 1 pupils is 0.10. See U.S. Department of Education, Office of Policy and Planning, *The Chapter 1 Implementations Study* (Cambridge, MA: Abt Associates, 1993).

17. U.S. Department of Education, *Digest of Education Statistics*.

18. The adjusted pupil/teacher ratio formula is similar to the formula in footnote 16.

19. For a discussion of issues in applying the production function idea to education, see Eric Hanushek, "Conceptual and Empirical Issues in the Estimation of Educational Production Functions," *Journal of Human Resources*, 14, no. 3 (Summer 1979), 351–388.

20. Congressional Budget Office, *The Federal Role in Improving Elementary and Secondary Education*, p. 22.

21. Eric Hanushek, "The Economics of Schooling: Production and Efficiency in Public Schools," *Journal of Economic Literature*, 24, no. 3 (September 1986), 1141–1177. The results cited are for only the "statistically significant" associations—those which are so strong that they could not have happened by chance. If all positive associations between student achievement and per pupil spending are included, then this occurred in 58 percent of the studies, and if all positive associations between stu-

dent achievement and the teacher/pupil ratio are included, then this occurred in 30 percent of the studies.

22. Frederick Sebold and William Dato, "School Funding and Student Achievement: An Empirical Analysis," *Public Finance Quarterly*, 9, no. 1 (January 1981), 91–106.

23. Gary Anderson, William Shughart II, and Robert Tollison, "Educational Achievement and the Cost of Bureaucracy," *Journal of Economic Behavioral Organization*, 15, no. 1 (January 1991), 29–45.

24. Scott Callan and Rexford Santerre, "The Production Characteristics of Local Public Education: A Multiple Product and Input Analysis," *Southern Economic Journal*, 57, no. 2 (October 1990), 468–480.

25. Ibid.; E. M. Hetherington, K. A. Camara, and D. A. Featherman, "Achievement and Intellectual Functioning of Children in One-Parent Households," in J. T. Spence, ed., *Achievement and Achievement Motives: Psychological and Sociological Approaches* (San Francisco, W. H. Freeman, 1984).

26. U.S. Department of Education, *Digest of Education Statistics*.

27. U.S. Bureau of the Census, *Statistical Abstract of the United States, 1992* (Washington, DC: U.S. Government Printing Office, 1993).

28. Twenty-eight percent of two-parent families reported never or seldom helping with homework compared to 36 percent of one-parent families, see U.S. Department of Education, *Digest of Education Statistics, 1993*.

29. Congressional Budget Office, *Educational Achievement: Explanations and Implications of Recent Trends* (Washington, DC: Government Printing Office, August 1987), p. 66.

30. C. D. Haynes and S. B. Kamerman, eds., *Children of Working Parents: Experiences and Outcomes* (Washington, DC: National Academy Press, 1983), p. 221.

31. Congressional Budget Office, *Educational Achievement: Explanations and Implications of Recent Trends*, p. 68.

32. Ibid.

33. U.S. Department of Education, *Digest of Education Statistics, 1993*.

34. Eric Hanushek, "Teacher Characteristics and Gains in Student Achievement: Estimations Using Micro Data," *American Economic Review*, 61, no. 2 (May 1971), 280–288.

35. U.S. Department of Education, *Digest of Education Statistics, 1991*.

36. Academic courses are measured in Carnegie units, which give one credit for finishing a one-hour, one-year course. See Congressional Budget Office, *The Federal Role in Improving Elementary and Secondary Education*, p. 31.

37. U.S. Department of Education, National Center for Education Statistics, *The Coalition of Education, 1993* (Washington, DC: U.S. Government Printing Office, 1993).

38. Yao-Chi-Lu and Luther Tweeten, "The Impact of Busing on Student Achievement," *Growth and Change*, 4, no. 4 (October 1973), 44–46; and Barbara Zoloth, "The Impact of Busing on Student Achievement: Re-analysis," *Growth and Change*, 7, no. 3 (July 1976), 50–51. See also Robert Hornick, "Out-of-School Television and Schooling: Hypotheses and Methods," *Review of Educational Research*, 51 (Summer 1981), 193–214.

39. U.S. Department of Education, National Center for Education Statistics, *The Condition of Education 1993*.

40. Ibid.

41. See any standard microeconomics text such as Robert Frank, *Microeconomics and Behavior* (New York: McGraw-Hill, 1991), pp. 370–413.

42. This result holds even after accounting for higher salaries in public schools and the fact that public schools must deal more with students having disabilities, language problems, and other disadvantages. See Robert Genetski, "Private Schools, Public Savings, *The Wall Street Journal*, July 8, 1992, p. A10; Randall Fitzgerald, *When Government Goes Private: Successful Alternatives to Public Services* (New York: "Educational Achievement and the Cost of Bureaucracy." Universe Books, 1988), pp. 139–148.

43. Anderson, Shughart, and Tollison, Bergstrom, Roberts, Rubinfeld, and Shapiro [Theodore Bergstrom, Judith Roberts, Daniel Rubinfold, and Perry Shapiro, "A Test for Efficiency in the Supply of Public Education," *Journal of Public Economics*, 35, no. 3 (April 1988), 289–307] have also found evidence of inefficiencies in the provision of public education.

44. Voucher systems are in practice in several states, including New Hampshire and Wisconsin.

45. Thomas D. Cook, "What Have Black Children Gained Academically from School Integration?: Examination of the Meta-analytic Evidence," in Thomas D. Cook, David Armor, Robert Crain, Norman Miller, Watter Stephan, Herbert Walberg, and Paul Wortman, *School Desegregation and Black Achievement* (Washington, DC: U.S. Department of Education, May 1984).

46. William Niskanen, Jr., *Bureaucracy and Representative Government* (New York: Aldine, Atherton, 1971).

Appendices

Table A   Money Income of *Households*ª % Distribution

| | ALL HOUSEHOLDS | | |
	UNDER $15,000	$15,000–$49,999	$50,000 AND OVER
1970	25.7%	57.5%	16.8%
1975	27.2	55.5	17.3
1980	27.5	55.0	17.6
1985	27.4	52.5	20.1
1986	26.6	51.8	21.5
1987	26.2	51.4	22.3
1988	26.1	51.2	22.7
1989	25.3	51.1	23.5
	AFRICAN-AMERICAN HOUSEHOLDS		
1970	43.3%	49.8%	6.9%
1975	45.5	47.9	6.6
1980	47.1	45.8	7.1
1985	46.0	45.0	9.0
1986	45.7	45.0	9.4
1987	45.6	44.3	10.0
1988	45.6	43.3	11.1
1989	43.2	45.4	11.5

ªRanges are in 1989 dollars.

Source: U.S. Dept. of Commerce, *Statistical Abstract of the United States, 1991*, 11th ed. (Washington, DC: U.S. Government Printing Office, 1991), Table 721.

Table B   Money Income of *Families*° % Distribution

| | ALL FAMILIES | | |
	UNDER $15,000	$15,000–$49,999	$50,000 AND OVER
1970	17.5%	62.8%	19.6%
1975	18.4	60.5	20.9
1980	18.8	59.3	21.8
1985	19.7	55.5	24.7
1986	18.9	54.5	26.6
1987	18.3	54.2	27.5
1988	18.4	53.5	27.9
1989	18.0	52.9	29.0
	AFRICAN-AMERICAN FAMILIES		
1970	36.6%	55.5%	8.0%
1975	38.1	53.7	8.3
1980	40.3	50.6	9.2
1985	40.0	49.1	10.9
1986	39.7	48.4	12.0
1987	39.1	48.4	12.6
1988	39.7	46.1	14.3
1989	38.5	47.6	13.8

°Ranges are in 1989 dollars.

Source: U.S. Dept. of Commerce, *Statistical Abstract of the United States, 1991*, 11th ed. (Washington, DC: U.S. Government Printing Office, 1991), Table 729.

Table C   Income Distribution of Households, Following the Same Households (1989 $)

	UNDER $15,000	$15,000–$49,999	$50,000 AND OVER
1967	26%	59%	15%
1970	25	57	18
1975	26	55	19
1980	26	54	20
1981	27	54	19
1982	27	55	18
1983	28	52	20
1984	27	52	21
1985	27	51	22
1986	25	52	23

Source: Greg J. Duncan, Timothy M. Smeeding, and Willard Rodgers, *W(h)ither The Middle Class? A Dynamic View*, paper prepared for the Levy Institute Conference on Income Inequality, Bard College, June 18–20, p. 5.

Table D   Total Government (Federal, State, Local) Spending in Millions of 1989 $

YEAR	DEFENSE AND INTERNATIONAL RELATIONS	EDUCATION	DEBT INTERESTS	UNEMPLOYMENT COMPENSATION, SOCIAL SECURITY, RETIREMENT
1960	$190,225	$75,450	$36,247	$67,875
1970	251,239	166,307	54,901	147,129
1980	220,782	212,466	112,316	299,179
1981	236,060	213,677	132,039	327,991
1983	281,121	217,080	163,282	370,828
1985	330,975	236,014	197,973	382,202
1987	341,297	257,441	201,057	398,010
1988	339,893	264,669	208,510	405,495
1989	346,338	280,713	220,845	414,624

YEAR	HEALTH	TRANSPORTATION	HOUSING	PUBLIC WELFARE
1960	$20,391	$44,906	$4,440	$17,349
1970	40,519	62,245	9,509	52,235
1980	63,977	62,181	17,936	95,669
1981	64,068	63,496	18,788	100,939
1983	69,425	57,247	22,761	103,110
1985	73,054	65,343	21,307	108,680
1987	77,535	70,587	22,787	113,676
1988	81,153	69,568	25,968	118,579
1989	85,091	73,576	28,230	126,132

YEAR	PUBLIC SAFETY	FARM, ENVIRONMENT, PARKS, SANITATION	OTHER
1960	$14,569	$37,265	$14,302
1970	25,752	50,008	33,840
1980	44,470	81,212	42,331
1981	45,369	88,657	42,227
1983	50,468	98,114	47,172
1985	57,763	101,504	51,035
1987	65,900	135,419	55,167
1988	69,568	131,291	58,685
1989	72,236	104,767	63,019

Source: Table prepared by the author from raw data taken from The Tax Foundation, *Facts and Figures on Government Finance*, Washington, DC, various issues.

Index